Introduction

THE editor of the New York Times was once asked why the paper used so few political cartoonists. "Because," he said, "they can't say *on the other hand*." His irritation (or perhaps envy?) is shared by many other editors. They hate the thought that a single political cartoon might be making a bigger impact than their carefully composed leader column.

Editors of Punch, as you might expect, have never shared that view. Cartoons— *all* cartoons—have been an important feature of each weekly issue since the magazine was launched in 1841. As usual I have included some of the past year's contributions by our principal cartoonist, Trog. He is—for me—one of the most talented caricaturists in the world today. But Punch is fortunate to have the loyal support of many other able cartoonists: Mahood, Heath, Thelwell, Tidy, ffolkes, Langdon, Handelsman, Graham, Larry, Albert, Hewison, Dickinson, Murray Ball and many, many more. It is a genuine pleasure to work with them all, especially for someone who is completely useless on the drawing board.

Punch gets several hundred cartoons each week and we select forty or fifty for publication. It means a total of more than 2,000 cartoons a year—more than you will find in any other magazine in the world—and deciding which to include in the "Pick" is one of the most difficult tasks I know. I have no doubt that you will find at least some of those I have chosen for this volume wildly unfunny; the first thing one learns in this business is that what makes one man laugh is liable to make another furious. Britain has 52 million experts on humour. But I sincerely hope that the majority will give you as much pleasure as they gave me when I first saw them as "roughs".

There are some articles too. The difficulty here has been to know what to leave out. We are a weekly magazine and aim to be topical. It means that much of our comment, particularly on political affairs, dates very quickly. There is much that I would like to have included, but the main objective of the "Pick" is to entertain— and, hopefully, to give you the flavour of a much-changed "Punch" in the process. I don't doubt that some people read us only at the dentist. But more than 100,000 readers buy the magazine each week. They *can* be wrong but it's nice to have 100,000 friends.

WILLIAM DAVIS

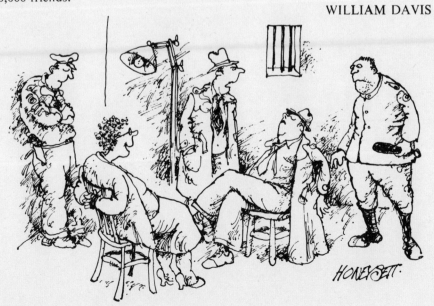

"*You got her to talk—now get her to shut up.*"

Love and Hate in the Sun

by NICHOLAS MONSARRAT

WHEN I was a young man, sun-worship, like sex today, had only just been invented. We now know that there was no sex to speak of until a few years ago, when certain energetic filmstars put the stamp of approval—indeed, quite a collection of stamps—on the copulative bed. In the same way, the sun was not really in the sky at all until English visitors began to arrive at Le Touquet, Antibes, Eden Rock and Biarritz in the late 'twenties, and there bared their bodies to an embrace warmer by far than anything to be found in S.W.1, 3, 5, or 7. Sun-bathing immediately became, as we said at the time, the done thing.

I was then an under-privileged young man, in the sense that, at the age of 19, I was still not getting anywhere with girls. What was the good of having a manicured, pencil-thin, hair-line moustache, just like Ronald Colman, if barbers were the only interested parties? Mr. Colman got the heroines, without fail; all I got was a chapped upper lip from over-cultivation.

Perhaps my approach was wrong. As a devotee of Dornford Yates and the "Berry" books, I had early been taken with a phrase containing one baffling metaphor and one ambiguous piece of syntax: "Being an old hand, he looked at her feet first." I always looked at their feet, first, wishing to seem a man of the world, but it did not work; the girls merely thought I was shifty, and as I looked at their feet, their feet would move away.

There followed a correspondence course in Body-Building and Repartee, but I remained tongue-tied and, presently, muscle-bound. Then certain newspaper advertisements started to plug the simple message: HANDSOME MEN ARE SLIGHTLY SUN-BURNED. Though they were selling sun-tan oil, my intention was to become very handsome indeed, and only the real thing would do. Thus there began a 45-year love affair with the sun, from which I have only recently grown estranged.

It started in St. Malo, where I was sent to learn French and, failing to make the recommended contacts, returned with a slight American accent and a sun-burn, product of hours of ritual cooking on the *plage*, which knocked them all sideways when I got back to my home town of Liverpool. Nut-brown, glowing like the very coals of desire, I emerged out of the Mersey fog as the biggest man-made threat since the tunnel.

But September came, and with it the customary slug-like hue. It was not cured until next year, when I was sent to Dresden (understandably, I was always being sent somewhere) and there enjoyed a blissful summer, wolfing Wiener Schnitzel and grilled *Fräulein* with equal appetite. By then I had lost, or at least mislaid, my innocence. Sun-burn, it seemed, really worked.

Then there was the war, which I resented because it was cold and wet, and then seven years in South

"*Okay, okay. We buy your religion. What about spares?*"

9

Africa where the sun was a permanent blessing, and fourteen in Canada, where the summers at least were blazing perfection, and snow-bound winters could be diluted with West Indian warmth. By this manipulation, a sun-tan lasted from year to year, and so did everything else.

Then, in search of a book—and just you wait for it!—I went to live in Malta, and the love-object in the sky became, by swift stages, the declared enemy. Like many another life-partner, it grew tyrannical.

If you *live* in the Mediterranean, instead of flying down as a refugee from West Hartlepool or Runcorn, the sun must be shut out from your house, with all the bolts and bars available. Small windows, solid stone walls (ours are two-feet-eight-inches thick), and overhanging balconies are the essential weapons against a fiery heat which can top the 100-degree mark and marinate the brain in half an hour. As for actually going out in the midday sun—mad dogs and Englishmen are still the only takers.

Of course, the warmth is welcome: when we read or hear of London "sweltering" in the high seventies, we are inclined to reach for an extra string vest. But the direct rays no longer charm. Last year we built a small screened patio, to make a bracket of a superb view, no mosquitoes, and a guaranteed sunshade. Introduced to this benevolent haven with pride, our first visitor could only commiserate.

She was one of a procession of lobster-coloured holiday-makers who include our house in their itinerary before they succumb to first-degree burns on the forehead, shoulder-blades, bared midriff, and see-through bottom.

"But it faces *north*!" she said, as if "north" were a combination of an abattoir and a glue-factory. "Oh well—you get a bit of morning sun, I suppose."

Since the morning sun hits you straight between the eyes like a red-hot sledgehammer, that's the only time the patio is empty.

There is a reverse side to English sun-worship, which is an atavistic fear of anything warmer than a banker's glass eye. Once I landed, in the middle of the night, at Abu Dhabi, which needs further identification as being at the front-burner end of the Persian Gulf, within a potato-crisp toss of the equator.

The temperature, at midnight, was still 94 degrees, and the price of cold lager 70p a bottle. We sat around in the airport lounge like stranded flying-fish breathing their last on the Skeleton Coast. An English couple, with one crimson-faced child, were having an almighty tug-of-love over their darling offspring. The man, in this equatorial oven, still wore a buttoned-up waistcoat, and the woman a coat of reliable, stylish tweed. The little boy, in addition to all else, had been topped off with a woolly cardigan. The husband wanted him to take this off. The wife resisted, clinging desperately to a panting child which must have been scalding to the touch. At the end of a long dispute, she produced a clinching argument.

"Do you want to kill him?" she screamed. "This is the *desert*! It's *treacherous*!"

Yet the sun is still a life-long friend, remembered with great affection, and now tolerated for all its simmering bad-temper. I recall, best of all, one time when it proved a singular ally on life's most important battlefield.

I once knew a most beautiful girl who decided to have a fling with an earl instead. She did not particularly like him—no one liked him, except a certain number of tailors, head-waiters, and gunsmiths—but she had been brought up to believe that her prime loyalty was to the marriage-market, and in this line of endeavour an earl was a considerable catch. A "trial honeymoon" might be the key to fortune.

But for her there was another catch. Though a belted earl was high on the list of social prizes, she was not really looking forward to the moment when he unbelted. When she came back from Marrakesh, we met in the cooler climate of Pimlico.

"How did the trial honeymoon go?" I asked mournfully. I was wildly jealous.

She gave me a gorgeous smile. "Saved by sunburn," she said.

"*American tourists.*"

All the World Loves a Tax Man

The Inland Revenue is badly under-strength. There is even talk of £100 million in taxes lying around ungathered. In its desperate attempts to recruit tax men, has the Government tried out all the psychological angles?

The Appeal to Curiosity

WHAT DO THEY REALLY EARN?

✱ Is it true that the Duke of Devonshire pulls in more than the Queen?

✱ Does the income of the Rolling Stones dwarf the National Budget of Luxembourg?

✱ Which newscasters gross £50,000 a year from fête-opening?

✱ What are Harold Wilson's literary and television earnings?

The answers to these and other urgent questions are known only to Her Majesty's Inspectors of Taxes. As one of this "happy band of brothers" you can be privy to the financial secrets of the great.

The highest in the land must show you their tailoring bills, their restaurant bills. YOU will decide what is a fair claim for depreciation on a throne. If a marquis overspends on gold leaf for his State Rooms YOU will explain to him the error of his ways.

Don't think of yourself as a nosey-parker. Somebody has to do the job and it may as well be you.

For an exciting career like this, bursting with job satisfaction, you will not expect an unduly high reward. Nor will you object to your salary being published in Whitaker's Almanack *for all your neighbours to see.*

HM Inspector of Taxes Sunningdale 21st District writes: As Assistant Deputy-Inspector of Foreign and Commonwealth Dividends I felt myself not sufficiently stretched. I can never thank you enough for giving me the Paul Getty file. He is a marvellous host, by the way.

For a Full, Satisfying and Eye-Opening Life, Join the Tax Gatherers!

BOARD OF INLAND REVENUE,
Somerset House, London, WC2

The Appeal to Humanity

Meet Jim Hake, Friend of the People

Jim Hake is a tax man. He spends his days handing out income tax refunds to what he sometimes calls "a shower of bloody strikers." But that is just Jim's little joke. Jim knows that strikers are human beings and— who can tell?—perhaps he will want to join them some day.
Meanwhile Jim does a job for humanity, cushioning the greedy against distress. In his courteous, unassuming way he helps to keep the wheels of Britain motionless.
You'll be proud to work alongside Jim!

CALL AT YOUR NEAREST INLAND REVENUE OFFICE NOW!

The Appeal to Virility

Are You Man Enough for this Job?

We mean to toss you into a sea of financial sharks! Every day you will do battle with sharp-toothed accountants and their blubbery parasites who squirt ink into your eyes.

Seek out the hidden lairs of the asset-strippers, stuffed with illegal gold! Pursue them to the farthest tax havens! Then scoop up the great shoals of petty fiddlers and leave them gasping for very life!

Tax men, real red-blooded tax men, are an international elite. Who tripped up Al Capone? Who toppled Spiro Agnew? It was a tax man. Sit still for a minute and think of the rogues you could trip up.

Rush me your free brochure *Goliaths And How To Trap Them.* I am over 21, in good health and would like an MBE.

Name.................Address.................

The Self-mocking, Excessively Truthful Appeal

HELP BRITAIN'S DESCENT INTO THE ABYSS!
Fly-blown temporary tax office in S-W Wandsworth, above undertaker's Chapel of Rest, seeks not too ambitious recruit to help with VAT and general drudgery. Spottiness an asset. No luncheon vouchers. Car park half-mile distant. Ring Mr. Wilbur after 11.30 and before 4.0 pm.

American strong-arm methods in Britain's factories? JENSEN carves some interesting new scars on the battered face of capitalism

"Too bad your Union won't let us fire you."

"As soon as the factory is producing cars again we're going to take you for a ride."

"Head office has flown us over to join your work's band."

"That's half your pay. The Chief says you can have the rest in seven days if the job's completed . . ."

"A small-ad for tomorrow's papers. The Chairman wants a new moll."

"The Chief don't like guys what smoke in the loo."

"Our Executive's Refresher Course now includes the screening of old James Cagney, Edward G. Robinson and Humphrey Bogart movies . . ."

A World Without Telly

by ALAN BRIEN

I REMEMBER, I remember, the house before telly was born . . . But it takes an effort to recall just what we used to stare at, cross-legged, bare-kneed, fogged-eyed little yogis, lost to that domestic world where mothers shouted from the scullery, "I thought you were going to do your homework," "Who was that at the front door?" and "You might have laid the table," on the peripheral frontiers of our trance.

There was the wallpaper, of course; palisades of floral shrubbery in gangrene on green cheese, with slug-black tendrils joining one blotch of porridge to another, executed by a distant relative of Art Nouveau (fils) in Paisley, Scotland. By focusing-out your irises, you could see mermaids' hair, Roman chariots, dinosaurs, volcanoes and Egyptian mummies. But this was more of a bedroom panorama. And even there, it was more stimulating to lie on your back and watch the free-hand scrawls of the cracks in the ceiling, cross-hatched with damp stains—a form of art I was not to encounter again until I came across the erotic lithographs of John Lennon.

There was the wireless, a streamlined impression of a Greek temple in brown bakelite, somewhere between the Wurlitzer at the Regal and the radiator of a Rolls, but nobody, after the first week, ever gave a second look at its metallic webbing face. You spent more time gazing at the clock, with its curly hands like waxed moustachios, competing to see who could guess how wrong it was before the Greenwich pips. One of the advantages of the wireless, at least to grown ups, was that you did not have to give it the attention of more than one sense. Elder brothers and sisters, who seemed to spend most of any evening running up and down stairs in search of clean shirts or blouses, complaining that there were no towels in the bathroom, or combing their hair in the mirror above the sideboard, rarely heard the wireless except through two walls. My favourite listening post was under the dining room table. And I noticed my parents would actually look at each other across the room, and talk, when they sat down to a favourite programme. Come to think of it, this must be one of the major differences between radio and television. I know telly-addicted couples who have rarely seen each other with the lights on, except in profile, for ten years. Wireless never provided a centre of family attention, claiming all eyes or even all ears. It was a kind of aural atmosphere, a climate of words and music, with which you lived as you did with the weather.

The nearest equivalent to telly in those days at home was my grandfather—a living colour fixture, slightly heavy on the reds, in the corner, and a continuous anthology of sermons, anecdotes, lectures, songs, discussions, serials and short plays, until he was turned off at 10.30 after his Epilogue. He had the same passion for anniversaries, and repeats, as the BBC and would have kept abreast with any ITV company in his total recall of past wars and revolutions. I say "discussions" but, just like the telly, he provided all sides of the argument and it would have been as much a sign of mental unbalance to think of interrupting him in his armchair as it would be answering back to Muggeridge on the box. Though I will say this for him,

" *You adorable old swinger, you **do** care! You've had my phone tapped, haven't you?*"

he had no fixation about balance in his broadcasts. His side always won, and he never said, "Well, we could go on talking about this all evening but I'm afraid that is all we have time for."

A world without television, then, would not be one which lacks an essential crutch on which I have depended since infancy. The telly never entered my unconscious, and cut new tracks in my brain, as it did with my own children, one of whom once casually told me that her dreams always came in segments with signs reading "End of Part One." Telly came to me late, by the measurement of today's young, but now I think of it none the less powerful a drug for all that— on par with the other sensual indulgencies of the years of indiscretion, like smoking, drinking and sex. As with them, it took me a while to convince myself that such a pleasurable obsession was not actually illegal, or anyway only to be savoured in semi-secret behind the drawn curtains of a decent hypocrisy. There was an assumption in my youth, which I did not openly challenge for its manifest unfairness, that you could only enjoy yourself without guilt at home if you were willing to take part and contribute something. Entertainment of really sybaritic, pasha-esque quality, when you surrender yourself utterly to tingling manipulation by the multi-tentacled machine, like Jane Fonda in *Barbarella*, was always an external pastime.

Part of the price paid at the turnpike on the Road to Vanity Fair was having to go out into the windy night, wait at chilly tramstops, stand in rain-sodden queues, pay ready cash on the spot, in order to sit in the town music hall ("Remember Sunderland" oldstagers in the variety profession used to say to each other whenever they felt a rush of *hubris* to the head) with its packed cavern of laughing customers, gilded by the glowing limelight spilling over from the stage, like the emanation from the Ghost of Christmas Past, or in the local fleapit, three changes of programme a week counting the Saturday morning children's show, with its dark-plush funnel of heavy-breathing solitaries, alone together, faintly silvered by the radiance of the screen which almost touched your knees. You went singly and ended up in a mass, and from the second you bought your ticket the unrolling fantasy was beyond your control.

When I first rented my own telly in the early Fifties, I could hardly believe such a toy really existed. It was the first really solid benefit that had been conferred on me by the new, scientific, expanding, post-war society, and I hurried home, like a newly-wed, to sample my newly-acquired rights. And, like a newly-wed, I always had a sneaking fear that authority in some form would find a way to break in and separate us. It seemed a pity to waste it by non-use. It was only the Government, cutting off my supply at 10.30, that freed me from that nagging sense of a duty, which was also a privilege, neglected whenever I fell asleep during a late-night movie and woke again to a crackling, atomised screen. There was sense of shame that I never

felt about food uneaten and decaying in the refrigerator, or wine uncorked and left to turn vinegary, or cigarettes grown stale in an unworn suit.

In a world without television, I should never have known what those who rule us really look like. I should have been forced to rely, as voters had for generations, upon carefully posed portraits, usually twenty years out of date. However flatteringly made up, and impressively lit, we can stare blatantly at them without fear of being stared down in return. Few of us ever actually examine feature by feature our nearest and dearest (especially our nearest and dearest) the way we can the most famous and powerful in the world on TV. Except in newsreel shots, we had never seen Baldwin or Chamberlain, even Churchill. We had never seen them at all under conditions not controlled by them. Macmillan was the first Prime Minister to face questions on TV. Now we could watch the shifty flicker of the eyes, the accidental, revealing slip of the tongue, the windy evasions, the indignant bluster. And despite the alleged magic of TV in creating mythological celebrities, famous only for being famous but even more famous for all that, it has cut down statesmen to politicians, and politicians to careerists, and careerists to con men.

In a world without television, many subjects would have remained unmentionable, many social evils no more than objects of Christmas charity. From the beginning, it was more outspoken than the press— abortion, homosexuality, crime, birth control, corruption, drugs, police violence, property racketeering, pollution—all these became subjects of general attention in newspapers only after they were seen to arouse public opinion on the screen. Nudity was on television before it was in the cinema. Obscenities were heard being uttered by visible human beings and society did not degenerate into rape and arson. Even now a deputy editor of the *Sunday Telegraph* is allowed on television to utter a word in front of millions which he would not be permitted to print in his own pages. By staying at home, among his family, the viewer has been introduced to a wide, wide world he could not hope to see out of doors.

In a world without television, thousands of only slightly extraordinary people (me included) have had their nights on the box, tasting the splendours and miseries of being for a while a mini-celebrity. Now they know what they look like to others, they are able to be more critical of how others look to them. They have learned the tricks, the dodges, the effect of fake indignation, the use of phoney candour. Television in competition has improved itself, and also improved its rivals. Without it, we would be a twentieth century planet governed by nineteenth century rulers. Nevertheless, I find myself surprisingly quickly accustomed to a world without television after 10.30. When I do watch, I am gratified to discover that I can switch off and still have half an evening still free. And even before the emergency measure, I was already phasing the telly out of my life. Partly this is because I tapered off, with minimum withdrawal

symptoms, during my six months last year in the Soviet Union. There is nothing like watching programmes you only imperfectly understand to realise that you do not need, or want, to understand them any better. Russian TV is openly "educational", that is propagandist and manipulative, and it does not matter that the ends they aim to achieve are often ones I would support. Back home, I detect more obviously the bones beneath the beguiling flesh. Like the wallpaper of my youth, the pattern repeats too quickly to allow the mind freedom to spread its wings. Its mental diet relies too heavily on stodge, and I feel a reawakening of the desire to cook for myself and become both full and slim. I want contact with people who will answer back.

A world without television for anyone is now unthinkable, except as a humorous fantasy, to anyone who has experienced the world with it. But I am now ready for a world without television for me, except on rare occasions which may not be everybody else's rare occasions. I look forward to putting it back on the level, hour for hour, with the theatre, the cinema, books and magazines, conversation, public meetings, the radio, the pub, the record player, and, if I feel like it, gazing at the wall. If I can now do without it, it is only because it taught how much I missed it when it wasn't there.

"First the good news. Our mills have been responsible for less air-pollution than during any year in the company's history."

From Our Ugandan Correspondent

IT GITTIN' to look like I de only worl' leader wot ain't gittin' a visit f'om Henry Kissinger. I tell you, I an' de wives gittin' damn sick o' turning' down de bunk bed an' goin' over it wid de expensive Flit an' everythin', also ringin' up to top Kampala dolly, Miss Phoebe Ngaga, 38-39-44, an' bookin' a table fo' de lucky pair at de Entebbe Wimpey plus Wilfred Mbili, de well-known gypsy violinist—a Head o' State gittin' to look a right idiot, runnin' about an' gittin' everythin' fixed up jus' in case de trendy superkraut jettin' in fo' de informal natter, also it damn expensive wot wid de services o' de enticin' Miss Ngaga runnin' out at aroun' nine bob a hour includin' plastic rainwear, an' you gotta pay fo' de reservations irrespective o' whether de Seckertary o' State turnin' up, otherwise de lovely Phoebe li'ble to come roun' an' stick a stiletto heel in yo' bonce, not to mention goin' fo' de groin wid de ever pop'lar ridin' crop.

Dis abbersence havin' a marked effect on de loyal popperlace, especially on account o' havin' to fork out fo' de paper Stars an' Stripes wot gonna be waved on de ride f'om de airport, also gittin' up de noses o' de Kampala All-Stars Banjo Minnerstrels, formerly de Eluwigi String Quartet, who reckonin' it a bit of a comedown f'om de Ludwig Mozart, havin' to stan' aroun' at de end o' Runway One wid de banjos tucked under de chins waitin' to greet Kissinger wid de famous *Darktown Strutters Ball*. But de main problem is where de devoted subberjecks beginnin' to feel I gittin' a snub—dey see de worl'-famous Kissinger whippin' roun' all de rubbish, hob-nobbin' wid de wogs an' de fiendish Israelis befo' nippin' across to put de arm on de disgustin' Douglas-Alec-Home, coppin' de big Nobel gong fo'

knockin' de Far East into shape, rushin' home to de crazed Nixon, whippin' back to de Kremblin fo' a quick bortsch wid de Russians—an' wot happenin' to Uganda, nub o' Africa, while all dis goin' on? We jus' sittin' here on de bums polishin' de bes' EPNS an' starin' up at de sky fo' de fust glimpse o' de great silver bird.

Wot keepin' him? Dis de golden opportunity fo' a ambitious honky, he done de Middle East, he done de slant-eyed lot, he done de Commies, it about time he rollin' de sleeves up an' gittin' down to de coon question, an' where better to kick off than wid de top coon? Kissinger could colleck de entire set, could be de hottest property since Jesus Christ; if you ask me, de trouble is wid handin' out de Nobel item too soon, man git de ole Swedish cheque in de bank an' de Oscar on de mantelpiece, he boun' to go off de boil a bit, look at de famous W. S. Churchill, after he coppin' his Prize he stop declarin' war an jus' sit aroun' swiggin' de VSOP an' sim'lar, also E. Hemingway puttin' de shotgun in de mouf, likewise de famous Ian Fleming, wot he doin' after cobblin' together de penicillin? Nothin'!

Well, I ain't never bin one to push hisself, but I ain't takin' dis insult lyin' down, I can tell you! If Kissinger reckonin' there not bein' any percentage in jettin' down to Uganda, Empire o' de future, he gonna find hisself wid a worl' crisis on de hands. Dis de last intimation, if if he listenin', an' if I ain't gittin' a han'-written letter in de nex' few days, I gonna march on de vile Nyerere an' put de rat among de pigeons. If de peace negotiatin' de only way I gittin' Kissinger to come down here an' cough up a bit o' respeck', such as puttin' us bofe on de worl'-wide *Time* cover, dat de way it gonna have to be.

After all, neither of us is in dis business fo' our healf.

A Golfer in the House

by GRAHAM

"Oh God! Don't tell me you've dug out your back numbers again!"

"I clinched it with a twenty-footer on the last green."

"What d'you think? A three iron or a four wood?"

"The elastic broke!"

"I'm worried about you, Eric! Why not pop round to the surgery and have a word with Doctor Dixon?"

*"He's in the hall, hitting chip shots into my **best school hat**!"*

"Put it off? Because of a little shower?"

"I'll bet Mrs. Jacklin doesn't go on at Tony like that!"

My Years with Marilyn

As the Monroe bandwagon rolls on, lovely
(but temperamental) KEITH WATERHOUSE
grabs his scrapbook and scrambles aboard

THE enigma that was Marilyn Monroe will intrigue me all my life, or at least all the way through a full-length biographical investigation, serialisation of same, a TV documentary, and half a dozen one-off articles explaining how the enigma came my way.

My fascination with Marilyn goes back to a chilly December dawn in 1959, the year of *Some Like It Hot*. It was 10.37 p.m. Pacific Time, 6.42 a.m. by my bedroom clock (I kept it five minutes fast and still do: a reminder, now, of Marilyn). My phone shrilled. It was Ziggy Tannenbaum, then head of production at Unilateral, speaking from Beverly Hills. He was planning an updated re-make of *The Fall of the House of Usher*, but with lotsa laughs.

He saw Marilyn as the goil. The property was a very deep and very beautiful and very moving exploration of humanity trapped in its own consciousness, and there was already a screenplay by Hermann (*Cry, My Darling*) Pastrami which was truly a work of art. All it needed was the yoks. Given carte-blanche to throw Hermann's script out the window, would I work on the re-writes?

I said I would be delighted.

"I had a feeling, Terry. I had a feeling this was your kind of movie. Like I was saying to my very beautiful wife Wanda who loves your work, with Marilyn as the goil all right I'm happy, but with Terry's name on the credits I'm twice as happy. Now lemme ask you this, Terry. How soon can you get off your ass and come over here?"

I said I could come on the next plane, but why was he calling me Terry?

"Isn't this Mr. Terence Rattigan, the English writer?"

"No," I said. "You must have the wrong number."

"Chee! Telephone operators!" said Ziggy, and hung up.

So, in the end, I was never to meet Marilyn. I was never to meet Ziggy either, but I read in a fan magazine that the remake of *Fall* had been shelved. Marilyn was already on location for *The Misfits* and she had sent back Hermann's first draft unread. It was endearingly, infuriatingly, typical.

Marilyn was not the kind of girl you forgot, or ever wanted to. If she ever did stray from my mind for a moment, a glance at my bedroom clock, five minutes fast, would bring me back to cloud seven. The clock now stands on my desk as I write. It shows 4.58. It will be 4.53 in Newton Abbott . . .

A blazing afternoon in the autumn of 1973. I am standing on the up platform at Newton Abbott station, and I have just learned that the 4.53 to

"*You have beautiful eyes, Veronica.*"

Paddington runs only on Fridays. I have forty minutes to kill before the 5.30. (Funny how Marilyn, so crazily unpunctual, is forever linked in my mind with time.)

Browsing at the station bookstall, I picked up a newspaper. I don't know, will never know, why I should have chosen that particular paper but my instincts were right for it contained a full-page article on Marilyn. So, I think, did every other newspaper and magazine on the stall, so maybe it was not such a hunch at that.

Most of the stuff was old hat—the Monroe "legend" re-worked by someone who had never even known her—but there was one story new to me, that throws some light on the secret of Marilyn's charisma.

In 1953, when she was working on *How to Marry a Millionaire*, the girls in the commissary had clubbed together and bought her a birthday present—a tiny dime-store wristwatch. Some of Marilyn's "friends" thought it was a heavy hint to stop arriving for breakfast during the second lunch setting. Maybe it was. But Marilyn, with her heartbreaking naivety, was as delighted as a little girl with her first doll. She promised to wear the watch next to her wrist.

Her notorious unpunctuality had long been noticed on the *Millionaire* set. The morning after the presentation she had been running a temperature of 214°F, two degrees above boiling point. On top of that her studio car had been involved in a minor collision on Ventura Boulevard. She arrived on the lot, white and tense, an hour and twenty minutes late.

One of the extras, who had been hoping to get away earlier to keep a dental appointment, muttered, "What the hell time does she call this?"

Nobody heard him except Marilyn. Forcing a dazzling smile, she looked at the cheap little watch on her left wrist and pouted: "Twenty after nine."

Recalling that story now, it seems to me there is something missing—a haunting punchline, perhaps, some elusive piece that will never be fitted into the jigsaw that was Marilyn Monroe. Was the point, perhaps, that she kept her dime-store watch five minutes fast, like my bedroom clock? I like to think so.

I haven't explained what I was doing in Newton Abbott that day. It doesn't seem important any more.

The story of Marilyn and the motorcycle is maybe apocryphal, maybe not. Perhaps, as with so many of the legends that began to cling like barnacles to her siren personality, the truth lies somewhere between fact and fancy. For what it is worth, it was told to me by Bobby Avocado. He had heard it on a TV chat programme.

Bobby was a sometime partner of mine in a publishing project we had tried to put together in the spring of 1972. It was going to be a monthly pocket

"They used to be called Peter, Paula and Sophie, but Sophie split, and later so did Peter and Paula, now it's a different group altogether called Iris, Mary and Dave."

magazine called *Marilyn Monroe Digest*, reprinting the best of all that was being written about Marilyn. If we had waited another eighteen months we would have made a killing, but we were ahead of the market. The first and only print of *Marilyn Monroe Digest* went for pulp.

But Bobby and I kept in touch when we could, and one autumn evening in 1973 he arrived at my house unheralded. It transpired that he had been in the neighbourhood and thought he would drop in for a drink.

Over a JB (straight, with a twist of lemon), Bobby asked—abruptly, I thought—"Did you see A——— C——— (a well-known writer) on the box last night? I couldn't understand a word he said."

I'd missed the programme. I remembered that the previous night I'd been playing squash.

"He started to tell some rambling, pointless story about Marilyn Monroe and a motor bike, then he broke off in the middle and said, 'No, I tell a lie, it wasn't Marilyn Monroe, it was Betty Grable.'

Pie-eyed, completely."

"Marilyn? She was never a drinker."

"No, not Marilyn. A——— C———. Tight as an owl, if you ask me."

No studio that she ever worked for would have allowed Marilyn to ride a motor-bike. Yet the legend persists. Was it, like her friendship with Kennedy, one of Marilyn's "open secrets"? We shall never know.

In 1950 Marilyn made *Love Happy*, followed by *The Asphalt Jungle* and *All About Eve*. In 1951, *Love Nest* and *Let's Make It Legal*. The pace was fast and dangerous—five movies in two years; three of them in one year, two in the other. Two of them had two-word titles, one had a three-word title, and another no fewer than four. Any analyst of her mood at that time, who wanted to fill up space, could go on to point out that three of these titles began with the letter "L", of which two were the same word—"Love". No wonder the girl who had been born Norma Jean

Baker was confused.

Early in 1952 she spoke to a visitor from Denver, G. G. Potboil, who was on a conducted tour of the set. Potboil was fooling around with a "prop" stethoscope, and Marilyn thought he was a doctor.

"I feel dizzy," said Marilyn.

Potboil, who recalls the encounter in his book, *The Marilyn I Knew*, retorted: "Boy, you sure as all hell look dizzy!" He was escorted from the set.

"The tip of the iceberg" is the wrong expression maybe, but I feel that in setting down these memories I have only brushed fingers with the real Marilyn Monroe. Maybe there was too much to say, and too little space to say it in. She remains, as I said a hundred thousand words back, an enigma. Maybe the key to the Chinese box of emotions that was Marilyn Monroe lies in a very long narrative concerning a visit to her dentist in 1955, the year of *The Seven-Year Itch*. But that is another story, and another book.

"From the Promenade Concert at the Royal Albert Hall—hello Mrs. Ravens of Rotherham, and on this glorious but sweltering summer evening what is your request to the BBC Symphony Orchestra?"

Epithalamium
by the Poet Laureate

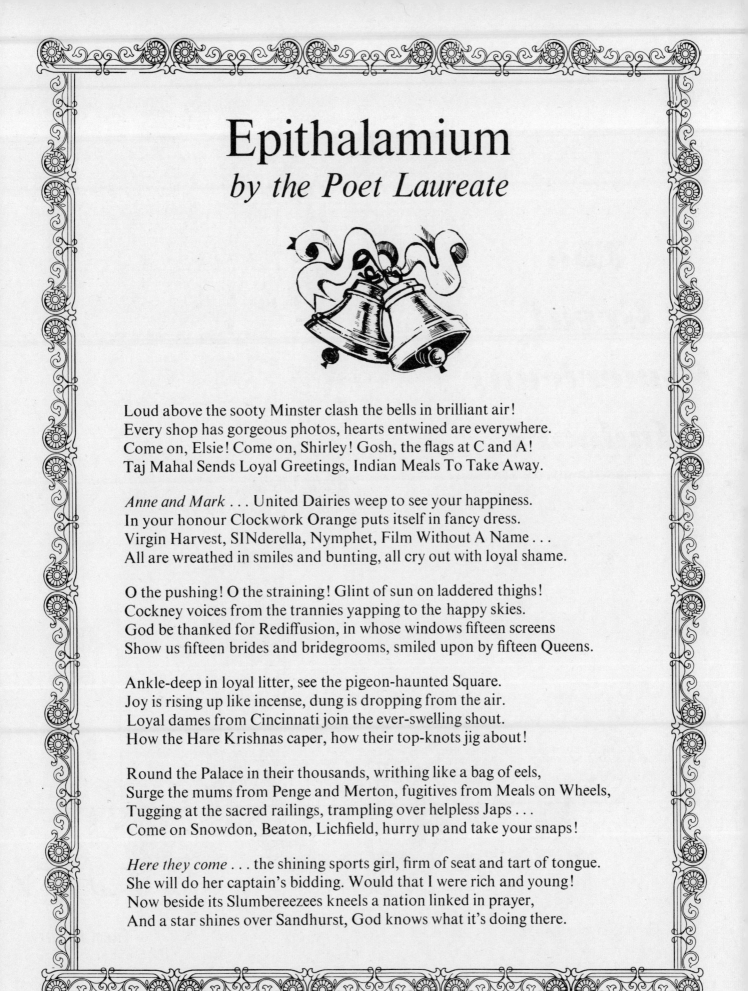

Loud above the sooty Minster clash the bells in brilliant air!
Every shop has gorgeous photos, hearts entwined are everywhere.
Come on, Elsie! Come on, Shirley! Gosh, the flags at C and A!
Taj Mahal Sends Loyal Greetings, Indian Meals To Take Away.

Anne and Mark . . . United Dairies weep to see your happiness.
In your honour Clockwork Orange puts itself in fancy dress.
Virgin Harvest, SINderella, Nymphet, Film Without A Name . . .
All are wreathed in smiles and bunting, all cry out with loyal shame.

O the pushing! O the straining! Glint of sun on laddered thighs!
Cockney voices from the trannies yapping to the happy skies.
God be thanked for Rediffusion, in whose windows fifteen screens
Show us fifteen brides and bridegrooms, smiled upon by fifteen Queens.

Ankle-deep in loyal litter, see the pigeon-haunted Square.
Joy is rising up like incense, dung is dropping from the air.
Loyal dames from Cincinnati join the ever-swelling shout.
How the Hare Krishnas caper, how their top-knots jig about!

Round the Palace in their thousands, writhing like a bag of eels,
Surge the mums from Penge and Merton, fugitives from Meals on Wheels,
Tugging at the sacred railings, trampling over helpless Japs . . .
Come on Snowdon, Beaton, Lichfield, hurry up and take your snaps!

Here they come . . . the shining sports girl, firm of seat and tart of tongue.
She will do her captain's bidding. Would that I were rich and young!
Now beside its Slumbereezees kneels a nation linked in prayer,
And a star shines over Sandhurst, God knows what it's doing there.

The Great (American) Indoors

by ARNOLD ROTH

Great Libraries

Great Playgrounds

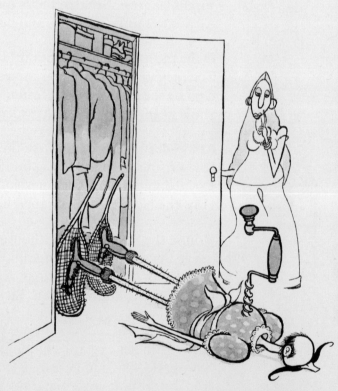

Great Mystery

Great Hunting Grounds

Great Wine Cellars

Great Prodigal Returnings

Great Intimacies

Roll Out The Barrels

ROBERT MORLEY strikes it rich at the bottom of his garden

"YOU mean to tell me," said my neighbour, "you have been living on top of an oil field all these years and mistook it for a vegetable garden?"

"That's right," I told him, "still, better late than never. They're coming with the equipment on Friday. A week, give or take, and I shall be in production."

He asked whether it might be noisy. "A sort of rhythmical tapping," I told him, "and of course a faint smell, but the gantry, I think that's what they call it, is pastel blue to match the shutters.

"I can give you a booklet if you like, they're the people who used to do the swimming pool, but now they've switched. Most people already have pools if they are ever going to have them. Oil is the new status symbol. They put it rather cleverly on the cover, 'Rig yourself out'."

He took the literature and went back to mowing his lawn, but I could tell he was no longer concentrating. I hope he decides to get a pump. My firm, they pay for introductions.

One of the leading estate agents prints small symbols under the photographs of the houses he has for sale nowadays, designating the amenities. A horse means stabling, a dog kenneling, a diver indicates a swimming pool, there's a radiator for central heating and now, lo and behold, a small derrick for you know what. We are keeping it pretty quiet in Berkshire, we don't want a lot of the big boys moving in, and among the crowd I go to cocktail parties with, a second derrick

"He's trying to raise the tone of the place."

is considered a bit much. Three oil wells on the property and you buy your own gin and go back to dusting the mantelpiece.

Most of us sell the stuff direct and just keep back enough for the Rolls and the radiators and a little for special needs, and to give to friends. Berkshire Spirit is that much richer and visitors driving down for Sunday lunch really appreciate a special fill-up.

Our neighbourhood oil prospector was a pleasant man, dressed in the traditional costume of worn denims and tin helmet; he might have stepped straight out of the celebrated TV series. He parked his van in the drive.

"If you will just show me where the boundaries are I can get down to it," he explained producing a survey map.

"Get down to what?" I asked. He looked round nervously, waited for a load of hay to pass the gate and uttered the magic word. "Oil. You're loaded with it here, didn't you know?"

"I had no idea," I told him.

"You're right in the middle of the biggest oil field between Marlow and Sonning," he went on, "there's no point in taking a soil sample really, just a formality, still it's all part of the service. Help us site the rig; I suppose you don't want it on the croquet lawn? Under the swimming pool, too, would be a bit awkward, come to think of it. We'd be better in the kitchen garden I suppose; anyway there's where I'll make a start, and Bob's your Uncle."

I hadn't heard anyone say "Bob's your Uncle" for a long time, but, come to that, I'd never seen anyone prospecting for oil among the raspberries.

"I'll be a fair time," he told me and asked if I was planning to go out to work. I explained I worked at home and would be available.

"You won't have to do much more of that once we've got rigged up," he assured me. "You can just sit in the shade and watch the old jigger go up and down and every time it comes up means another bob or two in the old pocket." He fetched a spade and a bundle of drain rods from the back of the lorry and marched off in the direction of the Brussels sprouts.

I don't quite know what I expected at this point, I am not even sure I believed the fellow but it was impossible not to admire his optimism. In any case it was justified. About an hour later he interrupted a short piece I was working on for a well-known travel magazine to bring me his report.

"First the good news," he told me, "you're stashed. I don't think I'd be far wrong if I called it half a million barrels give or take a couple of thousand. Now for the bad news . . . the rhubarb will have to go. For a time I thought we might save it but the pipe will have to come bang down the middle."

"Forget the rhubarb," I told him. We never eat it anyway.

"I like a bit of rhubarb myself, there may be a crown or two we could save, we'll have to see," he went on. "But the important thing just now is to order the equipment and find a day to install. Would next Friday suit? I shall be in the district, so if it's convenient for you it'll suit us both."

I told him Friday would do admirably and asked how long the operation would take. Apparently they'd improved the technique out of all recognition. He reckoned with luck, and given a fair crack of the drill, the whole thing would be accomplished in about five hours; in six we should be fully operational with the oil flowing, in the first instance into a static water tank which he was letting me have second-hand and siting by the garage. Later he proposed to connect the tank by pipes to an outlet point further down the drive.

"Much the same arrangement I see you already have with fuel for the central heating system, only this time in reverse. The tankers will arrive about twice a week to start with and instead of you paying them they'll pay you and give you a receipt."

I suggested that I might be the one to have to give the receipt but he demurred. Better not have anything in writing. "With this Government you never know, they'll try and get a piece of it, you can count on that. Barber screwed those North Sea boys, and he'll crucify you if he gets the chance.

"It's your land, it's your oil; I reckon you're doing them a service, making a patriotic gesture. In wartime we had to grow our own greens, now we have to grow our own oil. The only trouble as I see it is if we get too successful over here, we'll have another Uganda on our hands. Only this time it won't be one wife they'll want to bring in, it'll be the whole bloody harem!"

"I reckon," he went on, "it was a poor day for those old sheikhs when the Americans thought of Skylab. It was a poor day for America too, come to think of it. Didn't do Texas much good."

"You mean," I asked him, "the Berkshire Oil Fields were spotted from Gemini?"

"Where else? That's what they were looking for. That's what they found. Anyway, you don't have to pay for that little caper, all you have to pay for is the rig and installation and that you can do on the never-never if you wish. A cheque for a hundred pounds and your signature is all I'm asking at present, and whether

you'd like the rig any particular colour. Any particular colour that's on the card that is."

I chose blue and wrote out the cheque to cash. I spent the rest of the day trying to find out the asking price for crude oil and how many gallons are in a barrel. That sort of information is hard to come by, unless you are in the oil game. Finally I rang Paul Getty. I met him at a party, nearly met him that is. Just as I was going to walk over to his table and say, "Hullo, Mr. Getty, I'm Robert Morley," he got up and left.

I wasn't more fortunate this time, apparently he doesn't care to speak on the phone, or else it's a trade secret. I made up my mind, I'd have to wait until Friday.

I suppose you're thinking I was a bit of a mug; that when Friday came my neighbourhood prospector didn't turn up, and there isn't an oil rig at the bottom of my garden! I'm sorry to disappoint you. At two o'clock in the morning, if I open the window and listen, I hear, not as Kipling once wrote "the feet of the wind going to call the sun," but the tap, tap, tap, tap of the well. Twice a week a plain lorry calls to collect and hands over the cash and I now know the price of crude oil; and how many gallons to the barrel. But it's a secret. In this part of the Home Counties we don't have to discuss money, we just count it.

"We're all unethical now and then, Charlie, but some of us have the grace to deplore it."

TARTAN TAKE OVER:
The Biggest Oil Threat Yet!

If Scots Nationalists seize the North Sea oil profits, estimated at £4,000 million a year by 1980, what will happen to England? And to Scotland? These extracts from the newspaper files of six years hence are far from reassuring.

From the Daily Express

THE WORST CITY IN THE WORLD

(By Clapham Bowser)

Today I hopped on my left foot into the Wicked City of Wick, the fabled Gomorrah of the North, the blackest sink of infamy since Port Royal, Jamaica was engulfed in an earthquake.

My right foot had been cut off by drunken Excisemen at the Border.

Here in Wick debauched tinkers richer than Croesus boast of breaking all Ten Commandments before breakfast. The old law which forbids the giving away of women as Bingo prizes is openly defied.

Outside the harbour the luxury yachts of drillers from Cromarty lie at anchor. They cannot enter because the port is choked with Cadillacs, many of them with their drowned drivers still at the wheel, the victims of murderous sprees.

Scenes like these are the price Scotland pays for her new-found wealth in the North Sea—wealth she refuses to share with her ancient enemy, England.

I was told that in Wick surgeons can no longer perform operations, even when they are sober, because revellers have stolen the last reserves of blood to drink at unholy altars.

"It is the greatest hangover in our unhappy history, but at last we have found ourselves as a nation." The speaker, who described himself as the Moderator of the Free Church of Scotland, applied a match to the potion in the skull he was holding and drank the contents flaming.

"D'ye recognise the skull?" he asked me, as he extinguished his beard. "Aye, it's Harold Wilson's. He tried to nationalise oor oil, ye ken."

Outside rose hellish cackles as bands of ruffians and their drabs hanged each other on the lampposts.

"If he thinks this is bad," said the self-styled Moderator, "ye should hiv bin here at Hogmanay. Here, laddie, drink this. Let me light it for you."

I made an excuse and left.

Free-spending oil workers relax with their tiara-topped women at "The Jolly Calvin," the vast recreational complex covering one hundred acres at John o' Groats, "Las Vegas of the North."

From The Daily Telegraph

OIL TYCOONS ORDER CLEARANCES

THE Scots have long memories *(writes our Property and Estates Correspondent)*. All over England the new oil tycoons from the North are buying up big estates and driving out the impoverished inhabitants to make room for sheep. This is their belated revenge for the Highland "clearances" of last century.

"The real difficulty is to distinguish Englishmen from sheep," joked Jock McCarfare, president of the mammoth Tartan Oils. He has just acquired Chatsworth, ancestral home of the Dukes of Devonshire. "Some of the estate workers were slow to move," he said, "but they soon shifted after my agents put a torch to their roof timbers."

Mr McCarfare is having a giant granite statue of himself built on the highest peak in Derbyshire, rivalling the one erected at Golspie to the Duke of Sutherland who emptied the Scottish glens.

Mr Mick McGarble, who heads the £2,000 million Caithness Oil Consortium, told me: "I have just been looking over Lancashire, which seems to me a county suited neither to sheep nor men, so I propose to turn it into a deer forest. There will be a number of well-paid jobs for ghillies, if they keep their noses clean."

Asked what he proposed to do about Liverpool, he said: "There is no room for sentiment in these matters. It will have to go."

From The Guardian

ENGLAND ON HER KNEES

The days when England will be no more than a despised puppet of Scotland are rapidly nearing (*writes our Political Correspondent*). It is not inconceivable that the affairs of "South Britain" will be settled in a couple of afternoons every year by the Edinburgh Parliament, thus reversing completely the system which has hitherto existed.

It is even possible that the other nations of the European Economic Community will be taking their orders from Scotland, once the difficult problems of communicating with the "Arabs in Kilts" have been overcome.

With her stranglehold on the two most precious liquids known to man—oil and whisky—Scotland is now the most powerful nation in the West.

Under the newly-concluded Gleneagles Treaties, oil from the North Sea piped to Scotland is supplied only to those nations willing to concede moral, intellectual and spiritual superiority to the Scots. This poses a cruel challenge to the conscience of civilised man, but the choice is inescapable. The more oil a nation needs, the more Burns Nights it will have to hold.

Unofficially the Westminster Parliament has let it be known that it is willing to truckle and cringe without reserve. If the Scots demand a restoration of the Stuart dynasty, or the universal adoption of the glottal stop, it is unlikely that any serious obstacles will be put in their way.

NEWS IN BRIEF

Among would-be tourists turned away by the Scottish immigration authorities at Gretna yesterday was Mr Paul Getty, at one time the richest oil man in the world. Officials were not satisfied that he had sufficient funds to maintain himself.

*   *

On the field of Bannockburn the former memorial commemorating the Scots victory over the English has been replaced by a 100-ft gold obelisk, from the top of which leaps an Eternal Flame, fuelled by North Sea oil.

*   *

No further bulletins are being issued about the Loch Ness Monster, which has recovered from oil poisoning contracted after its recent escape into the North Sea.

*   *

Mr Hughie McTooth, the well-known public house drag artiste and street busker, has been appointed the first Lord Rector of Oxford University.

Believing that the dying city of London is sitting on limitless reserves of oil, Scots prospectors—not content with their North Sea bonanza—have erected this giant rig in Piccadilly Circus (note Eros statue). Hardly a word of protest has been voiced by apathetic Londoners.

From The Daily Mirror

FAN'S TRAIL OF HAVOC

THOUSANDS of fabulously rich Scots football fans roared into Heathrow yesterday in their executive jets. At one time the aircraft were so thick that they darkened the sun.

The chaos was such that all international flights were grounded for twelve hours.

At the airport the tam-o'-shantered fans were mobbed by well-dressed Englishmen begging alms.

"Ye didna want to know us when we came by coach and were sick all over the Underground," said a fan from Aberdeen, tossing a bundle of fivers contemptuously into the crowd.

The Scots piled into taxis for Wembley, but most cabs ran out of petrol before they were half way there and their occupants missed the Cup Final.

"It's a reet poverty-stricken country," said Rob McKeeler, a pipe-layer from "Millionaires' Row," Peterhead. "Why can ye no' find oil fur yersels?"

On their return flight to the North the fans buzzed every town and village in their path, stampeded herds of cattle and tried to set fire to forests with home-made incendiary bombs. "It was like a thousand-bomber raid gone berserk," said a police official.

"Even Everton fans were never like this," remarked a Football Association spokesman. "But if we want our trickle of oil from the North, we must learn to live with it."

Former Clydeside Red rebel and television philosopher, Jimmy ("The Sheikh") Reid, Scotland's £250,000-a-year overlord, has a spending problem. "We've built houses, schools, hospitals, nurseries, gaols, universities, motorways, recreation centres and marinas," he says, "and now it looks as though we'll have to start putting up office blocks for the bosses." No wonder Jim looks grim.

"*I think we'll dispense with the bowing.*"

PENSIONERS HIT BACK

American 'senior citizens' are being taught the ungentle art of karate, to help protect themselves. HONEYSETT provides a short refresher course

"*I said 'HIAAAAAAAAAA—SO!'*"

"*There he is, dad—that's the one that pushed me yesterday.*"

"*And this is Mrs. Scrottle, my bodyguard.*"

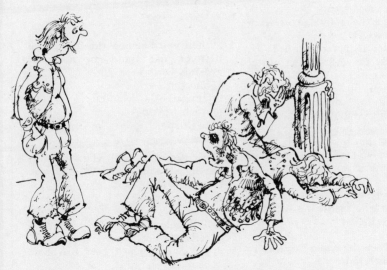

"*We've just been mugged by a bleedin' old age pensioner.*"

"*He's never liked wearing a belt, can he wear black braces instead?*"

"*Why can't you practise on your own balsa wood?*"

Test Your Own Corruption Level

Every man has his price—what's yours? We offer a small post-Watergate
quiz to keep you worried through the winter months

1. **When you heard about Vice-President Agnew's resignation, you thought:**
   a) This strikes a blow for honesty and morality
   b) He should have played for much higher stakes
   c) I thought he was dead
   d) I wonder how much he got for that

2. **You think the police are:**
   a) Wonderful
   b) As human as the next man
   c) Subject to terrible temptations
   d) Given wonderful opportunities

3. **Finally fed up to the back teeth, you throw in your resignation. To your surprise, they offer to double your salary if you will only stay. You reply:**
   a) I must think it over
   b) Make it three times and I'll stay
   c) I am not interested in the money. I merely wish you to understand that I am working in impossible conditions with impossible people. But now that I have had time to think, I accept your offer
   d) Get stuffed

4. **Back from a holiday in Scotland, you pay for your paper with a Scottish £1 note. Confused, the newsagent gives you £4.95 change. Your immediate reaction is to:**
   a) Point out his mistake
   b) Keep the change
   c) Say "I gave you a tenner, I think"
   d) Dash back to Scotland for more of the same

5. **When you are offered a company car, you say:**
   a) As it is hardly essential to my work, I cannot accept this kind offer
   b) Surely you don't think I would seriously consider adding to the traffic and pollution?
   c) Thanks
   d) That's all very well, but what about the company parking space to go with it?

6. **When a motoring correspondent writes, "If I have one word of criticism against the fantastic new Laguna Mk V, it is that the glove compartment is too roomy", you think:—**
   a) But not too roomy for a little present for the motoring correspondent, I'll wager
   b) This man is never satisfied. He didn't like the cigar lighter on the new Rolls either
   c) When you find a man actually bothering to walk round to the passenger's seat, open the glove compartment, put his gloves in it, waggle them around—well, it just goes to show that British motoring correspondents are the best in the world
   d) You don't need gloves in Tunisia, matey, or wherever it was they flew you to test the car

7. **When you see the word Poulson in the headlines, you:**
   a) Yawn
   b) Rage
   c) Blanch
   d) Put in a secret telephone call to a town clerk in the north

8. **When you are offered a drink, you say:**
   a) No, no, let me buy you one
   b) Sure it's on expenses?
   c) All right, but the next one's on my firm
   d) I'm sorry, I never accept gifts in the course of business

9. **When you read that a managing director has been heavily criticised for taking a £15,000 rise, you think:**
   a) Silly fool. No-one's worth that
   b) Silly fool. There are more discreet ways of getting the money
   c) About time I had a rise
   d) About time our managing director had a rise

10. **When putting down a taxi ride to expenses, you write:**
    a) Taxi from Euston to King's Cross, 48p plus 10p tip, total 58p
    b) Taxi, £1.50
    c) Travel, £4
    d) General expenses, £18.90

11. **When you learned the difference between tax avoidance and tax evasion, you were:**
    a) Shocked
    b) Anxious to learn more
    c) About $8\frac{1}{2}$ years old
    d) In Brixton

12. **You discover that your boss is having an affair with Wendy, the telephone girl. You:**
    a) Tell everyone
    b) Tell only your wife
    c) Tell only the boss, in return for certain favours
    d) Tell Wendy she'll have to choose between you two

13. **You are helping a blind bank manager across a lonely street when a large bundle of fivers falls out of his pocket. You immediately:**
    a) Tell him what has happened and put them back in his pocket
    b) Tell him what has happened and put half back in his pocket
    c) Look in his other pocket
    d) Change your voice and say: "OK you two, this is a hold-up"

14. **You consider yourself:**
    a) Honest
    b) Comparatively honest, considering the current state of morals
    c) More honest than Richard Nixon, anyway
    d) A successful businessman

TABOO

BARRY HUMPHRIES ventures into unmentionable territory

SPIDERS were a delicacy in the sixteenth century. They wriggled and jiggled inside many an epicure of that epoch, as we know from a contemporary folk song about an old lady who swallowed one. Arachnophagy was a commonplace of Shakespearean cuisine, and when Anne Hathaway packed her Bard off to rehearsal of a morning his cut lunch might well have included a juicy round of spider sandwiches. (This was before the theatre at Stratford provided an adjacent cafeteria.) Like oysters, however, spiders should correctly be devoured live, and only when there is an ARRGH in the month.

I have not sampled them, but the ant is no stranger to my palate. No-one who has attended an Australian picnic or barbecue can be unfamiliar with the taste of these crunchy termites, although I have also swallowed them voluntarily in Japan where their acrid corpses are heaped on crackers like caviar with legs. I have quaffed the spittle of birds, which is the chief ingredient in a famous Chinese soup, and the webbed feet of ducks, *sauté* in ginger, have trodden my oesophagus.

I have yet to savour the delicate comb of the rooster, but not seldom have I gobbled the pedal extremities of sheep and pig. Offal, which many gourmets relish, has never been to my taste, and butchers have in vain proffered me the iridescent violet and magenta fruits of animal viscera.

However, it is not for me to deny others the gastronomic delights of bowel and lung, and on a recent holiday in Czechoslovakia I fled a restaurant famished while my hardier companions glutted themselves on stewed bull's glands which came, suspiciously, in pairs, and swimming in a viscid broth. Likewise, in Bulgaria and North Africa, I have rejected a meal of sheep's eyes in response to some strange and ineluctable Australian taboo.

Wide travel has taught me that people will eat anything that moves, or has ceased to move, yet my protected Melbourne upbringing with its conservative, and let me admit it, unimaginative diet, oftimes interposes between me and an exotic morsel.

Surprising that I who have prized the succulent whitchetty grub from its gumtree cranny and devoured its walnut flavoured flesh straight from a rude bush-land grill, should be revolted by the thought of jellied eel. When, as a kiddie, I fell voraciously upon a meal of bandicoot stewed in milk or a roast saddle of wallaby served with crisp Melbourne pancakes, I little thought that I would blench at jugged hare,

black pudding or a cartilaginous goulash prepared from horsemeat. Kangaroo tail soup à la Qantas is a delicious beverage, so why should I despise a recipe incorporating the flesh of another less agile and picturesque domestic animal?

Prejudice, of course, since the tufts of khaki fur and wisps of exotic plumage which so often garnished my childhood meals are no less unappetising than the thought that one's London curry might have stalked the rooftops. Prejudice, and a curious form of culinary chauvinism.

Australians are privileged carnivores and so far have not found it necessary to regard their stables and kennels as anterooms to the larder. The grim conditions which obtain in Calcutta and Kensington have not yet obliged us to ingurgitate our pets, and our taste-buds are no doubt the poorer thereby. Similarly, the price of a sheep's wool is such that we have yet to esteem the gastronomic properties of their orbs of vision.

No-one in heaven-blessed Australia is going to bother acquiring a taste for snails when the land— indeed, every suburban garden—is aswarm with edible reptiles. A savoury decoction of snakes and lizards may seem wantonly luxurious to the esurient European, inaccessibly in the Fortnum's class perhaps, but to an Australian child it is a dish taken for granted and often not truly appreciated.

"Eat up all your iguana!" is a common cry in antipodean nurseries.

Australians are often puzzled why shark meat fails

"Well, that way is the prettiest . . ."

to enjoy popularity in England. The macabre octopus has a tenacious hold on the European palate, but the shark is still the Cinderella of seafood. On reflection it is odd that no taboo seems to inhibit the average Australian's taste for this fish, since it has played a grisly role in our history and the presence of multiple amputees in our city streets bears vivid testimony to the shark's reciprocal taste for human Austral flesh.

The groper fish is not enjoyed outside Australia, one surmises, because it is unknown in other waters. In *Mrs Beeton's Australian Cookery*, published last century, there is a delicious recipe for Boiled Groper, from which I quote: "Serve with parsley or any other fish sauce. Great care should be taken of the immense gelatinous lips, as these are considered the best part. In serving, a portion should be given with each helping." When there's a groper for dinner, cook can give as much lip as she likes.

One may be less lavish with braised terrapin, however, and in the same volume Mrs Beeton recommends that after the animal has been boiled its " . . . liver, gall and sand-bag *must* be taken away . . .". Odd that Australians should be deprived of a terrapin's sand-bag, which in other lands is doubtlessly regarded as a tasty, if abrasive, morsel. A rare blend of delicatessen and dentifrice.

But if one man's groper is another man's sand-bag, the consumption of human flesh is prohibited by a taboo which is as potent in England as in its dominions, with the exception of isolated cases in New Zealand and Canada. Long-pig rarely makes the white man salivate, except on very long and arduous excursions, and only when it is made very clear to the unfortunate travellers involved that they really *are* down to the last leg of their journey.

So much for the dietary caprices of healthy humans. Taboos being what they are, I cannot, in this essay, probe too deeply into the debased appetites of the coprophrage, or self-sufficient. Somewhere in the Bible Isiah alludes to loathsome practices of this sort, and elsewhere perhaps, Krafft-Ebbing documents these gourmets of the cess-pit who, were it not for psycho-analysis, might have popularised their vile discoveries and closed every restaurant in Vienna.

It is true that lobsters, those most succulent of all marine insects, thrive in excremental waters, and the finest clams sup on the unspeakable; indeed, the undrinkable. In ancient Egypt the scarab, or dung-beetle, was a talisman of good fortune, so we may deduce that these delicacies were never served without an accompaniment of pungent sauces.

From America comes the exciting news that a large agricultural company has introduced a new method of feeding cattle on their own manure. Free of condiments and other spices with which man is wont to camouflage his scarabs and his *moules napolitaines crues*, this remarkable new fodder neither looks or smells like manure, ". . . it looks like green sawdust or a powdery grey concentrate." For a manure menu, this certainly looks appetising for starters. Confronted with this bill of fare, the livestock of America will soon be bending over backwards to place their orders.

"The stuff is beautiful, but I know it'd be just too butch for me."

The Furry Male

With man firmly established as the furrier sex, QUENTIN BLAKE casts an eye over some of the wilder fringes

"What a bit of luck! It's a perfect match."

"Just a little higher and to the left."

"Plastic moths! Just how phoney can you get?"

"Can't sleep at night . . . worried about the office . . .
now he's started moulting."

"I suppose we could send out for some
carpet shampoo . . ."

The notorious one-time gaol of Alcatraz in San Francisco Bay is being thrown open to tourists. It's the thin edge of an exciting wedge . . .

Her Majesty's Prison Service offers . . .

THE
OF A
FOR A

FOR years people have been saying that life in British prisons is nothing but a pampered holiday, a refuge of luxury and indolence far removed from the stresses of the rat-race.

They are absolutely right !

Now that Wormwood Scrubs, Parkhurst, Albany and other legendary coolers have been released for tourist purposes, you can test out their delights for yourself.

We have tried to preserve as much of the prison atmosphere as possible. For as little as £29 you can enjoy a winter mini-holiday on bracing Dartmoor. For no more than £10,000, at the age of sixty, you can "sentence" yourself to a life stretch in storied Pentonville, an enclave of peace deep in the Concrete Jungle.

Why go to the Costa Brava, and risk a Spanish gaol, when your travel agent can book you overnight into frowning Barlinnie, with a free hair-cut thrown in ?

Life is never dull in a British gaol. If you are the hearty type, who must always be up and doing, why not try one of our tunnelling contests, armed only with a sharpened spoon ?

Or pit your wits against a brace of eager bloodhounds, out there on the lonely swamps.

If you are the withdrawn, quiet type, our solitary confinement cells are ideal for meditation. Their rigours exceed anything to be found in the caves of Tibet.

Tease yourself by trying one of our Open Prisons. You will never want to leave !

A gaol holiday is a perfect respite from family, Watergate, Robin Day and every kind of annoyance. The chances are you will find an Exercise Wheel, modelled on the old-time treadmill which kept our forebears healthy. If not, learn to shuffle round the Exercise Yard in single file, smoking surreptitious fags—it's like the conga, but much less wearing.

REMEMBER :

Only in gaol can you be sure of receiving visits from titled ladies.

Only in gaol can you be sure of a hospital bed.

Only in gaol do you have a psychiatrist on constant call.

Naturally, we require something from you in return. Say, a few hours in the prison laundry every day, or a brisk session of mail-bag stitching five or six times a week. And, of course, you will carry out your slops in the morning.

Is that too much to ask ?

HOLIDAY LIFETIME... LIFETIME!*

YOUR OBJECTIONS ANSWERED

Q. Why should I spend fourteen days cooped up with total strangers in a small steel cell into which daylight never enters ?
A. You pay £20 a day to do that on a cruise. At Dartmoor it costs you far less and your cellmates are not being sick in bags all the time.

Q. I am told that in prison people stab and strangle each other in disputes over which television programme to watch. Is this true ?
A. Yes, but it happens just as often in boarding-houses.

Q. Why should I allow myself to be ordered about all day by loud-mouthed disciplinarians ?
A. You will find the prison regime distinctly more relaxing than that of a holiday camp.

Q. How can I be expected to pick oakum when I don't even know what it is ?
A. We have ways of teaching you things.

Q. If my wife visits me, can I be forced to exercise my conjugal rights ?
A. No. You come to us for a complete change. If you wish, you will be able to joke with your wife through a mesh partition, as in the cartoons.

Q. Is it true that difficult guests are put on bread and water ?
A. Yes; but at a health farm you would get only an orange a day.

Q. Are there any organised excursions to places of interest ?
A. Yes, to the quarries for light recreation daily, at eight a.m. sharp.

Q. Must I make my own bed ?
A What bed ?

SOME SPECIAL ATTRACTIONS

READING GAOL: Have you literary gifts ? Write your own ''Ballad of Reading Gaol'' and compete for the Oscar Wilde Solid Pewter Cup. All the fun of an Eisteddfod without the Welsh.

BRIXTON REMAND WING: A holiday for the gourmet ! While staying here you enjoy the privilege of sending out to neighbouring hostelries for *pâté*, caviare, choice wines and all the other delicacies favoured by the rich embezzler having his last fling. If you have never drunk port wine from a mess tin, start now.

HOLLOWAY: ''A well-filled guest never complains'' is the slogan of Holloway. Its dedicated staff stand by to force-feed finicky women guests, as they once force-fed the Suffragettes.

LONG KESH: If you have a touch of the bigot about you—and who hasn't ?—why not strut for a week or two, or a year or two, behind the wires of this notorious compound, whose every stone is steeped in the bile of frustrated martyrs ?

---

* Or for seven days—it's up to you.

LIBERAL LINE-UP

The Liberal Party, always mindful of the appeal of the well-known personality (vide Ludo Kennedy, Robin Day) are cock-a-hoop that their policy has at last paid off in the persona of Clement Freud. Now Des Wilson has been roped in for Hove, and there is no dearth of other media men wanting to get in on the act.

HORNER is able to reveal some candidates still to be named

The Rt. Hon. member for Huyton will be up-staged by a fellow-North-countryman, fellow Pipeman-of-the-year with an even better sense of timing.

The Chancellor will be challenged by a disenchanted former Labour Stalwart with a shrewd head for figures.

Ardwick, Blackley, Cheetham, Moss Side—he can choose his own seat, all Manchester is at his feet.

The Minister for Aerospace will be eclipsed by one even trendier, shaggier, and with the edge in technology.

But there is a limit to the cult of personality—there is no truth in the rumour that a former disaffected Tory will be challenging the member for Wolverhampton, S.W.

I'll Sing Thee Songs of Araby

"Who was the Arab who disrupted the Stock Exchange last week?" cried Fleet Street. "Just a casual visitor", replied the Stock Exchange. "Oh, really?" asks SHAIKH ALAN COREN

AT 10.43 a.m., on Monday, January 14, 1974, the London Stock Exchange came to a halt. Who knows what fortunes faltered in those short seconds while the attention of the hundreds of dealers upon the floor was called elsewhere, what rough winds shook the darling buds of sterling, what ramifications rippled through the Western capitalist world, and, indeed, beyond? Some who were there likened the strange time to those fearful October moments in 1929 when Wall Street turned into Queer Street: uncertainty first, then disbelief, then hysteria, then . . .

That night, the *Evening News* put it succinctly: "An Arab visitor appeared briefly in the Visitors' Gallery. The man, swathed in traditional burnous and djellaba, watched impassively as dealers cried 'Give us oil!' Who was he? 'Just a casual visitor', says the Stock Exchange."

Nor, upon the following morning, could *The Times* shed much more light on this bizarre affair, despite an increase in both the finer details and the literary elegance: "An Arab shaikh appeared on the Stock Exchange visitors' gallery yesterday morning to see how western capitalism operates. With his entourage of chauffeur and personal photographer, and in flowing Arab robes, he was soon recognised and a chorus of boos arose from the trading floor. He left hurriedly, but according to the Stock Exchange information service, calmly. Another £500m of foreign investment lost forever?"

Not quite. The £500m is safe; but no thanks to the baying, middle-aged schoolboys hurling their insults up from the centre of Britain's economic structure, or, as some might currently put it, collapse. The fact being that while the Arab shaikh in question was soon recognised, he was not soon recognised at all. For beneath those flowing robes was none other than—— but let us begin at the beginning . . .

Our story opens, effendis, a few days earlier, with a four-year-old boy shrieking the panes from the windows in a normally tranquil London abode.

"Mummy, mummy, there's a filthy old man in a sheet in your bathroom!"

Whereupon the patter of two feet becomes the patter of four.

"God Almighty!" said his mother.

"You are to me like the new moon over the wadi, like the fresh date from the green palm," I murmured, "like the . . ."

"It's only your father," said his mother.

"What's that stuff growing all over his face?"

"What's that stuff growing all over your face?"

"There is nothing growing all over my face. What you are looking at is a gummed beard."

"What's he got a sheet on for?"

"What have you got a sheet on for?"

I walked again before the mirror, stately and slow.

"Sheet?" I said. I curled a lip, expertly. I did not sit through three hours of *Khartoum* for nothing. "These happen to be the dress robes of an Arabian shaikh, as worn by ace BBC bit-players, whence they were scrounged. It is my intention to spend the next few days strolling the streets of the Metropolis and

"... an Arab visitor appeared briefly in the Visitors' Gallery ..." *Evening News*

gauging public opinion. I am sick and tired of Fleet Street hacks telling me that the great British public hates the Arabs, or loves the Arabs, or does not give a toss for the Arabs! I aim to see for myself."

"*What's* he doing?"

"He's asking for a poke in the conk, darling," she explained.

"Is it Daddy's work?"

"That's what he calls it."

"Jeremy's daddy's a chemical engineer. He goes out in a suit."

"It wouldn't do if we were all alike," she lied.

"I nearly din't stop," said the cab-driver.

"I'm sorry?" I murmured.

He shoved the partition back a few more inches, and shouted, as one does with foreigners.

"NEARLY DIN'T STOP," he yelled. "Know what I mean?"

"Not exactly," I intoned. I had debated the question of a forged accent, but had decided, a fair number of Arab luminaries having left their engravings on the desk-lids of Harrow and Sandhurst, that a dignified *sotto voce* would sound as authentic as anything else. To the heavy beard and the hand-embroidered coveralls, I had added a quite legitimate, indeed characteristic, pair of dark specs, so that the blue eyes would be concealed, along with most of a skin unburnished by desert suns. Such pallor as remained visible, I hoped, might pass for the by-product of an over-enthusiastic harem. As events were to transpire, no-one ever gave it a second look, having seen everything they believed they had seen at the gawping first. Which would lead us into some very sober reflections about appearances and stereotyping, if we had time to indulge in moral speculation; which, fortunately, we haven't.

"Werl," said the cab-driver, "you can't expect your, er, people to be popular, exactly, can you? I mean, some might say—I'm not saying I do—that the Israelis should've gorn in and finished you off. Might even say *we* should've finished what we started at Suez, know what I mean? Instead of queuing up for two gallons here and two gallons there, and no telly after half-past bloody ten, am I right?"

"It could also be argued," I murmured, "that the oil happens to be our oil, under our land. I would not dream of insisting that you should not be allowed to sell your house when you wanted to, at whatever price you choose to fix."

He thought for a while. A few cars passed us, and a V-sign or two was flashed hospitably at me.

"Yes, werl, I wun't know about all that, I don't get involved in politics, do I? All I know is, what's right's right, and what's wrong's wrong." He paused, suddenly, and turned around. "I'm not Jewish, in case you were wondering," he said.

"I was not."

"Only a lot of people think all cab-drivers are Jews," he said. "I'm not biased against you people. I'm not prejudiced at all. As a matter of fact, it's my personal opinion the Jews would've been a bloody sight worse if they *had* got their hands on the oil. Money, money, money, know what I mean?" He waved a hand to indicate Golders Green Road, down which we were passing. "They all live down here, you know. As a matter of, you know, fact, I thought it was a bit funny you wanting 111, Golders Green Road. I thought: they'll have him, and no mistake! What is it?"

"Cohen's Smoked Salmon Ltd.," I said.

"*What?*"

"There it is," I pointed.

We stopped, and I got out, and paid while he goggled, and I went into the delicatessen. Which, you're no doubt thinking, was a rather silly and a rather provocative thing to do, and just the sort of facetious-minded trick a journalist would pull to get copy. And perhaps it is; but if the object is to elicit response and reaction, one must also not dodge

"... to stack an extra odd or two in my favour, I borrowed a Rolls-Royce and ..."

"...and before I could stop him, one of the PC's pressed the magic doorbell, the door opened, and a footman..."

extremes. Especially when the result is so curious.

"*Is there any point to which you would wish to draw my attention?*"

"*To the curious incident of the dog in the night-time.*"

"*The dog did nothing in the night-time.*"

"*That was the curious incident,*" remarked Sherlock Holmes.

The great detective should have been in Cohen's last week.

I walked to the salmon counter.

"A quarter-pound of the eighty pence," I said, "please."

"I'll start a new salmon," said the assistant. "I'm getting to the brown on this one."

"Thank you."

"Funny thing, people don't like the brown. Personally, I think it's the tastiest bit. Also the most nourishing."

"People are funny," I murmured in my beard.

"Believe me," said the assistant. He finished the delicate slicing. "Anything else, sir?"

I shook my head, and took my paper bag, and of the thirty-odd people in the shop, perhaps half a dozen gave me a second glance, and at least as many smiled. There was no nudging; and the manager opened the door for me.

Now, let us not be too naive. Everyone was fairly clearly on their best behaviour. But it is also true that there is a wide range of other behaviour for people to be on, should they choose.

Ribald, I think, is the word for the mood at the Blue Star Garage on Finchley Road.

I sat in the queue, in a large Mercedes. A man in a Marina in front of me watched me in his mirror for as long as he could stand it, then got out and walked over.

"You delivering, then?" he said.

Fortunately, the frightful gumming of the beard held my face intact. Shaikhs don't break up and roll about at jests.

"Seriously," he said, "seriously, I blame the oil companies. They screw everybody. Serve 'em right if we all went back to bloody horses. Or camels!" He threw his head back, and roared. "Camels! Get it?"

"What did he say?" cried a head poking out of the Cortina behind.

"It was me, I said he'll be back on his camel if this keeps up!"

The Cortina head shrieked.

"Don't mind me," said the Marina, "no offence, I'm a bit of a humorist, well, you know how it is on the road, I'm in builders' sundries."

"None taken," I said. "I am a bit of a humorist myself."

"'Course you are, 'course you are," said the Marina. "Well, you have to be, these days."

A mile further down Finchley Road, I swept into the Duke of York public house. It was lunchtime, and the place was full of labourers. But instead of uproar, there was, once again, a ripple of grinning, a polite whisper or two, and the sort of gentle banter to which none could take exception. Like the barman's slight bow, and

"Salaam, squire!"

"Salaam," I replied. "May I have an orange juice?"

"One orange juice," he said, snapping the crown cap. "Pity you blokes don't drink. You don't know what you're missing."

And beside me, an Irish navvy in a green slipover and a paint-splotched cap looked slowly up at him from his pint, and said:

"He'd like *your* stuff, mate. It tastes like bloody petrol."

For two more days, slipping gradually deeper into my new persona, such is the seduction of disguise and play, I did the town from Simpsons to Harrods, from Soho strip-joint to Queensway casino, flash neighbourhoods to council estates, white areas and immigrant. And it has to be reported that the average Englishman is a polite, generous, fairly incurious soul, whose worst excesses (we're talking of behaviour, here, not of what may lie deeper beneath it) are ignorance and a tendency to think in music-hall stereotypes and react with music-hall dialogue.

He is also incredibly gullible. One has only to appear plausible to be plauded. And that goes for more than just the average Briton, too. By Monday, I was ready to take on the expert.

To stack an extra odd or two in my favour, I borrowed a Rolls-Royce and its chauffeur (and a photographer; *The Times* misses nothing), and our first stop was Number Ten, Downing Street. Which turned out to have steel barricades across its entry, manned by a constable. Security being all.

We drove up to the said steel mesh, and the constable peered inside the car, and saluted, and let us through. He asked nothing. We pulled up at the PM's door, and two constables stepped forward. I am twigged, I thought. They saluted, wordless. The chauffeur opened my door, I got out, and before I could stop him, one of the PC's pressed the magic doorbell, the door opened, and a footman appeared, to usher me in.

It was at this point that I decided enough was enough, I had no wish for a long murmuring chat with the PM about smoked salmon, or the quality of keg bitter, much as we both might have enjoyed it.

"I wish merely for the souvenir photograph," I explained.

"Oh," said the handpicked security men, who had not even frisked me for the small automatic I might have placed behind the footman's ear once the door had closed, with a view to bigger game later.

Whereupon the shutter clicked, and we drove out again, and no-one ever thought to ask who this Arab was, or up to what he might have been.

Which brings us (we Eastern story-tellers have an instinct sense of unity and composition) to the Stock Exchange.

The Rolls discharged me, and I billowed in, and up to the Visitors' Gallery, and a young woman led me to the great glass panel that separates the lowly outsider from the financial wizards, peers of the fiduciary earth, who toil on the floor below. Great men, in whose capable hands this island's economic destiny is juggled, men of pith, integrity, wisdom and maturity.

One by one, these pecuniary paragons looked up; they nudged; they beckoned; they strode forward; they gathered. And, in a huge and univocal mob, they began to bay.

"Out! Out! Out!" they screamed. "Oil! Oil! Oil!"

And it was not at all funny. Even if the action was promoted by a misguided sense of humour, there can, I promise, be no doubting the end result of its ugliness and its offensive puerility. Which was, staggeringly, capped by the young woman's coming over to me and asking me to leave because I was "disturbing the members". They have a warm and winning way with guests, at the Exchange.

So I left. And had I been a Gulf shaikh, as sensitive to insult as Gulf shaikhs are?

Still, you know me, friends. Always end on an up-beat note, leave us not add to the tally of despair. There were less than a thousand on the Stock Exchange floor, and they had proved themselves to be atypical of the rest of London.

Although it has to be recorded that they would have been somewhat more significant than the rest of London, in what might easily have been the circumstances.

Teach us, O Lord, to bear the yoke–
For this is getting past a joke

Kipling's Barrack-Room Ballads have just been reissued, but that's not good enough. In these dark days we want to hear Kipling in recessional mood, Kipling on our failing fibre, Kipling on the nation's future, if any. E. S. TURNER has been through to the Master, on a private line.

"What are the bugles blowin' for?" said Private Lie-Abed.
"Come on, then, let's be 'avin' you!" the Colour Sergeant said.
"For Centre Point has fallen and the mob cries 'Good old Ted!'"
　An' they're hangin' 'Arry Hyams in the mornin'.

For they're hangin' 'Arry Hyams, you can 'ear the Dead March play.
The GLC's in 'ollow square—it's 'Arry's Judgment Day,
They've stripped 'is millions off 'im and they've took 'is yachts away,
　An' they're hangin' 'Arry Hyams in the mornin'.

*　　*　　　*　　*　　　*

'Ave you 'eard of the Sov'rin at Windsor,
　With a hairy gold crown on 'er 'ead?
She 'as run out of coal, she 'as kids on the dole,
　An' 'er 'orses are bloomin' well dead.

'Ave you 'eard of the Sov'rin at Windsor,
　With a hairy round orb in 'er 'and?
She just sits in the dark and the corgis all bark,
　An' she can't raise a tune from 'er band.

She is weary of wielding the sceptre,
　While 'er chamberlains 'iss in 'er ear.
O the things she has said both to 'Arold and Ted,
　They would shock you for many a year.

So 'ere's to the Sov'rin at Windsor,
　A Monarch of uttermost fame.
She 'asn't the sway what she 'ad yesterday,
　But mind 'ow you go, just the same.

*　　*　　　*　　*　　　*

The 'eathen in his blindness bows down to wood and stone.
A lot of good we've done 'im, for 'is 'ead is solid bone.
Give up the White Man's burden, pull out from 'eathen soil,
And altogether now, lads, bow down to coal and oil!

Land of our birth, we pledge to thee
To toil like ticks through the years to be,
Within the guide-lines as laid down
For shuttered shops and blacked-out town.

Teach us to add by candlelight,
Although we lose both sense and sight,
While holy Shahs and Sheikhs devise
The rules by which the nation dies.

Teach us to bear the yoke in grace,
Survivors of a master race,
That we may leave to some far age
A shred or two of heritage.

Throughout the anti-growth to come
Maintain us loyal, blind and dumb.
Now to hear us as we pledge to thee
Transcendent ardour for Stage Three.

*　　*　　　*　　*　　　*

If England was what England seems—
A sorry mess of thwarted dreams,
A nation that has lost its fizz,
How soon we'd quit her . . .

but she is!

*　　*　　　*　　*　　　*

O where are you going to, all you Big Tankers,
　With all that scarce oil, up and down the salt seas?
We are selling it off to the highest of bidders,
　And nobody cares very much if you freeze.

For the homes that you heat and the cars that you coddle,
　The signs that say "Sssssch . . ." and the mikes that go
　eeeeeeek,
They'll none of them function without us Big Tankers.
　We'd just as soon sell to Onassis the Greek.

O the Channel's as bare as a bottom already,
　And pilots are scarcer than yetis at Kew.
Come back, you Big Tankers!—Too late have you left it!
　Remember your coal mines. Get down there and hew!

"Stupid idiot! That mare could have broken a leg."

A God Called Horse

by THELWELL

" You little beast—you've been eating Tonto's peppermint creams."

"Catch the rope, Alice, catch the rope and tie it firmly round his neck."

"Keep calm, woman—you're making him nervous."

"I don't think I'd mind so much if it was another woman."

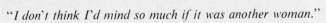

"Alison! *I think he wants a drink of water."*

The Second Homes of England

PAUL CALLAN
and MICHAEL HEATH echo the boom

Of late, I detect that the meaning of the second home is no longer the breathless search for a little place in the country—a Dulux-ed, Mateus-Roséd, Advertising Executive's Paradise. It is more sophisticated, more artful: it has become the second home in London.

Here, the essential man pares down his soul, surrounds himself with his own needs, is single-minded, the errant philosopher-vagabond, the unimpaired spirit. Or to put it another way, he has found himself a gaff away from the wife and kids, where he can get loaded in peace and even take the occasional bird, if necessary.

The character of Second-Home Man becomes quite transformed the moment he leaves first base. The alter ego leaps up to the surface.

Take the case of a highly successful barrister, I know. Call him A, as Edgar Lustgarten might put it. At weekends A is everything he seems: domestically attentive, slightly pompous, part of the local Tory Serfdom and all Old-Trousers-And-Two-Pints-On-A-Sunday.

But on those nights he cannot commute home—"Hello darling, I'll have to stay up for a couple of nights. It's a damned tricky case"—he becomes quite transformed.

"Never knew you liked Dizzy Gillespie," you remark on entering A's private world (a large flat off the Brompton Road) and staring up in mild amazement at a life-sized poster of the great trumpeter.

"Yes, well . . . we tend to adhere to some Palestrina and much Mahler 'down there'," he says dishing out a gin and tonic far more generous in size to any ever offered "down there".

I note that his old college oar, a beautiful, yellow tribute to an unflabby youth, stretches along a wall. "Somehow," he mutters, as I examine it and ponder on the whereabouts of all those coxless fours, "we didn't feel it fitted in with the Habitat curtains and the Finnish dining table. It didn't look right down there."

The furniture has that special sprawled-upon look, instant ease, with a tie draped just too casually over the back of the sofa and a sock that had happened along in the corner of the room.

It was as though, in an act of unconscious deliberation, they had been placed there as a tribute to bachelorhood.

Second-Home Man's concept of food is definitely Proustian: a clear case of Recherche de Fry-Ups Perdus.

It is not that he does not love his wife's cooking—or, indeed, his wife (a buoyant little brunette who looks like Googie Withers)—but the rules of the

"Being a developer—I developed the cottage."

game demand this kind of culinary preference. His taste buds may have been caressed by Robert Carrier and Elizabeth David down there ("Diana's boeuf strogonoff caused a sensation when we had the Matlocks down for the weekend"); here Vesta Prawn Curry is King.

Then, at precisely 10.05 p.m., comes the half-expected cry. "Good God old man, there's only 55 minutes drinking time left. Let's buzz round to the Lamb's Elbow and water the old epiglottis." I detect the self-conscious and desperate tones of false jollity.

Thus it is that we slurp at our pressurised beer, indulge in mild ogling at the sort of girls who call their fathers "Daddy", and murmur, well Enoch Powell does have a point. A garrulous gloom is setting in.

For A, being nudged by the spectre of middle-age, this second-property escape route, is making him happy enough.

But when we return for that final quick one, the telephone rings. "Hello darling" he yells, "how are you?" (It is down there calling up here.) "What about Matthew's tooth? He did what? I'll deal with it tomorrow . . . yes, I'll make the 6.45 easily. Oh, not much. Just a few drinks with old Callan. Callan—you remember . . . yes, that one . . .".

Somehow, I felt that there was more than a hint of relief in the voice of Independent Man.

But what of the reverse side of this extra property mirror? Those seekers of the Once-A-Week-Rural-Scene; or what the people of the little Sussex village

"We only come here weekends—we've got a bomb site in the City the rest of the week."

where I maintain a house meaningfully term as "Them".

Since I have been there long enough to qualify as "Us", I can just about judge "Them" with some objectivity. And having dissected A, let us consider B.

He is a young (37-ish) accountant, successful, possibly rather too good-looking, with a wife called something like Penny and the sort of children (horrific names—Ragnar, Kristin) who could appear on Heinz Baked Beans commercials with foul ease.

Every weekend B packs the whole crew into the Volvo estate car (what else?), leaving Penny's mini parked outside the house in Camden Town. They beetle down to the cottage—a beamed, low-ceilinged job, with a stone floor, wide, yawning fireplace (a must, a must) and an unkempt Amazonian garden for the children to vanish into.

They were damned lucky to get it, what with the

"I thought I'd buy a second home when I retired so I bought this place."

prices and all that. They are also "doing it up". And it is here that this particular brand of the Double-Residential—the Home Countryman, or Mix Your Own Yeoman Stock—first exposes itself.

For, however comfortably B lives in his blonde-furnitured, eye-level-grilled and water-bedded home in London, here he and his family unit seem willing to put up with the kind of discomfort that peasant farmers revolted over at the height of the Agricultural Revolution.

They seem to find nothing but joy in the rigours of the Elsan loo. And Penny, bless her, really thinks that lamb chops actually taste better for being cooked on a gas stove of variable flame-height and of great age.

Even B's drinking habits seemed affected by this move to Summer County. On Sunday morning they all zoom off to the village pub, an oddly-run affair which has the dubious distinction of having been visited by disparate Tudor monarchs.

Occasionally accompanied by similarly-attired friends from London—St. Tropez flared trousers, hugging shirts, John Lennon hats optional—he hurls himself into pints of bladder-damaging "local filth, old chap".

The locals themselves (a melange of inter-breeding across the centuries) sip steadily at Campari and Soda and "'er usual Tia Maria, please." It is a stunning reversal of roles, each section of this polarised community in some way playing one another.

"You mean you've forgotten to turn the gas off but can't remember which house!"

B and family even turned up the other weekend at the local Tory fete where he was a shade too successful at the hoop-la—and she bought rather too many locally-made jams ("Magnus and Veronica would love the green fig . . .").

And so it goes on, like property speculating itself. The second home gives birth to the second man.

As for me, I'm into the Third Property World: a darling little place in the back streets of the Gorbals, it's so ethnic, so close to the real people, and . . .

"Weekend squatters!"

How Patriotic Are You?

asks E. S. TURNER

1. Which of these do you regard as the prime duty of a patriot :
   (a) to share your bath water ;
   (b) to send threatening letters to Willie Hamilton MP ;
   (c) to make your own Châteauneuf du Pape from grass clippings ;
   (d) to encourage your children to send toffees to Princess Anne ;
   (e) to keep bloody foreigners out.

2. Talking of bath water, would you share your bath with :
   (a) reluctance ;
   (b) a couple of Afghan wolf-hounds ;
   (c) Miss World ;
   (d) Joe Gormley and his Executive ;
   (e) any good Tory ;
   (f) just about anybody.

3. Do you display the Union Jack :
   (a) tattooed on your chest ;
   (b) tattooed on any other part ;
   (c) on your flagpole ;
   (d) on the left buttock of your jeans ;
   (e) on the right buttock of your jeans ;
   (f) on both buttocks of your jeans.

4. You have been invited to dinner by a neighbour who makes a rich living speculating against the Pound. Do you :
   (a) refuse indignantly ;
   (b) refuse, and daub his walls with "Traitor" ;
   (c) accept, and maintain a frigid silence all evening ;
   (d) accept, and ask him how he does it.

5. Your wife wants you to put up shelves in the kitchen. You refuse, saying it is unpatriotic to use a power drill. She retaliates by refusing to grill you a chop. Would you proceed to :
   (a) order her to beat the carpets with a hand beater ;
   (b) bawl out your child for using his electric train set ;
   (c) bawl out your daughter for using a hair dryer ;
   (d) bawl out your eldest son for taking the last two toilet rolls to a football match ;
   (e) walk out on the lot of them.

6. The selfish Robinsons sit up reading every night until one a.m., or, if they're not reading, you'd like to know what they *are* doing. Would you :
   (a) pray to God to smite them ;
   (b) drive a pick-axe through their power main ;
   (c) refuse to lend them the mower ever again ;
   (d) complain to Lord Energy, whoever he may be.

7. Your 1960 limousine does only 15 miles to the gallon. Would you :
   (a) use your wife's Rover and let her walk ;
   (b) use your daughter's Mini and let her walk ;
   (c) borrow £3,500 from the bank and buy a 30 m.p.g. Swedish car ;
   (d) order a 45 m.p.g. British car for £1,999, available in eighteen months ;
   (e) take roller-skating lessons.

8. You have just remembered that you cheated the Income Tax of £50 forty years ago. Would you :
   (a) send Mr. Barber £50 Conscience Money ;
   (b) send Mr. Barber £50 plus 5% annual interest ;
   (c) send Mr. Barber 50p., "From a Repentant Sinner" ;
   (d) try to cheat the tax-man of another £50.

9. You happen to know that if the aged Duke of Bristol lives another seven days the State will lose £5,000,000 inheritance duties. Would you :
   (a) let Nature take its course ;
   (b) ring him up and say "Drop dead" ;
   (c) send him a letter-bomb, by first-class mail ;
   (d) send him some new books on D. H. Lawrence that will bore him to death.

10. Over the years you have lost £2,500 in Government War Loan and are still waiting for your Post-War Credits. The Government now urges you to hand over more of your savings, promising that it will be different this time. Would you :
    (a) send them all you've got, saying you have no hard feelings ;
    (b) send them all you've got, saying money will soon be useless anyway ;
    (c) send them £2 and see what they do with it ;
    (d) ignore them, and try to corner toilet rolls.

11. You occupy a house in which fifty per cent of the heat is wasted through the windows and fifty per cent through the roof, while another eighty per cent goes up the chimney. Would you :
    (a) turn up the thermostat, saying "To hell with economy" ;
    (b) turn off the heating and go to the cinema ;
    (c) use your wife's savings for double glazing and loft insulation.

12. On a last bus you are sitting behind two Americans who are saying that Britain is well down the drain this time. Would you :
    (a) stop the bus and strand them in some blacked-out suburb ;
    (b) say "Too right, mate" and cadge a cigarette ;
    (c) light the cigarette and stealthily burn holes in their clothing ;
    (d) initiate a full and frank discussion about Watergate.

Answers:
You are a good patriot if your answers coincide with those given below :
1. All of them. **2.** (f). **3.** (a) or (c). **4.** (a) or (b). **5.** All of them. **6.** (a). **7.** (a), (b) or (e). **8.** (b). **9.** (c) or (d). **10.** (a) or (b). **11.** (b) or (c). **12.** (a) or (d).

"They have a long tradition of brutality—this torture was perfected on the playing fields of Eton."

FALL IN, JERRIES!

The Germans don't like the BBC's Colditz series but they should be happier with the next one, set in a British POW camp. MAHOOD gives a preview.

"So far so good, Heinrich, all we have to fear now is being ravished by sex-starved Yanks."

"It's not RAF influence—Fritz needs it to gauge the width of his tunnel."

"Nein, nein! Mein Gott, Captain Smythe-Fosdyke, NOT ZE VERA LYNN AGAIN!"

"Brilliant, men! In their national costume you will be unobtrusive in any crowd!"

Alf Garnett was first adapted by American TV.
Now German television has its own version.
Next—Russia . . . . . ?

"Till Siberia Us Do Part"

by MILES KINGTON

THE living room of the Garnovs. Ilf Garnov is sitting in the big chair, reading Pravda. Mrs. Garnov is ironing. Their daughter, Nina, is ironing.

Ilf: (looking up) I'm trying to read the paper. (No answer). I said, I'm trying to read the paper. (No answer). 'Ave you ever tried to read the paper in the middle of a bleeding steam foundry? Well, I 'ave, and with you two carrying on like bleeding steam hammers, it's like trying to read *War And Peace* while swimming a bleeding length in the outdoor pool built for us by the far-sighted Moscow Committee for Citizens' Recreation and Sport.

Mrs. Garnov: What is your complaint?

Ilf: I'm not complaining. I've got no grumbles. Life is great in this Socialist paradise. All I'm saying is, couldn't you iron more quietly?

Mrs. Garnov: No.

Ilf: Well, couldn't one of you stop ironing?

Mrs. Garnov: No. We are determined to over-fulfil our quota of domestic work. So belt up.

Ilf: Right, that settles it. I'm going in the next room.

Nina: We haven't got a next room.

Ilf: That settles it. I'm staying here.

The door opens and in comes the Garnov's son-in-law, Mikhail, carrying a large bundle of books. He and Nina exchange kisses, and he sits down.

Mikhail: Sorry I'm late from college.

Ilf: You 'aven't missed much. A mass demonstration of ironing by the women of Russia and no bloody supper till it's over.

Mrs. Garnov: Stop swearing, Ilf. It's not comradely.

Ilf: And it's not comradely to starve a man neither. What's for supper anyway?

Mrs. Garnov: Fish.

Ilf: Steamed and ironed, I suppose.

Mikhail: (sitting down) Anything in the paper, Dad?

Ilf: Usual rubbish. Another space project. They want to find out if Mars is still there or something.

Mikhail: You disapprove of the Soviet space programme?

Ilf: (hastily) No, course not. But *he* never bothered to send up rockets (pointing to portrait of Stalin on the wall) and what's good enough for him is good enough for me.

Mikhail: But Dad, we've made progress since Stalin's day. Things are different now.

Ilf: I'll say they are. Holding hands with the bleedin' Americans and no oranges in the shops— call that progress? Old Joe wouldn't have sat in the back row of the stalls with Henry flippin' Kissinger. He'd have wiped him off the face of the earth.

Mikhail: Any other news?

Ilf: Only that Alexander Solzhenitsyn hates his country with a pathological fury born of true treachery, and Moscow Dynamo lost again. Bleedin' cripples.

Mrs. Garnov: Well, they should drop him from the team, then.

Ilf: Who?

Mrs. Garnov: Solzhenitsyn.

Ilf: You stupid cow! He's not a footballer, he's a writer!

Mrs. Garnov: What's he doing playing for Moscow Dynamo, then?

Ilf: He's not, he . . . You tell her, Mikhail.

Mikhail: He writes books criticising Russia, Mum, and gets them printed abroad by our enemies. They are a bundle of lies and propaganda.

Ilf: 'Ow do you know? Stands to reason, you can't know; if they're not printed here, you haven't read them. Maybe he's got a point. Maybe he says in his books that you can't get oranges in the shops. Maybe he's stood out fearlessly and told the truth about Moscow Dynamo, that they're a load of old ladies who couldn't hit the back of the net with a machine gun. If we'd sent that lot into Czechoslovakia in 1968 they'd still be asking the way.

Nina: So you support an enemy of the country, do you, Dad?

Ilf: I'm not saying that. That's not what I said. What I said was, *if* he complains about the orange shortage, then I'm with him. Course, the whole trouble is the Jews.

Mikhail: How do you mean?

Ilf: Well, stands to reason, dunnit. They're keeping the oranges out of the shops, aren't they? Jews got a stranglehold on distribution, haven't they? Well, they're holding back the oranges, trying to wreck the economy so's we'll let them go to Israel.

Nina: I thought you said it was the Chinese.

Ilf: The Jews *and* the Chinese. How's the ironing coming on?

Mrs. Garnov: Very well, no thanks to you. Why don't you do something?

Ilf: I will. I will. I'll have a drink. (Goes to the cupboard). It's gone! Someone's been and gone and nicked the vodka! It's a bloody liberty, if

you'll pardon the phrase. Who's took it?

Mrs. Garnov: I 'ave.

Ilf: You what?

Mrs. Garnov: I took it for the cooking. We're having fish cooked in vodka tonight.

Ilf: You stupid git! That's a waste of good vodka, that is. What's the use of having good Russian vodka and then dropping cod in it? (Goes out to the kitchen).

Mrs. Garnov: Try and keep him off politics, will you, Mikhail? Talk about football if you must, but not politics (Ilf comes back).

Ilf: One glassful left—one glassful! What do I drink when that's finished? I'm going to look bloody stupid at supper, aren't I, raising a spoon of fish juice in the air and saying "Cheers"? I was saving that vodka just in case Russia won the World Cup.

Mikhail: Well, we won't now, will we, because we've withdrawn as a protest.

Ilf: Protest? Don't give me that. They withdrew because they knew we hadn't got a hope of beating Chile. All that rubbish about protesting against the Chileans using the stadium as a detention centre—blimey! modern footballers are used to bodies lying about the place. Don't tell me it would have worried them, dribbling past a few political prisoners. I'll tell you what it was, mate. We would have been murdered by Chile. Five nil. Russian

"She's washing her hair tonight."

52

football has gone to pot. You ask Solzhenitsyn—
he'll tell you. Now when Stalin was team manager ...

Mikhail: He wasn't team manager, Dad!

Ilf: Course he was. He was everything. He looked
after everything personally—football, defence, the
arts ...

Mikhail: ... prison camps, pogroms, massacres ...

Ilf: And why not? Got to weed out the rotten element,
'aven't you? Stands to reason. Russian football'd be
a sight better if we had a bit more savage reprisals.
Being shot at dawn does wonders for a man's
game, I'm telling you. Now, this present lot—
they're your actual layabouts aren't they? In the
old days it was just Joe Stalin standing up there on
the Kremlin walls watching the tanks go past,
waving to them because he knew them all
personally, see? but now there's fifty of them in a
line all standing stiff and solid and no-one daring
to take charge.

Mrs. Garnov: There's not fifty in a football team, is
there?

Ilf: I'm talking about the flaming government! The
Russian football team doesn't stand on the Kremlin
walls! They'd fall off if they did. It's the government
up there, hundreds of them, so far away you can't
see their faces. You wouldn't know if they were
Chinese, you wouldn't. Maybe they are at that.
Maybe the Chinese have taken over the government.
That would explain the shortage of oranges. They've
all gone to China. What are you writing there?

Mikhail: I'm ... I'm making some notes for my work.

Ilf: You're not writing one of those books, are you?

Mikhail: What books?

Ilf: You know. Scribble it out in an exercise book and
pass it from hand to hand. So's it doesn't get in
the hands of the government. Not that they'd
understand it, being Chinese. Then smuggle it out
to Paris, make a fortune, get the Nobel Prize.

Mrs. Garnov: 'Ow do you know about them?

Ilf: 'Cos I got one, ain't I? Chap down the committee
passed me one. Boring, if you ask me. Life in a
cancer ward. Blimey, you could write a more
exciting story about life in Moscow Dynamo
reserve team. Always assuming they got any.

Mikhail: Can I see it?

Ilf: All right, but don't read it at supper. Nothing
worse than a book smelling of fish. (Hands Mikhail
a book. Mikhail goes to the door and opens it).

Mikhail: Right, you can come and get him.

Two KGB men enter and pinion him, taking the book.

Mikhail: (referring to his notes) There will also be
charges of sedition, questioning the Russian space
effort, libelling the government, undermining the
national sports programme, nursing ambitions of
printing foreign propaganda and doubting the
cooking value of State vodka.

Ilf: You bloody moron! Them's not my beliefs! That
was what was in the script! I only *said* the words!

Mikhail: Your explanation will be considered at the
trial. Take him away. (He is taken away).

Mrs. Garnov: What do we do now?

Mikhail: We carry on with the show, which will
consist of my telling you about the new engineering
works in Pomsk. Our glorious comrades in Pomsk,
by heroic effort ...

THE END

NOT QUITE RIGHT FOR OUR LIST

Spiro Agnew, one time Vice-President of the United States, has written a novel, but who is going to publish it?

Dear Mr. Agnew,

We return your novel with regrets. It is our policy to publish books solely on the strength of their literary merit and/or sexual content, and we would not wish to be accused of cashing in on the public reputation of an author.

You might, however, care to submit your MS to our subsidiary Cully and Trull, which casts its net widely and has recently had a runaway success with some droll stories by Charles Manson.

Yours very truly,
ROD NERTZ
Editorial Director
GOPHER PRESS INC.

The Editor of ASTOUNDING FICTION presents his compliments and returns with thanks the enclosed MS, which is unacceptable for the reason ticked hereunder:

Not astounding enough	Probably an Irving hoax ✓
Too astounding	No four-letter words
Grammatically written	Has English spelling
Requires reader effort	Has trick ending

Dear Sir,

I regret the extensive dilapidations to your MS, which I now return with thanks.

Yours truly,
J. C. GLUCK
GLUCKBOOKS INC.

PS. Since the above was written, the MS can no longer be found. *No responsibility can be accepted for damage to, or loss of, any unsolicited MS.*

Dear Mr. Agnew,

Mr. Hefner asks me to thank you for letting him see the enclosed, but he says that PLAYBOY needs—and I quote—"something with a stronger philosophical content and a touch of logodaedaly (I hope that's spelled right) to run between the full frontals." I am sure you know what he means. Do drop in again next time you are in town.

Love,
LULU
Assistant to Hugh Hefner.

Dear Mr. Agnew,

I regret that by inadvertence the MS of Senator Sam Ervin's SAY IT AGAIN SAM was sent to you with a rejection slip instead of the MS of your novel.

It is probable that your novel has gone to Senator Ervin, or alternatively to the President, who also has a book of *pensées* going the rounds. This is something you will probably be able to sort out yourselves.

Assuring you of our best attention at all times.

Yours very truly,
ROD BLINDWURST
PRAIRIE PRESS INC.

Dear Sir,

I regret that your novel is not quite suitable for condensation in READER'S DIGEST.

We have, however, taken the liberty of lifting from page 115 the phrase "He wriggled palely away, as a tapeworm might shy from its sixth brunchburger" which we hope to use in our "Picturesque Speech and Patter" department. A cheque for $25 should be reaching you shortly.

We are always on the look-out for good fillers and pay generously for all we use.

Yours truly,
WALT GLUHEIM
Editorial Assistant
READER'S DIGEST

Dear Mr. Agnew,

Our Editorial Board have read your MS with great interest. Why don't you try your hand at a novel some time?

Yours sincerely,
LEW LEWIS
Editorial Director
VULTURE PRESS INC.

Dear Sir,

We will be happy to publish your novel, but let us have cash on the table first.

Our fees are: $5,000 payable by you on publication, followed by $250 every six months for life.

Yours truly,
J. C. CUSTER
VANITY BOOKS INC.

The Scenario Editor of Metro-Columbia-Paramount thanks you for submitting the enclosed, which is returned unopened in accordance with policy.

Sorry, old man — why not get yourself an agent?
—Jim

Dear Mr. Agnew,

We like the general idea of your novel, but feel that the central character—a lovable, unacquisitive, patriotic, Red-baiting, vice-president of the United States, with a gift for colourful alliteration—is too like a figment from Batman Comics. In these difficult times it is vital that all characters in high places should have feet of clay, otherwise we lift off into the realms of fantasy. We feel sure you will have no difficulty in making the vice-president a more scabrous, and therefore more credible, figure and will not need our editorial board to suggest ways in which this might be done.

When re-submitting, perhaps you will be good enough to give us your assurance that, if the novel is published, you will not sue yourself, or us, for libel.

Yours sincerely,
MILTON FLINT
Editor-in-Chief
PEEWIT PRESS INC.

Michael Parkinson

7 Go Easy on the Dressing

RECENTLY I was voted the seventh best dressed man in television which says little for the six above me and nothing whatsoever for those in 8th, 9th and 10th position. Being both colour-blind and impatient of shopping I make an unlikely candidate for any fashion contest. Truth be told, I never did get on with clothes, particularly hats.

While not being huge my head is certainly larger than the national average, a fact first remarked by my father who was constantly urging me as a child to fetch two stones of potatoes in it. The only hat I ever wore because I wanted to, as opposed to being obliged to, was a pearl grey snap-brimmed trilby. I was sixteen at the time and just starting work on a local newspaper. The hat was homage to my hero, Humphrey Bogart, who used to wear it in movies where he played a hard-boiled newsman forever cradling the phone under his chin and telling the boss to "Hold the front page!" I never did master the art of phoning without using my hands but I did manage to find a Bogey trilby to fit me. That I was sixteen, as frail and spotty as a stick of young rhubarb with greenfly, made no difference to my fantasy. I was Mike Parkinson, ace reporter, looking at a cynical world from under the brim of my trilby.

Attired thus, I cycled my daily beat on a rusty Raleigh, wearing trilby, Burton's raincoat and polythene bicycle clips. Fearlessly I reported the births and deaths, the soccer results, the whist drive winners, the visiting speakers at the local Methodist Church Bright Hour. Apart from suffering a certain amount of ridicule as I went my way about the pit village I discovered certain practical problems about wearing a trilby and riding a bike. The most obvious of these is keeping the trilby on your head, particularly when tearing downhill into a headwind. I therefore devised a simple chinstrap made from knicker elastic, making a unique headpiece. Sadly it failed. The first time I tried pedalling downhill into a headwind the trilby billowed backwards like a brake parachute and nearly took my head off. I sold the hat to our local bookie, who wore it at funerals. As I mentioned earlier, I am colour-blind and this has often caused me deep distress in matters sartorial.

Shortly after my escapade with the trilby and still within my Bogart fantasy period I entertained ambitions to become an actor. I enlisted in the local drama group and was given the lead in a production of *Captain Carvallo*. My sudden rise to stardom had nothing to do with my talent but with my size. The leading lady was 5 ft. 11 in. in her stockinged feet. I was the only member of the group who came anywhere near her. We presented the play at a local drama festival and I must say I thought I cut a dashing figure in dress uniform and Sam Browne, passionate in the clinches, suave in the comedy bits. The adjudicator praised everything about our production and saved me to the end. What he said was: "And now to Captain Carvello. A dashing romantic figure, or so the author intended him. As played by Mr. Parkinson he was less than the author intended and the illusion of glamour and romance would have been greatly enhanced had not the actor been wearing odd socks."

"First the good news. His temperature has gone down."

Formal dress, by which I mean getting all tarted up like a head waiter, has always been a source of embarrassment. The worst was the time I was working in Doncaster and found myself saddled with the job of organising secretary of the Press Ball. My intention was to organise the event and then resign on the eve of the ball which would prevent me having to hire or buy a dress suit.

This plan was scrapped when it was brought to my notice that organising secretaries were allowed free drinks all evening. My thirst got the better of my principles and I set out to get myself a suit. Being the last of the big spenders I decided I would buy one. I went into a shop in Doncaster, noted for its cheapness rather than its quality, and demanded a dress suit. One was brought and I tried the jacket. It was one of those huge double breasted affairs and I looked a bit like Dillinger. I couldn't bear to try the trousers.

"Wrap it up, I'll have it," I said with that negligent swagger which has so often been my downfall.

"What about the trousers?" said the man.

"They'll fit," I said.

I didn't meet my suit again until one hour before the Press Ball. I laid it carefully on the bed along with the shiny black dancing pumps I had borrowed from my girlfriend's father.

"You'll look devastating, Parky old son," I said to myself. I started whistling *You Were Never Lovelier* as I dressed.

It was then I suffered my first traumatic experience. I slipped into my trousers and found that the waistband came round my chest and that they would have accommodated at least three of my largest friends with some room to spare. They looked and felt ridiculous. Desperately I thought of a solution and rapidly came to the conclusion that there wasn't one, that the choice was very clear: either I went with the

trousers or I went without them.

Having decided to wear them I felt much better until I came to consider how I might hold them up. I did not possess a pair of braces, and finally solved the problem by tying a piece of string around the waist. This seemingly sensible move was complicated by the fact that the top of the trousers fitted around my chest and the string restricted my breathing. Nonetheless, resourceful fellow that I was, I managed to parcel myself up and headed for the press ball. When I got there the secretary of the committee, a very dear friend, said, "Christ, you look like a bag of worms tied in the middle."

I said, "That is approximately what I feel like."

Nonetheless by propping myself against the bar all evening, holding my trousers up with the counter, bending myself so that I camouflaged my ridiculous shape, I managed to survive with only the odd curious look and faint snigger.

I was congratulating myself on my presence of mind when I was approached by the editor's wife.

"It is time we danced," she said.

"Sorry, I don't speak English," I said, looking for a getaway.

She laughed. "Charming, funny boy," she said. "But we must dance because I so want to talk to you about all the hard work you have put in."

"But you see I'm tired. I've got severe cramp in both legs and I think I'm developing lockjaw," I said frantically.

"Silly boy," she said, as she dragged me on to the floor.

I do not propose to give you a detailed account of what followed. All I will ask you to imagine is the difficulty of dancing a quickstep with a large and elegant lady when one is wearing a large and drooping pair of trousers which had come adrift from their moorings.

I managed to survive by dancing very close to her and holding my pants up in that way. I think she liked it. She'd be horrified if she knew why I did it. I gave the suit away straight after the ball. The last time I saw it my old man was wearing it to get a ton of coal in.

Given all the aforementioned proof of a sartorial shambles, the question remains: how did I become the seventh best dressed man in television? It's no good looking to me for an answer. Indeed I offer my services to those who believe that television distorts the truth as living proof that the camera lies. The next time you see me on the box, remember that under the smart suit there is likely a yard of string holding up the trousers. It is more than possible that one sock is purple and the other white. And if you look closely you can see the marks the knicker elastic made all those years ago, everlasting evidence of my losing battle with the dictates of fashion.

"*You don't have to be so generous.*"

Bringing Them Back to Religion

by McMURTRY

"Godfrey—just how long can we afford to give everyone an apple, a balloon and a piece of cake when they leave?"

"Oh, I know it pulls in the crowds, but I still prefer the old baptisms."

"Okay, okay you win!—We'll come to church on Sundays if you stop ringing the bells all night."

"I don't believe I saw you in church on Sunday, Mr. and Mrs. Oakley."

EXCLUSIVE— FOUR UNPUBLISHED EARLY MASTERPIECES

Now thats it's becoming the fashion to dig out the juvenile works of famous writers, MILES KINGTON jumps on the bandwagon with a quartet of previously unknown works of genius

THE CASE OF THE MISSING NAVY

Conan Doyle's first story (age thirteen)

"What do you make of this, Watson?" said Holmes, throwing a paper dart at me across the room. I unfolded it and saw that it was a letter.

"It has a message of some sort written on it," I said. "Gosh! Is this a new case?"

"Read it and find out," said Holmes, filling his mouth full of the liquorice all-sorts which he always stuffed himself with when he was hot on the scent of another villain.

"WATSON IS GETTING TOO BIG FOR HIS BOOTS," it said. "WE SHALL GET HIM."

"Well," I said, "I would deduce that it has been written by someone who thinks that I am getting too big for my boots and they are going to get . . ."

At that moment the door burst open and in came Queen Victoria, the Prime Minister, the First Lord of the Admiralty and several crowned heads of Europe. They were all disguised.

"Please sit down . . . Your Majesty," said Holmes. "Have an all-sort."

The Queen gasped.

"You recognised me!"

Holmes smiled.

"I could not help noticing the little marks on your forehead, which can only be caused by a crown. Perhaps you have read my essay on 'Marks made by Hats'. You are not the Kaiser, therefore . . ."

They all gasped.

"Wow, you certainly have an incredible gift for deduction," said the Prime Minister. "But let us get on with the story. We are in great trouble, Mr. Holmes. The First Lord of the Admiralty has reported that the British Navy has vanished. If some German spy sneaks on us to the Kaiser, it could mean the end of civilisation as we know it, or at least it could mean the German Navy coming and shooting our holidaymakers."

"Have *all* the ships gone?" said Holmes to the First Lord of the Admiralty, his keen eyes (Holmes's eyes, I mean) looking out from under his keen eyebrows. "Even the Zeus class destroyers with twin fourteen-inch turrets?"

"Unfortunately are they all disappeared," said the First Lord. With one stride, and then another one, Holmes leapt forward and pulled the moustache, beard, spectacles, hat and false nose from his face.

"Gentlemen," said Holmes. "Otto von Krempel, the German spy!"

* * *

"But how did you know?" I asked Holmes later.

"Jolly easy," said Holmes. "Any

chap knows that Zeus class destroyers have a sixteen-inch turret, also he spoke in a German accent. I am writing an essay on German accents. They only have one, the Umlaut. I thought of that joke this morning."

"One thing more."

"Yes?"

"Who wrote that threatening letter to me?"

"Who do you think?" said Holmes, throwing a cushion at my head.

DEATH AT TEA TIME

Ernest Hemingway's first story (14 years old)

Haley went out into the school yard. The first leaves of autumn were falling and it was chilly. The teacher told Haley to get his coat on or he would freeze to death. Haley went and got his coat. Then he went out into the school yard. It was a school yard much like other school yards, or I suppose so as I have not seen other school yards yet. Even if I had I would say it was much like other school yards as I have just discovered the expression "much like" and I like it.

"Hello, Haley," said Andersen.

Andersen was a huge Swede, standing well over five feet. He had blood on his chin where he had tried to shave himself. His shoulders were much like big shoulders.

"Hello, Andersen."

"I am going hunting in the woods. Are you coming?"

Haley knew what he meant. They were going to look for rabbits. They had never caught one yet and Haley was glad inside himself because they said that when you cornered a rabbit it was much like a mountain lion and tried to bite you, only lower down, about the knees.

When they were in the woods, Andersen stopped and shivered.

"It is a funny feeling, hunting rabbits. It is like the feeling of the thing between a man and a woman."

"What is the thing between a man and a woman?"

"I am not sure. I thought you knew."

"No, I do not know. But I thought you knew."

"No."

They went on a way further and they watched the leaves fall from the trees and hit the ground, which is the way of

leaves when they fall off the trees. Haley shivered and said it was cold. Andersen said nothing. Haley said it again. Andersen said that it was not too cold to hunt rabbits. Haley said he did not mean he was trying to get out of hunting rabbits, he only thought it was cold and that was all he thought.

"Look!" said Andersen. "A rabbit!"

"Where?" said Haley.

"Over there."

"I cannot see it."

"It has gone now. It does not matter. Perhaps it was not a rabbit at all. It is very cold."

"Shall we go back to school now?" said Haley.

They went back to school and did some more lessons and then Haley went home but he did not tell his parents of what had happened.

◆◆◆◆◆◆◆◆◆◆◆◆◆◆◆◆◆◆◆◆◆◆◆◆

DR EVIL

The first James Bond story
(Ian Fleming, 14½)

James Bond strode into the hallway of Dr. Evil's house, wearing an immaculate school blazer which had been made for him by Jacob Schneider of Lucerne, which I think is in Switzerland, and asked the receptionist to tell Dr. Evil that James Bond had come to see him.

"Dr. Evil?" she said into the phone. 'There is a boy called Bond to see you."

"Who is almost 17," said James.

"Who is only 17," she said. "Yes, sir. Will you take the lift to the third floor?"

When Bond left the lift at the third floor he found himself face to face with Dr. Evil, a squat, ugly, horrible little man who was uncannily like a certain schoolmaster.

"What can I do for you, Master Bond?" he said leering.

Bond felt in his pocket casually to

check that his 2½lb catapult, made of choice elm wood by a master craftsman in Bond Street, which is a very important street near Piccadilly, was loaded. He only used the very best conkers, imported from his aunt in Ireland, which was better than most aunts who only sent you book tokens.

"I think you know what I have come for," he said coolly, no, icily. "You have my replica authentic Japanese destroyer which fires real hara-kiri aeroplanes, which you confiscated for your own devilish ends. Sir."

The face of Dr. Evil went pale and he reached for his poison gun, but before he could pull it out Bond had pounced. At lightning speed he fastened the evil man in a half-Nelson, gave him a Chinese burn, did a quick knuckle-crusher and punched him in the nose. Dr. Evil sank lifeless to the ground, only he wasn't really dead. Like a flash, Bond entered the nearest room. There, on the bed, was the most fantastic blonde, really smashing, with no clothes on at all, if you know what I mean, like in books. There, on the table was his authentic Japanese destroyer.

"Who are you?" she gasped huskily gazing at the handsome stranger.

"I am James Bond and I am 16¾," he said in as low a voice as possible. "I have just killed your friend Dr. Evil, but he will live."

He strode to the table and picked up the destroyer. Before he left the room he turned to the girl, well, woman, and said:

"You will get cold lying around with no clothes on, anyway it looks silly, whatever they say in books. I would get a dressing gown on if I were you."

Moments later there came the distinctive sound of Bond's super three-speed-gear Raleigh as he pedalled away down the drive.

LORD ARTHUR WENTWORTH'S BLACKBOARD

Oscar Wilde's first play
(age fifteen)

(The scene is a richly decorated room, hung with damask curtains, rich brocade and the finest tapestries, but if you cannot get this your mother's dresses would do. There is a pale scent of incense and also the furniture is sumptuous. It is the Fifth Form at St. Topaz's School. A young man is seated at a desk, which is Arthur, who is the pupil. Standing by the gem-encrusted blackboard is a young man, which is Basil, who is the teacher. As the curtain rises, Arthur is lighting a slim, delicate cigarette.)

Basil: You know it is against the school rules to smoke, Arthur.

Arthur: What is the point of rules if we do not break them?

Basil: You have just made an epigram. Do you know the derivation of the word "epigram"?

Arthur: Like most words in English, it comes from the classics. Without the help of the Romans and Greeks, Englishmen would be hard put to it to express their contempt for foreign languages.

Basil: I sometimes wonder who is giving this lesson—you or me. Now, where was I?

Arthur: You were trying to persuade me that a knowledge of Canadian wheat production will enrich my career as a poet and artist.

Basil: My dear boy, one does not have a *career* as a poet. Poetry is too important to work at. One must content one's self with devoting one's self to it.

Arthur: Exactly. I shall write a play and with the proceeds withdraw to an exquisite house where I shall dedicate my life to a poem.

Basil: It is a charming thought. What will your play be about?

Arthur: It will be about two wonderful young men sitting in a classroom talking about art, poetry and Canadian wheat production. One must show the public one has taste and also has done one's lessons.

Basil: And how will the play end?

Arthur: Suddenly, without any warning at all.

(CURTAIN)

◆◆◆◆◆◆◆◆◆◆◆◆◆◆◆◆◆◆◆◆

Why I Am Not Rich

by AL CAPP

THE financial world has never been able to figure out how anyone who has made as much money as I have, for so long, could have managed not to become rich. Yet any imbecile could have done it. The secret is an old one, and a boring one. It is "MAKE YOUR MONEY WORK FOR YOU".

I immediately began investing in real estate. Over the years I bought a large house in Cambridge, Massachusetts, a larger one in the New Hampshire countryside, a mid-town Boston building that I converted into a studio and an apartment in New York City. I invested astronomical sums decorating and furnishing each place.

Yet never, even when we have spent half the year travelling, have I ever rented any of them. My money is working for me, you see, not for some bunch of vagrants.

I invested in exotic cars, and, later, in dangerous ones for my children. I invested in innumerable trips abroad, accompanied by children, and, later, by their children, and their husbands and wives. My money, instead of working for Polaroid or Xerox, was working for me.

I invested in an increasing horde of indigent relatives. I never consulted my accountants about these investments, since money is their business and non-working relatives had become mine. I simply sent them names, addresses and sums. I knew from their Christmas cards the money was getting to them, and so I was serene in the knowledge that my money was not being squandered, but working for me and mine.

And so now, in the sunset of my career, I, unlike so many chicken-brained artists, can look back at a lifetime of shrewdly using my capital. Not a penny of it ever worked for some soulless corporation. It all worked for me. But not, I confess with some chagrin, quite all. I didn't look at the small print in a contract I signed some years ago and now I discover that about a third of my earnings were channelled into some dreary little savings account, and so I haven't wound up with tens of millions, but just a few.

Yet it could have been worse. About twenty years ago I created a character—an animal—called The Shmoo. It was knee-high, shaped like a marrow, it reproduced with any company, or encouragement. It eagerly followed humans around, ready instantly to provide anything they wanted.

At the slightest sign of hunger, they flung their happy little selves into the nearest broiler or oven. Fried they came out chicken, broiled they tasted like steak. Shmoos laid eggs, in rows, all labelled "Grade A", and the finest type of milk in handy carton sizes. For dessert they produced chocolate cake, and for birthdays, chocolate cake with lighted candles, regardless of the wear and tear on their little insides. Shmoos made interesting companions, could improvise shmoosical comedies. There was no upkeep since they were nourished solely by human delight.

"Very interesting I'm sure, sir. Now if I could just expound the monetarist argument . . ."

60

People loved the Shmoo, especially my brother. He was convinced that there was a fortune in Shmoo dolls, Shmoo wristwatches, Shmoo colouring books, Shmoo wallpaper. I poo-pooed the idea, but he kept pushing, and finally I yielded, on condition that I never be asked to draw another one, since I was now sick of the little beasts.

A year later, the Shmoo craze subsided and *Time* magazine reported that 26 million dollars of Shmoo novelties had been sold. It wasn't all profit of course, but enough of it was, to make my brother a captain of industry, and me an idiot.

He then announced that he intended to plough our profits into an even grander venture, one that was none of my business since I had shown I had no head for business, but which required innumerable mysterious trips from New York to California to purchase certain mysterious rights from an old gentleman who turned out to be Cecil B. de Mille.

Once those rights were ours, my brother revealed to me that our Shmoo profits were to be invested in the Minoan craze, which would sweep the world, after the release of de Mille's *Samson and Cleopatra*, starring Victor Mature and Hedy Lamarr, and set in the Minoan period. We, and we alone, would be ready with warehouses full of Minoan dresses, Minoan sweatshirts, Minoan tennis-shoes, Minoan toys and trinkets, for the millions who would pour out of cinemas maddened for something, anything, Minoan.

As you recall, nothing swept the world like the Minoan craze except the Edsel craze, and so I did not take my brother's advice when he came up with another stinker: a TV series in which my hillbillies suddenly got rich, and moved into a mansion in Beverly Hills. I predicted to him that this would be an idea we would always regret, and when someone else came up with *The Beverly Hillbillies* which, now in its twelfth year, still makes ten million a year, there is, as I predicted, quite a bit of regret around.

I also personally handled the matter of a company which, because it is still celebrated in the bankruptcy courts, I will call the Celebrated Artists School. After a lifetime of failure, a hard-luck pal of mine organised a method of teaching cartooning by mail and asked six celebrated cartoonists to write the text-books, for a thousand dollars in cash, or a percentage of the School. We couldn't turn the poor guy down, and knowing that he didn't have a thousand dollars, and never would, we agreed to take the percentage, since, in that way, we wouldn't lose any money, merely a worthless piece of a doomed company.

Within five years, the School had grown to the size of the University of California, was teaching Portrait Painting, Mural Painting, Fashion Design, Brain Surgery and Embalming, all by mail. My percentage was now worth considerably over a million dollars, my hard-luck pal died, and the School was taken over by brilliant young executives, with stunning records of success.

Free from interference by its plodding founder, they

"We're prepared to overlook it this time since it's only your fifteenth shoplifting offence, Your Grace."

announced plans to expand all over the world, jetted everywhere, buying land, contracting for buildings, hiring faculty, and, a year later, my million dollars worth of stock was worth two thousand dollars and sinking fast. So I sold it for that. My incredible luck had held. I had doubled my money.

Hugh Hefner has the reputation of being a financial genius but little is known of the time I outsmarted him. *Playboy* was struggling through its first year or so, when he asked to see me. He was determined to attract well-known names, and proposed that I do a cartoon series. He couldn't pay me what it was worth, but he hinted that an arrangement could be made to give me an interest in *Playboy*. *Playboy*, I could see, was a bust, but I was interested in Hefner. I advised him to go into some other business. I hated to see a smart kid devote the best years of his life to a magazine which consisted mainly of pictures of bare bosoms. One bare bosom, I assured the young enthusiast, was so much like another that the public would eventually grow bored with them. His talents should be devoted to a magazine with a future, like *Life*.

The public's interest in bare bosoms has not, I admit, been satiated yet, but some day it may be, and you can bet Hugh Heffner will look back at the advice that shrewd old cartoonist gave him, with certain emotions.

I am one of those fortunate people whose financial wizardry is matched by his political acumen. In 1972 a certain President asked me what he ought to do about the election. I said don't do anything. I have heard your opponent's campaign. Don't interrupt him and he will elect you. Don't get involved in it, Mr. President, I said, and don't let any of your buddies get involved in it. Well, the President was re-elected, and I was sure it was because he had taken my advice. Now I am not so sure. Turns out his buddies did get involved in it, and, as to whether he did or not, John Dean says yes, and 34 other Watergate witnesses say no, so according to the *New York Times* the score is a draw.

Softly, Softly

The Government is urging Local Councils to tighten up on Noise Abatement. GRAHAM tiptoes into one of the proposed new Quiet Zones.

"*I declare this a noise abatement zone.*"

"*. . . and now we come to the question of jumbo jets.*"

"*Psst! . . . Late final.*"

"Sarge . . ."

"I'm afraid my wheels squeak."

"Certainly not around there—that's the mayor's sawmill!"

"And emitting noxious fumes while exceeding the speed limit!"

MEMOIRS OF THE NINE-DAY WAR
(TAX AND SERVICE INCLUDED)

Everyone likes a place in the sun, especially the Germans currently holidaying at the Hotel Miami in Ibiza. And it has led to a bitter feud with British holidaymakers who, arriving at the swimming-pool after their leisurely bacon and eggs, find all the deckchairs on the sunny side already occupied by Germans glistening with tan-oil. "The two groups aren't on speaking terms and at one point looked as if they might start fighting," said a hotel spokesman *Daily Mail*

(Author's note: I have left this journal exactly as I wrote it during those tense, far-off days last summer. The narrative may seem a little scrappy, but I think it preserves the atmosphere and vividness of the campaign.)

June 11
Arrived Hotel San Antonio for routine summer manoeuvres—pool training, bar deployment and so on. About 150 of us in the 3rd detachment Royal Holiday Tours, under our leader Courier Chambers who seems a good sort though not very decisive. Food good, but foreign. My room has a fine arc of fire, with splendid views over the main road to the town and vital access to the beach.

June 12
There are about 150 Germans here also. Presumably their intentions are peaceful but they seem very well armed; they have bigger and heavier beach towels than us and their supply of sun-tan oil seems almost limitless. Chambers says they mean no trouble. Bill Church, a fellow tourist, doesn't agree; says they need watching.

June 13
Clock golf practice going well.

June 14
The Germans have occupied the ping pong room. No violence involved, but they have definitely moved in. They are playing non-stop—every time one game ends, another pair of players moves in with more ready to start. Now, the ping pong room is neutral territory and although I myself have no interest in it (as Chambers says, "It's a silly little game, a long way from the main hotel"), Bill Church quite rightly insisted that a principle was involved. We tackled Chambers about it.

"Look, lads," he said. "Who needs ping pong in weather like this? Let the Germans have it. Now, who's for a trip to the cathedral?"

"That's not the point," said Church. "If we let them get away with this, what will they grab next?"

Chambers unhappily went to see the German Courier. Came back looking pleased. Says he has his personal assurance the Germans will make no further demands.

June 15
The Germans have occupied the swimming pool. They have moved in overnight with their heavy towels and sun-tan oil, supported by sunglasses and newspapers. There is not a pool-side deck-chair left for us. Chambers went to see their leader. Came back waving a piece of paper.

"It's all right," he said. "They weren't making any further demands. This is a copy of international hotel regulations, which says that anyone who gets a poolside seat is entitled to it. They will not do anything more to annoy us."

"Not much they can do, is there?" said Church. "There's only clock golf and writing postcards left. We must fight back!"

"For heaven's sake, don't let's do anything that might annoy them," urged Church. "Who's for a walk through the old town?"

Church and I and several others agree we must start planning against the Germans.

June 16
War has been declared. The Germans have flagrantly broken the international agreement that breakfast starts at 8.30. They were all seated at 8.20, ordering. We sat for almost an hour, waiting for cereals. They have gone too far. Chambers has been ousted by Church, who called a first meeting in the morning.

"We shall fight them," said Church. "We shall fight them on the beach, we shall fight them on the clock golf, we shall fight them at the bar."

We are not yet strong enough to challenge them at the pool. Our supplies are pitifully small. Some of us have not even got bathing suits. But morale is magnificent.

I am in command of the first campaign, to regain the ping pong room. Spent the day reconnoitring. Frontal attack out of the question—must cut supply route. Only two sources of ping pong balls in the town: Gomez's shop and the kiosk. Dealt with. Tomorrow we strike.

June 17
Operation went like a dream. At 0100 hours I and a detachment of six men entered ping pong room as spectators. The men located the box of balls and quietly put them out of action. Meanwhile I waited till the ball they were playing with rolled towards me. When it did so, I bent forward and stepped on it.

"I am terribly sorry," I said.

"It does not matter," said the German.

Frankfurter Goldnertours leaves on a day trip to the Malaga bullfight

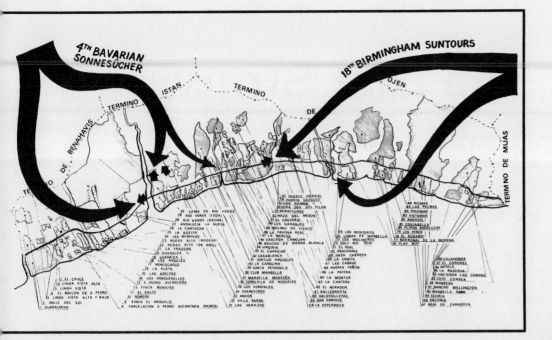

4ᵀᴴ BAVARIAN SONNESÜCHER 18ᵀᴴ BIRMINGHAM SUNTOURS

How wrong he was. The box of balls was out of action and when they sent a party for more supplies, they found that Gomez and the kiosk had completely run out. Not surprising. We had bought them all. At 1100 hours, the first British ping pong players were in action.

Afternoon deathly quiet. Too quiet. Feel they are planning something.

Bill Church intends to send an agent in to discover what he can.

Mrs. Price hit by German beach ball. Not badly hurt.

June 18
Tomkins, who is dark, has borrowed a Spanish waiter's uniform and gone behind their lines to their HQ, near the lager pump in the bar. Pray God he makes it.

(Later) Tomkins is back.

"What are they up to?" said Church.

"Not sure. I don't speak German."

We groaned.

"But the operation code name seems to be Clokolf, or Clogulf."

"Clock Golf!" said Church. "Their next objective!"

We were ready when they came. Over the brow of the hotel garden they marched and I must say there are few sights to rival a trained squad of German tourists armed with putters. They seemed puzzled to find no opposition, then started playing. The first man put his hand in the hole to retrieve the ball. Then he put his arm in. Then he reached in to his shoulder. Not surprising, really; we had dug the hole five foot deep.

June 19
A bad defeat today. The supplies of English bitter in the bar have been sabotaged by enemy action—all pipelines cut. We are reduced to living on lager and wine. Morale has suffered.

June 20
This is it—the long-awaited swimming pool offensive. I write this at 0600. In half an hour we attack. If anything should happen, my medical insurance policy card is in my wallet . . .

(Later) Well, we made it. We simply moved in at 0630 and pushed the German seats back a distance of fifty yards. We have occupied the whole of the pool area and entrenched ourselves.

But there was one casualty. When we were regrouped, Tomkins announced he was going swimming. He jumped in. No splash, only a crash and a scream. The Germans have emptied the pool.

(Later) The ping pong table has collapsed. Three of the

A holidaymaker advances on the poolside barbecue

legs were sawn through. Thank God, no-one seriously hurt. Bill Church has ordered the classic answer to a setback, and we are to mount an all-out counterattack, to occupy the dining-room and bar.

(Later) The war is over! The Germans have gone! There is no sign of them anywhere. Their sabotage was a last despairing gesture before the retreat. We have won at a terrible cost to ourselves (no ping pong, clock golf, bitter or swimming) but we have defended freedom and made the hotel safe for breakfast, lunch and dinner.

*   *   *

(*Author's postscript:* I have one thing to add to this war journal. Several months later I found myself sitting next to a German on a plane who turned out to be the leader of the clock golf detachment. We started chatting about the war and how it had looked from our different sides and I ventured to mention our final victory.

"By no means were we beaten," he said. "We were also due to leave the hotel that day and so we went because our holiday was finished." Then he smiled.

"But do you know, I think that was the best and most exciting holiday I have had. Now today we have a great respect for each other."

I think anyone who lived through those dark and awful days will know what he means.)

The Last Straw

WILLIAM DAVIS reports from the Caribbean

Antigua

"WHAT HO!" he cried, in a voice that had no need of microphones. "Ready for elevenses?" He had the flushed, freckled, dried-out look of a long-time, white dweller in the tropics and he was, without doubt, a splendid specimen of that entertaining creature—the last-straw Englishman. I said yes, elevenses would be fine. "Goody, goody," he boomed, and snapped his fingers. A black waiter appeared at his side. "Bullshots," the 1-s Englishman said. "On the double."

The bullshots—beef consommé, vodka, Worcester sauce and lime—appeared with astonishing speed. American tourists at nearby tables, accustomed to being told "soon come" after a half-hour wait, nudged each other and commented enviously on the unusual sight. In the tropics hurrying waiters are as rare as snowflakes. The 1-s Englishman paid no attention. "All right, Nelson," he commanded. "Set up the other half."

I hadn't expected it. Not really. I mean we lost the Empire—well, *how* many years ago? And we were in Jamaica, where they are inordinately proud of their independence. People like him would look utterly phoney in a modern film or novel. Clearly, though, no-one had ever told him that he lacked credibility. Or if they had the message had been ignored. He ran a farm, had black servants, wore a bush jacket, drove a Land Rover, and was partial to a noggin. And, of course, he had nothing against the midday sun. Independence? "A lot of damned nonsense."

He'd left England when Attlee became Prime Minister—the last straw. Jamaica, of course, was a colony at the time. He stayed on after 1962. Life had become more difficult since—there is, he complains, "a lot of racial discrimination"—but he is determined to "hang on, old boy, until the booze runs out."

I had heard that before, in Kenya. Indeed I shouldn't have been surprised at all: there are last-straw Englishman all over the world. Some left England when Eden made a mess of Suez, and when the Government abolished hanging. Others went off when Harold Wilson moved into Downing Street, when the Beatles got their MBE, when *The Times* put news on its front page, when cigarettes went up to two bob for twenty, when the dustmen went on strike, when women were allowed into the Garrick, when Kenneth Tynan used four-letter words on TV. I dare say there are even people who decided they had had enough when the 8.30 to London Bridge was late three days running: the last straw is often small.

Abroad, they become more English than they ever were at home—just to make sure that no-one could possibly mistake them for anything else. They live in houses called Broadstairs, Worthing, and Falmouth, and congregate in ancient but exclusive clubs where the menu highlights are Brown Windsor soup and angels on horseback, and where the reading matter consists mostly of ten-year-old copies of *Punch* and the *Illustrated London News*—plus, in the more with-it establishments, three-weeks-old copies of *The Times*. They wear blazers and old school ties, drink

"He's got toothache, a sprained ankle, a bad back, gout, influenza, a broken arm and an ulcer and he's just hoping someone will ring him up and ask him how he is."

66

the Queen's Health on her birthday, and are fiercely patriotic about the country they have left behind. England (always referred to as "home", even by grandchildren who have never actually been there) is "the greatest country in the world". Puzzled Americans are sometimes heard to ask why, in that case, they chose to leave. The question is usually ignored—or, if they are tactless enough to repeat it, dismissed with some vague reference to the weather, death duties, the trade unions, and Harold Wilson. Local politicians, too, occasionally ask why, if we are so efficient, Britain staggers from crisis to crisis. The correct answer to that one, it seems, is "will you have another drink?"

Here in Antigua—a rather barren but delightful island with superb beaches—you can see an intrepid Englishman walking through the streets of St. John's in solar topee and long, khaki shorts. But he is nowadays regarded as an eccentric, mocked rather than respected. And although British influence is still apparent in many ways—notably in the bureaucratic set-up—it is only skin-deep. Ministers (Antigua has a population of less than 70,000, but maintains a Governor, a Prime Minister, and a full Cabinet) are determined to prove that they can manage on their own. As everywhere else in the Caribbean, it makes them excessively touchy.

Officially Britain remains in charge of foreign policy and defence. But the only military base on the island is run by the US Navy, and our status is largely meaningless. It certainly doesn't guarantee newcomers a warm welcome.

If, like many expatriates, one simply wants to have a comfortable life in the sun, financed by dividends from stocks and shares, there is no problem. Land is still reasonably priced, despite growing American interest, and the booze is remarkably cheap. You can get a bottle of Scotch for less than a pound, and a bottle of rum for 30p. (Food, on the other hand, tends to be expensive and Englishmen here talk longingly about fresh strawberries and mushrooms—both unobtainable.) I have always rather fancied being a remittance man, but that fine institution seems to have gone out of fashion—perhaps because black sheep are no longer the social embarrassment they used to be. The nearest thing to it, today, is the teenage hippie, and I'm too old for that.

It's only if one wants to work in Antigua, or start a business here, that life becomes frustrating. One Englishman who made it is ex-pilot Peter Deeth, and he says that "at first, it was a nightmare." Deeth used to fly tourists around the islands, and like many other people concluded that "it would be bloody nice to have a hotel right on the beach." A detached retina forced him to give up commercial flying at 35, and he set about building his hotel. Britain was then still

"Cleat the sheets, aye aye! Soon as I finish trimming the jib."

trying to create a West Indian Federation, and he managed to get a long-term, low-interest loan. He drew up some plans and went to see the Chief Minister, who brought his entire Cabinet down to the chosen site. After much argument they finally told him to go ahead.

Deeth opened his hotel in 1960, with only six rooms completed, and found the going harder than he had bargained for. Nearly everything he needed—including food—had to be imported and there were frequent power cuts. Once the whole island went without power for ten days. (Imagine *that* happening in London.) There were strikes, too, and a couple of years ago he was threatened by riots—though, he says, "it all blew over by teatime." But Deeth persisted, and today his venture—The Inn, overlooking the splendid English Harbour—is a well-deserved success. Deeth earns enough to send his three children to boarding schools in England and Switzerland, and to maintain a yacht in Majorca, where he spends his summer months. Not everyone, though, has fared as well. Another British-owned hotel went bankrupt not long ago, and was sold off to an America-owned chain.

There are still colonies—the remnants of Empire—where Englishmen can feel very much at home. And of course islands like Bermuda and Barbados remain unmistakably British. If our latest economic crisis has proved the last straw for you you could do worse than fly out on the next available plane. But explore before you settle: reality is invariably less appealing than the tourist bureau literature, and you might simply find yourself exchanging one set of problems for another. The Caribbean has much to offer to the visitor—sunshine, beaches, warm sea, brilliant vegetation. But the resident also sees another side—high unemployment and the resentment that goes with it, growing crime in towns like Kingston, impetuous decisions made by inexperienced Governments because of some real or imagined slight, irritating red tape, and racial hatred stirred up by a small but noisy and aggressive minority.

Having spent a most enjoyable three weeks in the Caribbean I would certainly not dissuade anyone from going. Whether I would settle here is another matter: I am not a last-straw Englishman and if I were I think I'd prefer a farm in Normandy or a bar in Cannes.

Bung ho. Cherioo.

TARGET PRACTICE

TRIAL RUN

"JUMP!"

. . . AND IN THE MORNING HE WAS STILL A FROG

VERY WELL, THEN—ALONE

Publish and Be Damned!

"I needed the money very badly. I took it on as a two-month commitment. Writing it that way, I had to take certain dares and certain gambles, because there was no time to go out and interview people."

Norman Mailer replying on TV to criticisms of the accuracy of his Marilyn Monroe biography.

When R. G. G. PRICE read this report in *The Observer*, he somehow guessed that Mailer's frankness wasn't unique.

William Shakespeare: I know full well that some of our city wits have cavilled at the Third Murderer in my Tragedy of *Macbeth*. Who was he? Had I fallen into error over him? Such light scoffings, such currish flouts are what fall to the playwright, his lot. But I will waste no time trimming my plays to a shallow neatness. A player myself, I know how little count the jots and tittles of a drama. I do not spend my hours on blotting lines. 'Tis hard for the keeper of a playhouse to find an idle hour to scribble words for his players.

John Milton: I wrote *Paradise Regained* in four books because for the twelve of *Paradise Lost* I was paid but £5. To justify the ways of God to men is no mean labour but a high endeavour which deserves rather a foretaste of the gold of heaven than such paltry journeyman pay. Let the firmament rain fire upon the bookseller Simmons, that gutter-quaffer, that slavering maggot, that spawn of Ahriman . . .

Edward Gibbon: It has been objected that the Roman Empire did not, in fact, decline and fall in steady declension from the Age of the Antonines. The title of my history appealed to me as an author: as an historian, I gave place to the claims of art. I took care that the books which I perused diminished neither the strength of my argument nor the vivacity of my style. Had I permitted myself to advert to periods of recovery, I should have brought ruin on the booksellers and derision upon myself. To sustain a single argument through the labour of twenty years is to provide Mankind with an exemplar of industry: alas, I can expect no reward in this world or in the next.

William Wordsworth: I am aware that my *Lyrical Ballads* lack politeness and must appear rude beside the poetical lucubrations of Gray. But that gentleman was admitted to the society of the nobility and to the sodality of the fellows of two colleges. Far different is my world—for the heady draughts of Eton converse, trudging the lakeland fells with, at best, an ignorant shepherd or idiot boy for company. Such is the constriction of my rural circle, that the toil of correcting my lines and exercising the nice ingenuity required by the heroic couplet would be wasted upon them. Nay, the more time I devoted to prosodical labours, the less I should have for keeping our pot well stocked at the expense of our local landowners. He who spends his days by meadow, grove and stream need never go hungry.

Queen Victoria: The Queen is *most* annoyed with critics who complain that her *Leaves from a Journal of our Life in the Highlands* appears to be aimed at the tepid pieties of lodging-house keepers. This was the audience that The Queen had *always* hoped for. The Queen is so *maltreated* and *put upon* that she hardly knows how to meet the cost of a cup of tea. If she wrote in an elevated style addressed to the intellectual classes (which she is *well* able to do), she would have to forgo the few pounds which her literary efforts enable her to lay aside for her old age. Bowed with sorrow like some . . .

A Headmaster: I regret that certain users of my *Arithmetic for Middle Forms* have presumed to complain that the Answer Book is not invariably correct. The amount of work that a man placed at the helm of a school has to undertake is unbelievable, quite unbelievable. I sometimes think that the lightminded do not realise that the composition of textbooks eats deeply into one's leisure hours. My only thought in their composition is to contribute towards the Guidance of Youth and to save my dear wife from penury, should I have the privilege of being summoned before her.

Robert Browning: I cannot help it if my poems seem obscure. As Sheridan said: "Easy writing's vile hard reading." I have a running wager with Tennyson on which of us can produce most lines in a year and I need my winnings.

Thomas Hardy: The reason that my works are accused of pessimism is low sales. Readers who wish me to cheer up have only to buy my works prodigiously.

The author of Etiquette for Today: I know, I know—marriages aren't white tie. But I was on the run from my creditors and just lifted an 1898 French handbook from a barrow. I did translate it, though.

James Joyce: I reckoned that I wasn't going to make enough out of *Finnegan's Wake* to justify wasting a lot of time on proof-reading. In fact, having the little tale set by a Peruvian monoglot turned out to be the making of the book.

I'll Drink to That

by JONATHAN ROUTH

I'M glad to read that at last the drinking man has corroboration (or corrobary diagnosis, as we'll henceforth refer to it) that his activities are purely unselfish and in the interests of his loved ones and the community at large. Social drinkers, according to a California survey, "are less prone to heart attacks than teetotallers." Yes, but I bet if they're on those incredibly heavy, sticky Californian wines "bottled by Brother Timothy, Cellarmaster to the Xtian Brothers, Vintners since 1932", as I once read on one of their labels, they're prone to one or two other things the following morning, perhaps more temporarily painful but also more easily curable than coronary thrombosis.

Of course, we serious social drinkers have always known that we wouldn't have to wait forever until society acknowledged its debt to us. That's why you see us seated—or lying—in our pubs and our clubs with that faraway look in our eyes—*bleary-eyed*, I believe the ignorant refer to us as—*we* know what we're up to, we're just looking ahead to the day when the Vatican does too and decides to canonise Jack O'Rednose of Pewsey (downed 124 pints of Russian Stout, 6-8pm March 13th, 1632), and that English King who euphemistically "drowned" in a butt of malmsey, and—who knows?—maybe even one of us.

You see, it works like this: alcohol makes the heart beat faster, and blood pumping twice as fast as normal gives you twice as much energy as normal. Where do you see the most extraordinary feats of energy performed? In pubs and clubs of course. People dancing on tables, talking to total strangers, kicking each other. And these feats—seen not in Stock Exchanges, nor Churches, nor offices—all being performed by persons who have unselfishly imbibed more alcohol than the dull lemon-barley-sipping rest of the human race.

True, every now and then one does fall down dead, he falls impaled on the point of an old cheese sandwich, or withers under a barmaid's disapproving glare, or is bored to death by having to listen to the one about the Japanese buying a kilt for the 100th time. But when did you last see anyone clutching a treble Scotch have a heart attack?

What we have to do is think of ways of harnessing this incredible source of energy, putting it to greater use than can be found for it within the confines of pub and club. For instance, it could well become Britain's secret weapon at the next Olympics. Don't just give our performers a pat on the back and a glass of diluted champagne for being good losers *after* the event, but fill them with the hard stuff two hours *before* they're due to go on, and then watch the staggering results. I don't know how it happened that somewhere along the line we got it all wrong and considered that *after* the event was the time to let up and drink. What's the point of all the red corpuscles racing twice as fast, giving you twice, thrice the energy *after* you've had the real need of it?

Drinking and the ability to hold his drink and make use of its effect should become part of every sportsman's basic training.—"We've got no room for a teetotaller in t' team, lad. Either you muck in with the others and finish your Martinis or else you're out."—Pour the stuff down the throats of the England XI before they take to the pitch—and none of this slices-of-lemon nonsense at half-time, what they're going to need is energy-replacing cocktails. Boxers, too, could be served with a Manhattan or a John Collins between rounds. And would-be Ballroom Champions.—At least there'll be a likelihood of their gaining points and

"Hello! Hello, Henry! Good luck! See him wave? He's not ignoring us."

awards for the originality of their steps. But it should be the most strict and stringent part of their preparation for championship to spend four hours before any event with their trainer at the bar.

I reckon that right and indiscriminate use of drink can revolutionise sporting events. Chess would become twice as fast and exciting a game if both participants imbibed the energy-giving liquids before-hand. Cricket might become even a tiny, tiny bit interesting—I daren't suggest exciting—if drinks were served between overs. Tightrope-walking and trapeze-swinging would become positively spine-chilling.

So it's up to the Government to do something about changing Drink's image. Slogans like "Gin—the stuff Champions train on," "Drinka Pinta Scotchaday," and "Brandy Fortifies the Over-Fortyfives" should be blazoned from every hoarding, every TV screen, to encourage the youngsters to take up the habit and not surrender to the blandishments of the Teetotalitarian State. Sporting celebrities will be shown, after eight double-whiskies at the bar, endorsing with indecipherable signatures the goods of spirit manufacturers. Every Bottle will Carry a Government Health Message: ADVICE From H.M. Government—DRINKING WILL IMPROVE YOUR HEALTH. Because, of course, the greatest boon, once drinking gains its new respectability, is going to be to H.M. Government itself, via its subsidiary the National Health Service. H.M. Government may at first have to reduce the price of gin and allied spirits to a penny a bottle, but even so the cost of subsidised gin and allied spirits, as opposed to the cost of subsidised tranquillisers and sleeping tablets, is going to put H.M. Government millions in pocket.

One thing we'll have to do is get rid of the word "drunk" with all its past unrespectable connotations. Maybe "drink-filled" would be the least euphemistic term, and one which could gradually breed respect. Because the person who in old-fashioned parlance is "tight" or "tiddly" or "absolutely blotto" is going to become the hero-figure of the new Drinking Age. Respect for him will be his natural due.

Come to think of it, why do the police so carefully conceal the statistics of drunken drivers who *don't* have accidents? It's my theory that nearly everyone driving with excessive care and attention is drunk, or drink-filled, and that's why they're making such a good job of it.

I remember in such a state myself—purely in the interests of research—I found myself driving very slowly along the pavement of Kensington High Street. I was on the pavement because I felt there were too many fast-moving hazards to a safe journey on the roadway. And I was driving so slowly because I was worried about meeting other cars travelling the other way on the pavement. But those are the sort of cautious, unselfish thoughts that drink can engender in a driver. No wonder the police don't want you to know, otherwise they'd be losing all that lovely Fine and Summons money.

I have to stop and go back now to taking precautions against having my first heart attack. It's hard and selfless work, but it's never been easy for the pioneer; and I feel I owe it to my family, and to myself, and most of all I owe it to the landlord of the establishment where I take my preventive medicine. Roll on the day when we'll all be able to get it on the Health.

"Yeah, they're all right, I'll take 'em."

Thus 11% Mortgage doth make cowards of us all...

GEOFFREY DICKINSON
appears by kind permisson of the
Halifax Building Society

"*I'm afraid our weekend of lechery in Brighton will have to wait until November 1994, Miss Frisby.*"

"*Lie down in the fifth, George—not for me but for 14, Addiscombe Avenue, Bromley.*"

"*What the hell's a Revolutionary Socialist doing with a £20,000 mortgage in the first place?*"

"*I suddenly realised that I should be communicating with a much wider audience...*"

"*On second thoughts, I'll wait until I'm 72 before I tell the old fascist where to stick his job.*"

My Dear Shah

The Shah of Iran offered a lucrative post as football manager to Brian Clough.
Are there any other good jobs to be had out there? A lot of people think there
is no harm in applying . . .

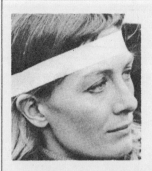

MOSSBUNKER AND ROTWURST
Theatrical and General Agents

**Wardour Street,
London**

His Imperial Majesty Mohammed Reza Pahlavi
Shahanshah of Iran
May it please Your Majesty:

We act for a Miss Vanessa Redgrave who has expressed herself
anxious to assist Your Majesty "to drag Iran kicking and
screaming into the Twentieth Century." She has been attempting
a similar task in Britain, where so many of her gallant sympa-
thisers have been dragged kicking and screaming into Black
Marias. The time has now come for her to seek a wider and more
rewarding field for her talents.

Miss Redgrave is of the opinion that Your Majesty's six-point
"White Revolution" of 1963 has run into the sand. She will be
happy to suggest a number of new points, about fifty-seven in all,
which could form the basis of a new Revolution, White or Red.

We are convinced that Miss Redgrave, whose photograph we
enclose, would be an excellent choice for the post of Political
Adviser and Counsellor Extraordinary to Your Majesty. She is
capable of a smart turn-out when occasion demands and would,
we submit, make a striking figure standing beside the Peacock
Throne.

We are authorised to state that Miss Redgrave would be very
willing to appear from time to time on the Teheran stage, either
in "adult" drama or in pantomime. She would appreciate the
opportunity to introduce the Theatre of Protest to backward
tribes.

Your Majesty's humble and ignoble servants,
MOSSBUNKER and ROTWURST

```
Shahanshah Iran
Rush rush will undertake to reduce
Thousand And One Nights entertainments to
twenty-six gripping Palliser-style
instalments for Iranian Television
incorporating up to seventy per cent of
own material and any amount of sauce.
              Simon Raven
```

Mr. David Attenborough is deeply grateful to the Shahanshah
for the offer of the following posts: (1) Hereditary Ranger of the
Caspian Forests; (2) Master of the Bulbuls; (3) Photographer-
in-Chief of All His Imperial Majesty's Game Reserves, Zoos and
Safari Parks South of Isfahan; (4) Extra Superintendent of the
Cheetahs; (5) Keeper of the Swans on Lake Azerbaijan; (6)
Conservationist-Royal and Lord High Falconer of the Sand
Desert; (7) Surveyor-General of the Salt Desert; (8) High Bailiff
of the Herat River; (9) Hereditary Consultant on Wild Life to
Television Iran; (10) Dog-Catcher Royal.

Mr. Attenborough very much regrets his inability to accept,
owing to a long-standing appointment with some yetis in Tibet;
but hopes His Imperial Majesty's gracious offer will still be open
on his return.

```
Shahanshah Iran
Peacock Throne too too vulgar my dear
Stop Humbly entreat your Majesty to allow
me to redecorate all palaces summer
retreats hunting boxes marine residences
Stop Estimates free Stop Easy terms
              Cecil Beaton
```

Shahanshah! Anointed Reza! Prince upon the Peacock Throne!
Scourge of all the Grasping Nations!
You can have me for your own!
Star of Shiraz! Lord of Meshed! Conquering Lion of Abadan!
If you need a new Court Poet, send at once for Betjeman!

Betjeman, the new Firdausi! Omar! Hafiz! Three in One!
Odes of every kind accepted, no commissions left undone!
Mosques defended! Tombs befriended! References from
Princess Anne—
Shahanshah, you won't regret it. Give the job to Betjeman!

Long Ago, and Far Away

Much talk is talked of the need for the Dunkirk spirit today. But suppose instead that we had had today's spirit at Dunkirk? ALAN COREN reflects

Up to his waist in the filthy sea, oil lapping his sodden webbing, bomb-blasted flotsam bobbing about him, he sucked his teeth, and shook his head.

"I'm not bleeding going in that," he said, "I'm not bleeding going home in no rowing boat."

"Right," said his mate.

"Eighteen blokes in it already," he said. "Conditions like that, they're not fit for a pig."

"Not fit for a pig, conditions like that," said his mate.

"Got brought here in a troopship, din't we?" he said. He cupped his hands towards the rowing boat, and the man leaning towards them over its stern, arm outstretched. "GOT BROUGHT HERE IN A BLEEDING TROOPSHIP!" he shouted, "Ten square feet of space per man!"

"Regulations," said his mate, nodding. "All laid down. Nothing about going back in no bloody rowing-boat. Get away with murder if you let 'em, some people."

A Stuka shrieked suddenly overhead, levelled, veered up out of its dive, back into the flakky sky. Its bomb exploded, drenching the two men.

"Not even got a roof on," he said. "What happens if it starts coming down cats and dogs halfway across? You could catch pneumonia."

"Get a chill on the liver," said his mate.

"*And* there's seasickness. It's not as if I'm a sailor. I'm not saying it isn't all right for *sailors*, am I? All right for them, open bloody boat. I mean, it's their line, know what I mean? But I'm a gunner. That's what I got took on as, that's what I am. If I'd wanted to be a sailor, I'd have got took on as a sailor."

"I'm a cook," said his mate. "Cook, I said when they asked me up the recruiting. I didn't say bleeding admiral. I didn't say, I want to be a cook on account of I'm interested in the standing up to me waist in water, did I?"

"Course you didn't."

An Me109 came low over the surface, strafing the scummy sea. A machine-gun bullet took his hat away.

"You'd have got more as an admiral, too," he said. "You get compensation, working in filthy conditions. I reckon they owe us special benefits. Nothing about all this in basic training, was there? Prone shooting and a bit of the old bayonet, dry conditions, two bob a day, all meals."

"When was the last time you had a square meal?" asked his mate.

"I never thought of that!" He took a notepad from his saturated battle-blouse, licked his pencil, scribbled. "I never thought of that at all. Three days ago, as a matter of fact. Bleeding Cambrai, if you can call two spoons of warm bully a square meal."

"FOR GOD'S SAKE GET A MOVE ON!" cried the man in the stern.

The two privates waded awkwardly forward.

"Not so bloody fast, mate," said the first. "I require a few moments with the brothers here."

The eighteen stared at him over the gunwales. Red fatigue rimmed their eyes, their bandages were thick with oil, their helmets were gone, leaving their hair to whiten with the salt.

"It has been brought to my attention by Brother Wisley here," he said, "that we are being expected to

"I thought it would be a nice gesture to include a member of the staff."

work in conditions unfit for a pig. Not only are we not being allowed to pursue our chosen trade, we have been dumped here in what can only be described as the sea, we have been required to leave our tools behind on the beach, we have not had a square meal for three days, and as for the statutory tea-break, I can't remember when. I won't even go into the overtime question."

"We won't even go into the overtime question," said his mate. "But may I draw the meeting's attention to the fact that members of the Kings Own Yorkshire Light Infantry can be seen on our left climbing into a cabin cruiser?"

The eighteen turned, and looked.

"Bloody hell," said a corporal.

"Well might you say bloody hell, brother!" said the first private. "Course, I'm not saying our brothers in the KOYLI are not entitled to what they can get, and good luck, but the anomaly of the heretofore mentioned situation currently under review before the meeting by which we of the Royal Artillery . . ."

"And the Catering Corps."

" . . . and the Catering Corps, Brother Wisley, thank you, by which we of the Royal Artillery and the Catering Corps do not enjoy parity is one which threatens all we hold most dear."

"RIGHT!" cried the man in the stern, "Get in, or shut up, we haven't got all damned day, Jerry's throwing . . ."

The private held up his hand.

"Just a minute, squire," he said, "just a minute. After frank and free discussions with my ad hoc executive here, we regret to inform you that deadlock has been reached in the negotiations, and unless you are prepared to furnish us with such basic requirements . . ."

"I'm getting out anyway, brother," said the corporal. He eased himself over the side. "Come on, you lot, I have no intention of allowing my brothers on the floor to be manipulated by a cynical management and subjected to actual distress to serve the whim of the bosses."

"Well said, brother!" cried the private.

The eighteen slid into the icy water.

The rowing boat came about, and sploshed off towards another queue. But a bomb, exploding between it and them, gave the private time to wade up to the head of the line, and the man on crutches leading it.

"I know these are difficult times, brothers," announced the private, "but let us not use that as an excuse to allow ourselves to be led like lambs to the slaughter. Solidarity is our watchword, brothers."

The line hesitated.

"We could be, er, needed back home," said the man at the front, "couldn't we?"

The private stared at him bitterly.

"Oh, got a troublemaker, have we?" he said loudly. "It's amazing, there's always one, isn't there?"

"Always bloody one," said a voice down the line.

"Thank you, brother." He poked a finger into the leader's chest. "You'll get that crutch across your bonce in a minute, son," he said. He spread his hands to take in the gradually assembling crowd of waterlogged soldiers. "Got a man here who believes all he reads in the newspapers! Got one of your *thinkers*! Doesn't know all this scaremongering is just put about by the gumment to screw the working man, doesn't realise that your *real* situation is all very nice, thank you, doesn't . . ." The private broke off as a couple of Heinkels came howling in from the dunes, their tracer slicing a red swathe through the crowd, drowning his words ". . . doesn't appreciate that gumment propaganda is being cunningly directed to militate public opinion on the side of nationalistic interests contrary to the welfare of the entire work force, does he?"

"I think we ought to vote on it," said a fusilier who had been standing next to a man dismembered in the last strafe.

"Oh, yes, and I don't think!" snorted the private.

"You won't catch me out with no snap show of hands, brother, contrary to the democratic secret ballot as we know it. I should cocoa!"

The men shifted their feet uneasily. The private had articulated it all so clearly, and, after all, the men who had brought the little boats were, for the most part, men of a class they had long learned to mistrust. Nor did they wish to betray their mates, with whom they had come through no small adversity; and it could not be denied that it was at just such fraught moments as this that advantage could be taken of them, with their defences down, and the odds in favour of those who sought to control them.

And after all, were things so bad that they should forget all else but short-term salvation? They were not yet dead, were they? which was rather more relevant than the emotionally-loaded evidence that others could be seen to be dying. They had, had they not, stuck it out on the beach up until then, why should they not continue to stick it out now?

Slowly, but with what certainly appeared to be determination, the entire waiting army turned, and began to wade back towards the littered dunes, and the devil they knew.

There were, of course, one or two who glanced over their shoulders in the direction of England; but, naturally, it was too far away for them to be able to discern anything, even had the darkness not, by then, been falling.

"I thought 'Godspell' was better."

Twelve Months Gone

Just a few of the letters from readers disillusioned by the first year of EEC entry . . .

Dear Sir:

Well, so much for all this mobility of labour rubbish, that is what I say! As a professional Coronation Day flagseller, I have been unemployed now since June 1953 and scraping along on the meagre National Assistance which is how this country rewards its sons who fought in two world wars, not to mention the rest of us.

Anyhow, hearing that opportunities were better in Germany, I hitch-hiked there at my own expense earlier this year, explained the nature of my profession, and asked the way to the Arbeitslosenunterstützung office, a word I had taken considerable trouble to learn, because this is where the unemployment benefit gets handed out. I was informed that Germany was a republic, and that in consequence they did not go in for coronations. When I pointed out that this was no fault of mine and that due to their reorganisation a lifetime of training and experience had now been thrown out of the window, I was thrown out of the window.

We don't know how lucky we are in this country, is the way I look at it, even if having a monarchy does mean a lot of extra work.

Yours truly,
Eamonn Parrott

Dear Sir:

After frank and free discussions with my executive, in which full cognisance of the ramifications was democratically and unanimously arrived at, I write to inform you of the unilateral decision of the Associated Union of Boilernailers and Allied Trades to co-operate no further in the farrago of Europe.

Our understanding was that, as of January 1 ultimo, we should be able to enjoy the full support and sympathetic co-operation of our European brothers. However, not one whit of this was forthcoming during our recent major industrial dispute which involved a cardinal issue of industrial policy, viz. the reinstatement of Brother Angus Wormold wrongfully dismissed for throwing the personnel manager into the grummling vat after the latter overstepped his authority in enquiring of Brother Wormold how he was feeling, which Brother Wormold quite rightly took as an unwarranted personal intrusion into his individual rights as a human being, and an implied criticism of his action in taking two months off to convalesce in Benidorm after the lancing of a particularly major boil.

We had hoped that our action would bring the ports of Rotterdam and Hamburg to a standstill, as it did those of Liverpool and London, and leave the Italian motor industry reeling after a blow from which it might never recover. None of this happened. It is our opinion, therefore, that the workers of Europe are nothing more than a bunch of money-grubbing wage-slaving tools of the ruling entrepreneurial clique, and that the action of the tyrant Heath in linking our great destiny to theirs is just one more typical example of the transparent lengths to which this loathsome capitalist is prepared to go to bring the country to its knees.

Yours,
R. F. Firkle, Hon. Sec.

Dear Sir:

A year ago, when Britain joined the Common Market, the *Daily Express* and similar were full of how foreigners were going to come swarming over here, many of them swarthy and even darker such as Algerians etc., and start sleeping with our women and so forth. Since then, I have kept a close watch out for the invasion, also spent £28 on various sets of records including Italian and Croat and a megaphone for shouting through in the relevant tongue. What I want to know is, where are they?

Yours faithfully,
Irene Maud Potter (Miss)

Dear Sir:

I hope my experience may be of some help to others who, like I, believed that a new era would be ushered in with Britain's entry into the Common Market, but who have been sadly led up the wossname.

Taking my annual holiday in the Fiat 850 I purchased to demonstrate solidarity with my new European brothers, also on account of the British car I ordered not turning up due to being recalled from the showroom owing to them putting the pedals on the passenger side, I travelled with the family to Portugal, where it conked out near Faro. What a stroke of luck, I thought, here I am in Europe with a European car, no problem! On pushing it to the nearest garage, however, I was told they had no spares. "Don't talk daft," I replied, "this is bleeding Europe, isn't it?" The mechanic purported not to understand, even though I shouted at the top of my voice, and slowly. I called the manager, pointed to him and the car very clearly, and said "You foreign, car foreign, you fix", which nobody in his right mind could fail to grasp; so imagine my surprise when in the ensuing discussion I got hit with the till.

I am now of the opinion we should never have let India go. That's where it all started. The trouble with Clem Attlee was he never got to places like Faro.

Yours faithfully,
R. J. Wharton, AMTPI

Dear Sir:

Queuing up for our own petrol, and no end to the tide of pornography, well, you can't say we at the Society Against Metrication did not warn you! Litres, kilogrammes, centimetres—it is a well-known medical fact that working these things out makes people go funny in the head and has spelt ruin to many a foreign culture, look at the Roman Empire, where is it now, also Napoleon and Adolf Hitler? Since going metric, Britain has plunged further and further into the abyss, and the decimal system has claimed more lives than smoking and VD put together, as they so often are. It is sapping our young men's vitality, and look at the price of beef! The milk-bottle has virtually disappeared. *Our* system, heptagonal for money, triangular for weight, and entirely ignoring the length of things (which is, for all practical purposes, irrelevant) not only irrigates the blood, removes unsightly facial hair, and adds valuable inches to your height *without painful surgery*, it can also be used to prove that the world is flat.

Do not allow yourselves to be hornswoggled and misled by Europe! You have seen what the last twelve months have brought. Send now for free illustrated cat (mark your envelope KORKY) containing full details, plus free instructions on how to grow macrobiotic tomatoes by pelmanism.

Yours faithfully,
Desmond Clin (Mr.)

Everything Must Go!

MYERS brings the house down

"He's a one-man business."

"We like to keep a photographic record of all the jobs we've completed."

"I believe it's a demolition company take-over bid."

"Of course I'm experienced—I've done one hundred
and twenty-seven phone boxes, eighty-five bus shelters
and twenty-three railway waiting rooms."

"Must you bring work home every night?"

How to Beat the Food Shortage

by EAMONN ANDREWS

IF you anticipate a frivolous piece, please turn the pages and go elsewhere. This continuing story of Poultry Place is not yet a tragedy, but it certainly has in it the seeds of disillusionment, if not disaster.

Like most situations of importance in your life or mine, it sneaked up as a matter of little moment, a ripple on the sea, a dropped handkerchief, a clearing of the throat.

It began, in a way, on the subject of sex and was only remotely connected with food in so far as I was at dinner at the time and sitting opposite an internationally known and beautiful woman.

The lady, whom I shall call Bobo, for want of no better, was interested, in a clucking sort of way, when I told her how envious I was of our host, who had six hens of his very own, and took warm brown eggs from the nest for his breakfast, and was totally independent of those cold pale offerings from the local grocer.

She was, however, openly disbelieving to hear that I, a lad from an agricultural land, did not know that a hen laid eggs without the aid of a cock. That chickens came only with the kindly intervention of the proud cockerel. That the eggs came anyway, infertile perhaps, but very much egg.

Finally she believed me (as I hope you do) and

taught me the Facts of Life about eggs. By the time the brandy arrived, I was clutching mine host by the lapel and saying earnestly "Bobo has told me everything."

Before the night was out, he had invited me to join the Chicken Club by promising me a present of six hens the moment I had a henhouse ready and available.

I could hardly wait for morning to implement my vision of sylvan serenity, grateful hens pecking up the left-overs, the odd cabbage leaf, the potato skins. I was only momentarily halted, and had no presage of the complicated world that lay ahead, to discover that the henhouse had to include a special feed dispenser, a special water dispenser, and, since I couldn't bear the thought of the birds permanently blinking in a dark little henhouse, a wire-covered run that would let them seek the sunshine and see the great world outside. The whole ensemble was purchased and erected within a week. A total bill of some seventy-two pounds cooled my ardour only momentarily. Cascades of eggs at 5p a time would soon amortise this.

I alerted my erstwhile host of the bounteous village awaiting its new inhabitants. Nothing happened. Reminders, but still nothing. Further reminders were in danger of bruising friendship, so Mairead, the only member of the household beside myself with the sudden passion for poultry, and a young lady well-versed from a childhood upbringing on a real, live, full-scale farm, was commissioned to purchase six hens.

By now the meal was rotten, had to be thrown out and a new lot purchased. The henhouse itself had to be repaired from the ravages of rain. Twenty-four hours after six beautiful, light-weight rangers were installed, my penitent friend drove up, opened the boot of his Jaguar, and produced six more. Now we were twelve.

Weeks passed. Meal disappeared, and my faith in Bobo's assurances that no male entrepreneur was needed began to fade. Then, suddenly, like dawn in the tropics, an egg. A small, modest, grey egg, but an egg nonetheless. I hurried across the city and presented it suitably inscribed to Bobo. A toast was drunk. Photographs taken. We were in production. Some days two eggs. Some days three. One glorious day, seven.

How many ways can you cook eggs? You'd be surprised.

"I mean, it's obvious. Replace them by microfilm and the table falls over."

"Do you haggle?"

Suddenly, trouble. One hen was wilting. Mairead diagnosed something I'd never heard of before. Coccidiosis. Which turned out to be an infection of the digestive tract, and required treatment with something I'd never heard of before either—Sulthamegatline. A slight improvement and then Aureomycin was called for, which, when added to the drinking water, had the desired effect, including a reported increase in egg production.

At this stage, a quick calculation showed that my emancipation from the grocer was now resulting in eggs costing me three times the going rate. Assuming all the hens lived, and the henhouse didn't fall down, I would break even by 1978.

A week later, mysterious forces struck again. One of the hens started to go bald at its nether end. The diagnosis was not disease but—wait for it—cannibalism. We had to find a quick refuge in an old shed, a large box, wickerwork baskets and a separate supply of meal and water. The hen recovered, and was re-introduced to its colleagues. Within twenty-four hours it was bald and bleeding again, and had to be rescued and returned to its wickerwork fort.

Death No. 1 was a macabre affair. We were sitting on the porch, in the Sunday sunshine, when some boys who'd been playing at the end of the garden came rushing up.

"One of the chickens is dead."

Not only was one of the chickens dead, its body was already partly concealed by cut grass. The hen house was locked. Eleven hens elbowed and kicked each other gently, safe behind the wire. The boys established their innocence. The only other spectators were my five-year-old daughter, her equally angelic cousin, and a Jack Russell terrier.

"Yes." Thirty minutes of questioning had finally passed the blank denials. "Yes," said cousin, "she did get the key to give me a peep at the hens; but nothing happened."

"Nothing?"

"Well, maybe one got out between her legs."

The case was closed. The Jack Russell acquitted on the grounds of nature.

A week later came tragedy Number Two. It had become the humanitarian custom to let the hens out on a closely-guarded daily walk. Seemingly, when the eleven were shoo-ed back into the pen, one managed to play hide-and-seek. At five o'clock that evening, our proud black Labrador came into the kitchen and gently deposited one dead hen.

Now we were ten.

In the way that nature arranges things, the latest casualty had at least one good result. We were able to re-introduce the isolated hen to its companions, who seemingly welcomed it with open wings. No more pecking.

By a stroke of good fortune, the Labrador had disposed of the cannibal.

Alas, it was by no means over. The Sulthamegatline and the Aureomycin appeared to lose their magic properties. One hen wilted and died. Within two days, another keeled over. Panic stations. Mairead consulted the appropriate Government department, and the services of a Poultry Adviser were promised. She arrived, fortunately, when I was away, but her report spoke of paralysis, worms, and, shamefully, over-crowding. I felt like a slum landlord. The size of the run had to be extended, topsoil removed and treatment provided with hot lime.

There are now eight happy hens, a fair trickle of eggs, and five, sometimes six, people doing shift work unpaid, watching, walking, cleaning, repairing.

Someone from the Farmers' Union said the other day that we might have to think in terms of eggs being 50 pence each. It fell like music. To hell with the unacceptable face of capitalism.

MONTY PYTHON'S TOUR of CANADA

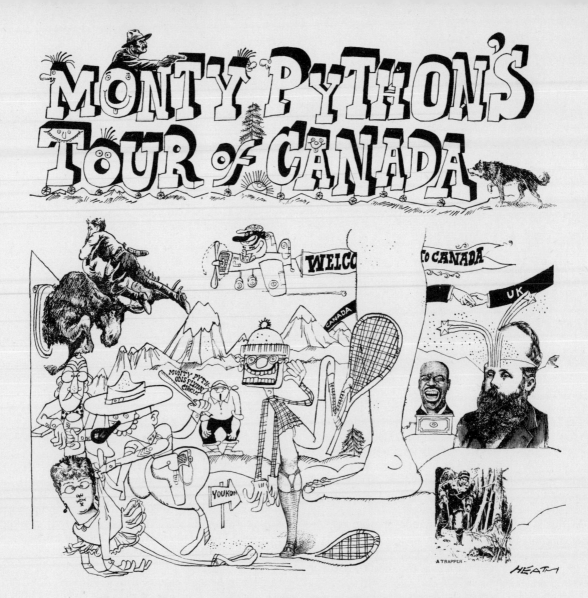

Reports from a galaxy of famous writers and journalists

June 2nd: THE TRIUMPHANT ARRIVAL IN TORONTO.
An on-the-spot eye-witness account of events as they happened by BERTRAND RUSSELL

Hello! I expect you thought I was dead. Well let's get one thing clear from the start: I'm not Bertrand Russell the philosopher, and quite frankly I'm getting pretty fed up with people coming up to me at parties and saying: "Oh I thought you were dead." It's the sort of joke that wears pretty thin, you know. I can't even go down to the Labour Exchange without some half-wit yelling out, "Here comes the famous dead philosopher!" Not that I need to go down to the Labour Exchange anyway . . . well . . . not a lot, but times are a bit . . . how shall I say . . . a bit . . . er . . . thin for us philosophers . . . Not that I'm a philosopher! That's the other one. *He's* the famous philosopher. I'm just a journalist trying to scrape a meagre pittance out of the filthy, degrading commerce of the gutter press and its ilk. Urgh! Oh yes! *My* thoughts on the meaning of life and the Development of Thought in the Western World didn't even make the About Town section of the *Toronto Herald*. 72,000 close-typed

foolscap pages—with practically no margin—on the Cultural Achievements Of The Modern World, and all I get is a rejection slip! All right—perhaps it *wasn't* good . . . perhaps I *had* got one or two little things—piddling little unimportant, pointless little things—wrong, but does that give someone else the right to pour scorn on two whole weekends of toil and labour? They could have just pointed out that there were a few inaccuracies in the text . . . like Bertrand Russell (yes—the *other* one) not being a dwarf . . . and asked me to change them. Heavens above, I can take a hint! Anyway, now we've cleared that up, and I do assure you that I haven't taken it quite philosophically, I can get on to . . .

June 4th: THE GLAMOROUS FIRST NIGHT AT THE ST. LAWRENCE CENTRE, TORONTO.
A report from WINSTON SPENCER CHURCHILL

Hello! Let's get one thing clear from the start: I'm not *that* Winston Spencer Churchill. Nor am I his son. I'm not going to go on about it like Bertrand Russell (not the famous philosopher) does about *his* name, because thank goodness, I've come to terms with it.

It doesn't worry me. Mind you it does become a bit of a bloody bore when people come up to you at parties and say: "What was Stalin really like at Yalta?" And I'm not saying I don't sometimes wish I had a perfectly ordinary name like Len Nol or Merlin Brando or Ben Rosewall. At least then I wouldn't have to waste my entire column explai

June 7th: MONTY PYTHON ARRIVES IN MONTREAL.
A report from our showbiz correspondent from the packed Place des Arts: HENRY KISSINGER

Hello! It's me, Henry! Yes! It's difficult to believe that in between negotiating new policy agreements with Red China, co-ordinating business interests in the new Soviet-U.S. Trade Agreements, consulting daily with President Nixon on a wide-ranging series of topics, constant liaison with the press and White House officials, keeping myself informed on the latest internal and external developments in the Far East, as well as doing all the shopping and helping with the housework, I still have time, as Showbiz correspondent, to see these whacky Python boys at the Place des Arts. I'd seen the show already in Cardiff, Glasgow (where I managed to see both performances), Manchester, Birmingham, Brighton, Southampton, Edinburgh, Norwich and Toronto, but then my mind was far too preoccupied with the truly awesome problems of East-West reconciliation for me to be able to spare more than a cursory glance at the stage. So this time, with the Chinese Commodity Controls Agreement virtually signed and sealed, and the Central Clearing Banks agreement ratified, I was determined to give the show my undivided attention. As the curtain went up on this zany sextet, I couldn't help thinking how pleasant international diplomacy can be in such a convivial and relaxed atmosphere. One of the funniest items in the Python repertoire set me to thinking how I had slipped a vital clause into the 1967 Cambodian Trade agreement, whilst watching Doris Day and Rock Hudson in *Pillow Talk*. My Cambodian friend was laughing so much that he readily agreed to an advantageous purchase of 127 Phantom fighters in addition to the ground control system I had clinched during the opening scenes. Yes! I thought to myself, as Marty Robbins Circus drew to an end, World Diplomacy *is* a wonderful thing.

MONTY PYTHON IN BOTSWANA.

Our correspondent writes:

Hello! Still no sign of Monty Python here in Botswana.

June 13th: WINNIPEG. FRESH FROM HEADY TRIUMPHS IN EASTERN CANADA, THE MONTY PYTHON TEAM ARRIVE IN THE PRAIRIES.
A report from the Centennial Theatre, Winnipeg. by YEHUDI MENUHIN

Hi! Wow! Zapee! Am I having the good time out here in Winnipeg! Zow! Bam! It's grrreat! These Python boys certainly can grab an audience! I haven't seen an audience so zonked since I played the Bartok unaccompanied violin sonata last month. I played as I've never played before. My fingers seemed possessed, dancing across the strings, as if each one had a life of its own! How the audience roared their approval! It was fantastic! They wouldn't let me leave! I took bow after bow and still they asked for more! Of course, these Python boys didn't get anything like that sort of reception, but the audience were pretty enthusiastic. If you can call a bit of applause enthusiastic. Personally when you're used to the sort of response I usually get from an audience it seems pretty thin. In fact I felt if only I could have leapt on the stage and given them a few bars of the unaccompanied violin sonata I could have raised them to a pitch of excitement little short of frenzy, then I could have led them across Canada towards the West Coast, and taken over Vancouver and so on to World Domination. But what was the reaction of a Canadian audience to this essentially British show? Well they certainly laughed. But what is laughter compared to the rapture of an audience maddened with the wild rhythms of the unaccompanied violin sonata, lifting them higher and higher, driving them to the very rim of self-control, when the pent-up passions of the human soul crave for expression, crave for a leader, a leader who will stand at their head and point the way to the future—the way to a better world, where the destinies of ordinary men and women are controlled by a musical genius with a distinctive name! I will triumph! I will succeed! All human life will be at my command!

June 11th: CALGARY. WITHIN SIGHT OF THE CANADIAN ROCKIES AND THE MID-POINT OF PYTHON'S TRIUMPHAL TOUR.
A report from the logging correspondent: LISA MINELLI (No relation).

It was 197 below, when the coach left Frozen Creek on the 4,000 mile journey to the Southern Alberta Centre for the Arts. Even the milk was frozen in our milk chocolates, and a pack of wolves attacked us as our tickets were being given out by the Drama Group Organiser, Red Larsen. Red, the strongest, most fearless juvenile lead north of Goose Bay, was lucky to escape with a torn ear and two broken legs—no one knew who they belonged to. Blizzards whipped the icy snow into 74-foot high drifts, as we drove south along the frozen Mackenzie River. Old-timers at the back of the coach said it was worse than the terrible journey of 1957, when only four members of the party survived to see *Blithe Spirit* at the Little Theatre, Saskatoon. On the 4th day out of Frozen Creek, I was finishing a Douglas Fir sandwich, when suddenly the glacier fell away, and our coach plunged a thousand feet into the raging waters of McMurdo's Gorge. I felt myself grabbed by Big Frank Kelly, who made such a fabulous Natasha at the Yellowknife Festival of Arts & Lumber in 1971, and together we opened the emergency exit of the bus, grabbed the nearest stalls tickets, and struggled out into the icy tide. I felt Frank's grip weaken, as the raging torrent hurled us past rocks and through vicious whirlpools. With our last breath we agreed to meet in the Foyer at 7.15. There was a sickening thud and all was black. Three days later I regained consciousness to find myself stranded in the weird subterranean darkness of the Athabaska Caverns, only 400 miles from the stalls entrance, I—K. Nineteen days after leaving Frozen Creek, I reached the theatre. I couldn't believe it. There, in the bar, were Frank and Red Larsen, Moosejaw Morgan, and the one-eyed trapper Fenson. Red was hurt so bad he could hardly hold his programme, and Moosejaw died of his wounds halfway through the first act, but I was just glad to be alive, even though I was sitting behind a pillar.

June 20th: VANCOUVER. THE END OF THE TOUR.
A summary by our medical correspondent: CHRISTIAAN BARNARD (A relation, but not of *that* Christiaan Barnard).

Hello! Medically the tour was a great success. Heartbeats remained fairly constant, and blood pressures were generally average. Minor skin irritations were an ever-present threat, but none developed into full-scale fungal infections. In fact it was bloody boring, medically. I just read most of the time. Once I was on a tour when the leading lady caught scurvy. Othello came off one night and said he thought Desdemona had badly swollen gums. I gave her an examination after the bed chamber scene, and she claimed that Othello had a severe neck rash. And, believe it or not, it turned out that *she* had scurvy, and *he* had pellagra! Iago refused to go on, until they were both on a vitamin diet, but one night an anonymous note was slipped under my door to the effect that Iago had worms. I later diagnosed belharzia not only in Iago, but also in Roderigo, his friend from Venice. Two nights later, anthrax decimated the chorus, Cassio's fight-scene had to be adapted because of this colostomy bag, and Brabantio couldn't go on without an enema. Shakespearean productions are by far the most interesting medically, but I have seen cases of Yellow Fever in the *Seagull*, some very unpleasant boils in an otherwise perfectly hygienic revival of *Private Lives*, and a severe foot and mouth outbreak in *Babes In The Wood* at Leicester, during which the chorus had to go on through a dip.

Written, produced, researched and spelling looked up by TERRY JONES and MIKE PALIN

"I can't help feeling it will lose something when we try to get it down on a memo."

90

Not a Drop to Drink

"Follow that cloud!"

MAHOOD forecasts
how we will cope
with the coming
water shortage

"God just isn't making rain like that any more."

"The '65 Lake Windermere is very
good, sir, but I would recommend the
Thames Valley '69."

"Not only is it not funny,
Henderson, it is damned
unpatriotic as well!"

"Some conversation pit that turned out to be! All they could talk
about was the damn water shortage!"

THE BETHLEHEM EFFECT

by Basil Boothroyd

Man I know hates
Waits.

Well, it would make more sense
To change tense
And say that he did when there used to be any.
Now, of course, you seldom see any,
Let alone hear 'em
Sounding off with the old goodwill theorem,
Cracked vocals
By unbidden locals
Wavering mittened torchlight
Under a perfectly adequate porch light,
Their approach so ingenuously grasping
That he never got more than half a verse of token rasping
Before they nearly drove him off his rocker
With deafening clouts at the knocker.

He so used to deplore
This sort of thing before,
That when, caught over a barrel
By a sudden carol
Such as Wenceslas,
He felt persecuted and defenceslas
And could only fling up his window on the line about
    "a poor man came in sight",
And yell, "That's me, mate, and when do we get a touch
    of Silent Night?"
Being misunderstood
It didn't do any good,
Or not much :
They just gave him a touch.
And though he sometimes scotched
A Shepherds Watched
Or We Three Kings
By throwing things,
They still seemed disinclined to go
Without treating him to a few sharp bursts of Christians
    Awake, as if they weren't awake already, or Dulce
    Jubilo.

Today
They've more or less faded away,
The lot of them.
He's shot of them,
Due in part
To being ousted by Billy Smart,
So they either stay home and watch it
Or imagine that this is exactly what he'll be doing, with a
    consequent reluctance to abandon his living colour
    with a glad cry and a hand in his potchet.

It's true
That a few
Full-throated hallelululations
Still survive on rush-hour main-line stations,
As members, say, of the Stock Exchange Operatic
Wax ecstatic,
Shouting down the BR's amplified apologies for each
    late arrival
By superimposing energetic descants on The Holly and
    the Ival :
And this — but me no buts —

Certainly takes guts,
Even if it's not
Linked all that closely with a certain Palestine event in
    the year dot,
Just try accosting someone missing his connection
And rattling a tin at him labelled for a somewhat
    tenuously accredited collection,
And you'll notice a marked, if localised, dearth
Of Peace on Earth,
Not to mention a couple of sharp knocks
From the new hi-fi system he's taking home as a present
    for himself in an enormous cardboard box.

Talking of which,
The only other rich
Source,
Of course,
These days,
For songs of praise,
Takes the shape
Of magnetic tape,
Either Heralding the Harks
Outside Marks and Sparks
Or planted by the UDC
In the polyurethane fronds of an artificial Tree :
No doubt it's municipally well-meaning,
Trying to strike a festive note for housewives in a last
    mad dash to collect the dry-cleaning,
But aren't things pretty far gone if a
Plastic conifer,
Burping bits of electronic *Messiah*,
Is all that's left of the one-time angel choiah ?

That's just the sort of question, incidentally,
That confuses this man I'm talking about, both
    rationally and sentimentally.
He used to detest every irrelevant accretion
Of the Christmas Setion,
And totally reject
What he snarlingly referred to as the Bethlehem Effect,
The yards
Of Cards
Both coming and going
Robined, belled, coach-ridden and determinedly
    snowing :
"Who the heck," he cried, burrowing in the heap on the
    table,
"Are Eric and Pam, or, worse still, Ron, Dot, Kevin and
    baby Mabel ?"
When he read quotations from Bob Cratchit
He was ready to go for his hatchet,
And cards designed for the Tiny Tim Society, registered
    as a charity, painted with the crutch,
Made him angrier, much.

But now that nearly all his greetings
Are of a business nature, e.g., from Amalgamated
    Stackable Seatings,
International Cement,
Federated Sewage Monitors, Hawkhurst, Kent,
Or the directors
Of United Convectors,

He'd confess, if you pressed him,
That he'd be quite relieved to see a return of good wishes
   from real people, even conveyed by snow, bells,
   robins, coaches and all the other stuff that depressed
   him.
And he actually states
That he could again take waits.
Oddly,
Since they disappeared, he feels less, rather than more
   godly :
Even stranger,
Though he abhorred the model, shop-window Manger,
Trying to look as
If it belonged amid the Useful Gift box-spanners,
   matching tie-and-handkerchief sets and
   pressure-cookers,
He now says he'd rather have that back, too,
Instead of the crew
Of assembled bodies
Of Sooties and Noddies,
Which he regards as being neither there nor here
When it comes to considering just what it was, way
   back, that Came upon the Midnight Clear.

And whereas he once worked dangerously choleric
   views up
About the domestic nosh-and-booze-up
Masquerading as Old Tyme Cheer,
He suddenly feels that he could take it this year :
It did, after all, happen in the home,
And not, as now, after cheap group flights to the
   Bahamas, Balearics, Algeria, Rome,
Or in the Merrie hell
Of the home-based, out of season
— But opened briefly for a profitable reason —
Hotel,
With Muzak in the air
And traditional Xmas (sic) fare
Served at the run
By waiters clearly having no fun
Despite their cut of the not inconsiderable corkage,
The clashing knife-and-forkage,
Crackers, hats, mottoes,
And, for the kiddies, improbable papier-mâché grottoes
Enshrining scenes so religiously hearty
As the Seven Dwarfs' country and the Mad Hatter's
   Tea Party.

So his thought,
In short,
Seems to be this :
That the things he found so awful about Christmas Past
   are the very things he's beginning to miss.
Mixed-up, crazy,
His feelings are now sharp, now hazy,
What seems to emerge is that the Good Old Days that
   once made him so mad,
Weren't half bad,
And the thought he finds most stinging
Is that if any waits came calling this year and were short
   of a wobbly baritone he might well be persuaded
   to join them and go round singing.

He doesn't quite know why,
And neither do I.

Which I ought to, you see,
Because he's me.

"*The telephone repair man came today.*"

"*I suppose it could mean having to make do with shabby,
underfed servants.*"

I'm so sorry...

A bedside manner is all important, especially if you've just taken the wrong bit out of a patient. RICHARD GORDON presents some medical apologies

APOLOGIES in medicine are newer than antibiotics. Thirty-odd years ago, doctors freely cut off the wrong legs, prescribed the wrong drugs, and sent mothers home with the wrong babies, without a word of contrition. None was necessary. Hospitals were then run on the principle that all diseases brought into them became the property of the doctors, the institution being no more responsible for the loss of the inmates' organs than for that of their hats and coats and other personal belongings.

The patient arriving in hospital was stripped, cleaned, pinioned between rough sheets, had his temperature taken twice daily and his bowels asked after solicitously, until one morning he got no breakfast, and was shortly lifted on a trolley to be wheeled into a small, smelly room where someone suffocated him. He would have heard his case discussed, literally over his head, by doctors and students. But this was a conversation he had no more opportunity of joining than an author hearing his book discussed by a panel of critics on television.

Occasionally some patient, braver or more despairing than the rest, would venture, "But what's *wrong* with me, doctor?" The reply was always a kindly reassurance, "Well, old chap, it's got a long Latin name which wouldn't mean the slightest thing to you, so just leave all that sort of business to me, and lie there quietly and do what Sister tells you."

Diseases were then matters capable of understanding only by classically educated ladies and gentlemen, and certainly not by the lower classes who suffered them in such abundance. Theirs not to reason why, Theirs but to do and/or die.

Some patients even in the old "voluntary" hospitals achieved a rough word of apology from the medical and nursing staff, but this was a minor concession unlikely to disturb the ward apartheid, because the biggest complaints came always from those with the slightest diseases. It is a well established clinical principle that sufferers from hernias, warts and such comparative trivia protest about everything, from their treatment to the cold food and the cold hands. Only those whom a series of clinical mishaps have led almost to the grave eventually leave hospital with nothing but touching gratitude for everything the doctors have done for them.

Then there appeared, more or less together in the late 1940s, the National Health Service, the Legal Aid Act, and the consumer society. Patients grasped swiftly that they could turn the little accidents inevitable in such busy and confused places as hospitals into hard cash. In this they had the benevolent co-operation of the judges, who invariably accepted that the youth whose finger had been unhappily removed in place of his toe was destined to be a top-flight violinist, and the young woman who was regrettably not cauterized but sterilized had no other desire in life but an enormous family. So doctors became

"I could give the whole damn thing up and make a fortune sponsoring ads for airlines, travel sickness cures, energy foods . . ."

immediately apologetic, even abject, and checked regularly on their banker's orders for the Medical Defence Union.

It is futile apologizing to a patient simply, "Dreadfully sorry, but I seem to have done the wrong operation on you . . . stupid muddle with the case notes, the filing clerk's been sacked." Some convincing clinical reason must be offered with impressive authority.

A common hazard of modern surgery is the anaesthetists' reluctance actually to give anaesthetics. Instead, their patients are injected with a derivative of curare, the arrow poison found by Sir Walter Raleigh in 1595, up the Orinoco. Every morning, citizens are lying about all over the country in exactly the same state of utter paralysis as the blow-pipe victims of primitive South American Indians.

The anaesthetist adds a little something to produce sleep, but occasionally this is not powerful enough. So the patient lies wide awake on the operating table feeling the surgeons rummaging about inside, and unable to raise a finger against it. This is inclined to bring post-operative complaints, which must be soothed with the assurance that dreams of singular vividness occur under the influence of powerful anaesthetics administered with such admirable deftness.

Hospitals trade in germs as banks trade in money, constantly taking some in and handing some out. Apologies are continually necessary to patients who come with one infection and catch three new ones, all resistant to antibiotics. This is described as "Cross-infection", which shifts the blame from the medical staff to the other patients. It implies them a filthy lot, teeming with bugs of all sorts, which they should never have brought into such a nice clean place as a hospital.

The profession's present avidity for hearts, livers, eyes, lungs and other bits and pieces of patients newly perished is a fresh source of embarrassed apology. The point when patients incontrovertibly have no further use for these desirable organs is difficult to pick. The Styx is a broad and sluggish stream, across which its boatloads can dawdle and eddy one way or another, and even put back to the familiar, nearer shores. Though there has yet been no case of the over-eager surgeon apologising the morning after, "I'm most awfully sorry I've left you with no kidneys . . . but really it's hardly my fault, as I thought you were stone dead. Just goes to show, doesn't it?"

If the overlooking of life itself seldom brings the doctor's blushing regrets, his mistaken asseverations about its remoter termination are common. One of the first principles I learned in medicine was never to tell anyone that he had only six months to live. The physician who instructed me was apologising at the time to an irate private patient who had drunk his cellar of claret, kicked out his wife, and spent the time taking showgirls to the races, to end up broke, homeless, thirsty, and feeling fitter than ever.

"It isn't ours!"

One royal pediatrician once had the sombre duty of informing a titled couple that their infant heir had, at the most, but a few weeks to survive. The time passed on, but the child didn't. Every visit, the doctor was obliged to apologise with increasing shame for his little patient's continued presence on earth. One afternoon, the saddened parents saw him kneeling beside the sickbed, and touched at the medical adviser's resorting to prayer on behalf of their loved one, they tiptoed up behind him. They could hear him muttering over and over again, "Why don't you *die*, you little bugger, for God's sake?"

Now our brand-new National Health Service Reorganization Act will "Provide for the establishment of health service commissioners for England and Wales to investigate complaints." So the doctor need never apologise again, having an ombudsman to apologise for him. This may not have been the Government's intention. But I know it will recommend itself to a profession bred in the idea that the mistakes which it makes upon earth are discovered only in Heaven.

This Article is in Short Supply:

Please Re-use Carefully

by MILES KINGTON

FINALLY, just to prove how bad things really are, did you know that the Civil Service now hasn't enough paper for all its paperwork? I'm not saying this is a bad thing for *us*, just a bad thing for the Civil Service, but it's a shock all the same. It's like suddenly learning that the only reason the Bronze Age came along was that the Stone Age ran out of stone. ("Stone Shares Hit All-time Low: Heavy Bronze Buying".) It certainly looks as if it's the beginning of the end for the Paper Age, and the Civil Service has reacted accordingly. Already some departments are being told to use single-spacing instead of double-spacing, to correct mistakes in pencil instead of retyping letters, to avoid all unnecessary background briefing, and to telephone wherever possible.

I'm with them. We writers have had it too easy for too long. Each week whole acres of woodland are chopped down just to provide the useless blanks of white between our lines, not to mention the otiose, self-indulgent and repetitive adjectives we throw in, to mention only three. I mean, only 3. I have already taken the first step by omitting a good deal of background briefing; this article in its original form started with a look at the effect of a bad papyrus harvest on Egyptian prose style, some speculation on the imminent disappearance of the monster American novel and an investigation into whether the English

"Excuse me, is this gallery just empty, or is this an exhibition?"

96

paper shortage could be cured immediately by getting Bernard Levin to write shorter. That's all gone now. It also explains why the word 'finally' sneaked in at the top there.

Next I'd like to ask the printers to set this piece a little closer together, just to see how it looks. Quite readable, I think. Thank you.

Now, if writers can learn to write more economically, it will not only ease the paper shortage. It will also mean that those writers who have learnt to economise on space will be more likely to be hired than the old-style, long-winded type. I've nil v. (nothing against) the conventional full-lgth novelist except that he's Xtinct. It's going to be people like me in demand—at this v. moment I'm working on my 1st 7 novels, which will all be short enough to get in my first novel jacket together. And that's why I'm going to experiment with a new way of writing, or rather, & th's Y Im going 2 xperiment w a nu wave writg. U dnt find it 2 hard 2 read, do U? U C, it uses ½ space & gets over OK. No prblm at all. Rlly. a X between sh'hand & est agts' lingo. V. economic, qte gd fun, and damned difficult to get the hang of till you've practised a bit, I find. Wm Shakespeare found the same thing too, otherwise he would have quite simply dashed off:

Hmlt: 2B or not 2B, that's the ?

And even Shakespeare practised some shorthand on the sly. Don't tell me (and if you do, phone, don't waste paper) that people in Tudor times really went around saying O, in't, i'faith, 'sblood, 'tis, as 'twere. What we have here is a

"You want me to believe, don't you? You want me to stop doubting? Get me the Cranbourn contract."

Pitman before his times, or rather a penurious playwright up from Stratford eking out his precious supply of paper. How else do we explain, from Act III of Hamlet:

—He poisons him i'th'garden for's estate.

If y'ask me, he writes short t'avoid the turn o'th' line. I don't claim, by th'way, to be the first person to think of this technique—typists and estate agents have for years been telescoping their prose to maximise economy and it's no coincidence that typists and estate agents are among the most highly paid of all writers. Nor is it any mere chance that the part of a newspaper which provides the most concentrated reading material, and absorbs the reader the longest, is the crossword. Even the good addict will take up to half an hour to crack the *Times* crossword, whereas the slowest reader can solve the *Times* leader in a couple of minutes. I believe the day will dawn when the average journalist, to provide value for money, will include a short crossword in each article.

In fact, the day has dawned. I proudly present the world's first telescoped Xword.

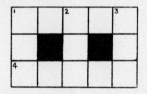

Across
1. "Tomorrow & tomorrow & ———" (Macbeth) (5)
4. Robot (5)
Down
1. "I'this a ——— that I C be4 me?" (Macbeth) (3)
2. Trombone (abbv.) (3)
3. Shakespeare's of it (abbv.) (1, 2)

It's worth noting that, as far as economy of paper is concerned, the lead was taken long ago by, as you might expect, the Scots. Not for them the cumbersome and wasteful use of big words like have, not, with, you, of and little; instead, the logical thrift of hae, no, wi, ye, o' and wee. The logical implications of this escape me for the moment; it could mean that crosswords to come will be more economical in Scots, it could mean that *Macbeth* could be reduced by a third simply by being rendered back into the rightful dialect or it could simply mean that the Scottish Nationalist MPs are going to cause an awfie lot o' trouble wi' yon Hansard.

I don't, in fact, have the time to work out the implications because altho I've asked the printers to close up the lines once again (ta), space's running short & I must use evry trick in the bk to sgn off, wi'out countin' gettin' the Xword answers in. Just want to say, firmly believe future journalism v. condensed and every word count. Amazing this article in just one, mean 1, page. Tolstoi wd be still ½way thru credit list, & Hal Robbins still on landing outside bdrm. For yr next compact, wee artcl, Y not write M Kington, c/o Pnch? Ye'll no regret it. Also lt gdning and local bike jrneys undrtaken, or wd consider forming nxt gvrnment. Tel (not write) 246 8091.

Xword solution. *Ac* 1. Ditto 4. Robot *Dn* 1. Dgr 2. Tmb 3. O'it.

"But I have it on good authority, Mayor, that there are pictures in the public conveniences already."

Support your Local Artist

More and more local authorities are taking on artists and sculptors, says the Municipal Journal. QUENTIN BLAKE joins the rush.

"We never done it."

"We thought we'd site it about here . . . ."

"You can tell it's a council job all right—hopelessly out of drawing, crude chiaroscuro, no sense of tonality . . . ."

"And this Francis Bacon, if we can get him—would he be right for the Sunnyside Old Folks Leisure Lounge?"

"I told you we should never have given the job to an R.A."

Bring me my bars of burning gold, Bring me my ingots of desire . . .

Great Poems of the Money Crisis

Darling, I am growing old, let us join the flight to gold!
Death is grinning at the gate—look at this conversion rate!
But, my darling, if we flee to a gold-based currency,
O how happy we shall be! We may yet survive Phase Three.

•

(In affectionate memory of a great monetary conference)
O Bretton Woods were heaven!
  And jocund were the nights.
In nineteen-forty-seven
  We talked the world to rights.

The structure we erected
  Is gone and hardly missed,
And here we stand rejected,
  Our knickers in a twist.

In Bretton Woods, half-witted,
  We quaffed the flowing cup.
Too bad that we omitted
  To string each other up.

•

The Pound is going it alone,
  Doodah, doodah!
The Pound is sinking like a stone,
  Doodah, doodah, day!
Goin' to sink some more,
  Goin' to fade away!
The Pound has fallen through the floor,
  Doodah, doodah, day!

•

I'm a silly little kroner.
I'm an outcast, I'm a loner.
No one wants to purchase me,
I'm as useless as can be.
Toora loora loora lee!

(Pivot on last line, with forefinger on head)
Repeat with:
  I'm a potty little quetzal,
  Frankly, I'm not worth a pretzel.

  I'm a dreary old escudo,
  Only fit for playing Ludo.

  I'm a randy little rand,
  Who will take me by the hand?

  I'm a drachma—yoo hoo hoo!
  Do I stink? I'll say I do, etc etc.

•

O say, can you see by the dawn's early light
  The vision we hailed as disaster seemed nearing?
The Dollar advancing with God-given might,
  Enfeebled no more by the Watergate hearing?
O say, do the dime and the quarter still flash
In the land of the tough and the home of the brash?
Does Europe still bow, as it did long ago,
At the sight of a greenback? Well, actually, no.

•

Just a dream of comfort, when the larder's low,
While the Central Bankers vainly come and go.
Just a sigh for prices soaring past recall,
Just a dream of ease, dear, just a dream, that's all.

•

Come all ye bold rascals and list to my lay.
I move my hot money by night and by day.
From pesos to guilders, from guilders to marks—
This short-term investment's the choicest of larks!

I'm two jumps ahead of the Council of Ten,
I laugh as they try realigning the yen.
The "snake in the tunnel" means nothing to me.
Let crawling pegs crawl—I am footloose and free.

So come, ye bold rascals, and heed not the rage
Of all the dull boneheads who work for a wage.
And lose not your nerve when the storm flags are blowing:
When the going gets tough, it's the tough who get going!

•

Children of a future age
Reading this immortal page
Know that in a former time
Thrift was punished for a crime.

Those who saved with might and main
Lost their money down the drain.
This was due to Market Forces.
Children, why not back the horses?

E. S. TURNER

The Last Australian Hero

The filming of "The Adventures of Barry McKenzie" by BARRY HUMPHRIES

MUCKY PUP ("*It's Hilarious!! Watch your friends' faces!!!*") is a curious substance sold in novelty emporia and Tottenham Court Road joke shops. Manufactured in Tokyo, it is a convincingly glistening dollopy scroll of bright brown plastic which people with an irrepressible sense of humour place mischievously on their friends' drawing room Axminsters. If there is a dog or a kiddie around you can imagine what a load of fun is in store for the Mucky Pup purchaser.

On a sunny January morning in Earl's Court a group of Australian film makers could be found scattering about twenty pounds' worth of factory fresh Mucky Pup on the immaculate pavements of kangaroo valley. A street scene in *The Adventures of Barry McKenzie* was about to be shot and our chosen location just didn't look authentically English. To make matters worse it wasn't even raining, and an adjacent phone booth was conspicuously operable. In fact, it must have been the last unvandalised public telephone in London. Clearly the person whose job it had been to discover film locations which typified English squalor and desuetude had blundered badly, and the Australian designer and his assistants were frantically sprinkling fish bones on the footpath and piling overflowing garbage cans in people's doorways.

In the back of a van our graphics designer was hastily writing a sign which said "Remember, Leprosy Inoculations are Compulsory" while highly paid extras attired themselves as bowler-hatted beggars and starving stockbrokers. Disguised as a Cypriot crone, an actress waited patiently at the upper window of a derelict dwelling we had requisitioned and suitably defaced, for the cameras to roll. When Barry McKenzie stumbled out of his taxi (which had taken him from Heathrow to Earl's Court via Stonehenge) it was this lady's task to deject the brimming contents of a chamber pot into the street below whilst another extra, picturesquely disguised as a beefeater, rummaged hungrily in a faked-up dustbin. But still it hadn't rained. The weather was positively bloody Australian, in fact.

The enormous cost of making the real England look really English was borne by the Australian tax payer. Long before, when it was first proposed that a major motion picture be made of Barry McKenzie's scabrous comic strip adventures the problem had been who was going to foot the bill. One of us knew the ageing whizz-kid who wrote the then Prime Minister's speeches, and a daring ruse was hit upon. Affairs of State in Canberra being what they are, it was rightly assumed that the P.M. rarely had time to check his copy before holding forth to the House, and so it was that one fine morning he overheard himself pledging a quarter of a million dollars of the taxpayers' money to finance a courageous new film venture which would spearhead the fledgling local cinema industry and put

"*Right, Watson, I'll keep a lookout, while you plant the bug.*"

101

Australia in the centre of the cultural map where it belonged. The money duly changed hands with a murmur of incredulity in the Press and a rancorous howl of protest from Australian film critics who all had the grubby and time worn screenplays of their own cinema epics stuffed in the bottom drawers of their copy desks and naturally resented two hundred and fifty thousand of the green folding stuff finding its way into rival pockets.

The Art of the Film is a serious business, even in Australia, and public monies should properly be spent on cinema dramatisations of aboriginal folklore, or "relevant" and "viable" social documents about the agony and the ecstasy of "real" Australians in settings of kangaroo-infested bushland or gleaming Sydney skyscrapers. Fantasy, humour and downright ribaldry were the enemies of antipodean culture. Barry McKenzie might achieve a cheap and contemptible success at the box office, but in doing so it would demolish our international reputation as a race of suave sophisticates. People might even think we were *all* common.

Hardly believing our luck, we leapt aboard the first plane out of Sydney to spend the money so generously entrusted to us, but not before a little man from the Ministry of the Environment, Aborigines and the Arts (a cinderella portfolio customarily assigned to the Party dunce) had rushed across the tarmac and uttered the amazing line: "I hope you won't be using any Australian *colloquialisms* in this movie of yours!" We assured him that our artistic intentions were impeccable, not to say ponderous, and that no-one viewing the finished product would thereafter suspect Australians of vernacular usage. We said something like that anyway, and privately wondered if any of those chastely spoken experts on the environment or the abbos had ever glanced at our script.

The yarn we were about to spin on celluloid concerned the vicissitudes of a foul-mouthed Australian virgin (or latent heterosexual) marooned in London and prey to a horde of perverted rapacious Poms. The hero, of course, bore the name of Barry, antecedent of Monty Python's Bruce and the popular forename of most likeable and intelligent Australians. According to an encyclopaedia of Christian names, Barry is Old Welsh for "a spear." Time and long usage have rusted and blunted its meaning, however.

In photographing Barry McKenzie's misadventures it was necessary for our expatriate film-company to acquire a London office and a vehicle. Thus, within a week of arriving in London, we bought a second-hand van which irretrievably packed up outside Harrods and might still be there, and we rented a flat in Soho which enjoyed the propinquity of Wardour Street without the advantages of hot water or electric light. Although the landlord was a Greek and the car salesman a fellow Australian, we were already experiencing at first hand the commonplace discomforts of English life. In a grisly fashion, life was beginning to imitate art, and Barry McKenzie's fictitious persecutors beleaguered his biographers. The pinguid landlord's name was, astoundingly enough, Mr. Damocles (which is old Greek for Barry) and the coin-operated telephone in our jerry-built high rise apartment jangled constantly with plaintive calls from previous Pakistani tenants demanding refundment of their £200 deposit.

One of the film's most important props was an elaborate meter which was to adorn Barry McKenzie's hotel room. Since it was supposed only to accept pound notes and emit flashing lights the machine had

"*Everything about the movie is nostalgic about the 30's except the price of admission.*"

"Live within our means! My God, don't say it's come to that."

to be specially constructed and a quiet and ingenious little Englishman was given a very large sum of the Australian taxpayers' money to build it. We never saw him again, though in all probability he went into the accommodation business in Earl's Court, profitably equipped.

It still hadn't rained. London had rarely looked lovelier in January. Short of shooting the film in our own flat we were at our wits' end to convey the ghastliness of English life, when Miss Undine Voide turned up at the Savoy. Miss Voide worked for the Dept of the Environment in Sydney and had been assigned the onerous task of flying over and checking up on how we were spending the cash. The heartbreaking pleas from the Pakistanis were now interspersed with telephone calls from this suspicious hireling of the Australian Government who was demanding to see our accounts and, worst of all, our rushes. Luckily we had a fair bit "in the can" as they say in Hollywood, but try as we might, a few proscribed colloquialisms had somehow crept into Barry McKenzie's dialogue. The next fortnight was spent hiding the film from Miss Voide and simultaneously granting her access to *some* of our impeccable book-keeping. Luckily she was more interested in staying at the Savoy and shopping at Fortnums on her expense account than sabotaging our work of art, so that she was somehow sent back to Sydney with glowing accounts of our progress and integrity without once meeting a single member of the production company.

Meanwhile there were ominous rumblings from a famous airline which has certain Australian associations. We proposed to film part of Barry's trip in one of their planes and they were deeply distressed by a line of dialogue in which the hero, in response to the hostess's "Is there anything I can do for you sir?," bluntly proposes a spot of dalliance in the airborne toilet. A celebrated Melbourne brewery was likewise apprehensive lest their distinguished product become linked in the public's mind with such a coarse and undesirable consumer as Barry McKenzie.

However, in the face of injunctions, boycotts, threats, and outraged protests a film was made. It opened in Australia a year ago to a scream of abuse from the critics. In eight weeks, thanks to our colonial customers, the government got all its money back and they have now made so much profit that the Department has been able generously to subsidise other film makers; our talented critics amongst them. *The Adventures of Barry McKenzie* is now unleashed upon an unsuspecting Pom public. Columbia Warner thought it might be a good idea to add subtitles: e.g.

BARRY (to irritating Englishman): "I hope all your chooks turn to emus and kick your dunnee down."
SUBTITLE:
"*I hope your poultry transmute into ostriches and demolish your outdoor earth closet.*"

We tried it but there wasn't enough room left on the screen for the picture. Alas, as for the Mucky Pup, it ended up on the cutting room floor.

Tales of Courage

King Furthermore of Morovia was puzzled by the word "courage". He summoned his six leading story tellers and ordered them to tell six leading stories illustrating courage—"which," said the King, "at this point in time I believe to be a short form of curried cabbage. Disabuse me."

THE FIRST LEADING STORY TELLER'S STORY

Skipper Leatherhead of the trawler *Fishface* grasped the helm and roared, "Damn the typhoon! We're here to catch fish, Mr. Brisling! Full steam ahead!"

Mr. Brisling, the first mate, pleaded with him. "We'll never ride out this storm, Captain. Let's head back to port, sir, pretty please with sugar and walnuts."

"Fish or cut bait, Brisling!" the captain thundered. "I am not changing course by one iota!"

"Permission to mutiny, sir," said Brisling, clutching the wheel, "and relieve you of your command, since you are suddenly as nutty as a fudge sundae topped with a maraschino cherry."

A blue whale named Dopy Mick then attempted to capsize the *Fishface*, but was harpooned.

"I don't buy that," said the King. "The whale, seeing two officers struggling, and having no experience of harpoons, misjudged the situation. You are telling me that ignorance is courage. Go and be decapitated."

THE SECOND LEADING STORY TELLER'S STORY

It was the night of the big fight. Jersey Jake's timing was off and he had become everybody's punching bag. This was his last crack at the heavyweight title and he knew it. One more horizontal finish and the promoters would write him off. He wouldn't get a fight with Hayley Mills. Harry Carpenter would cut him dead.

Jake stood impassively as the referee gave final instructions. Coolly, he met the Champ's arrogant stare, then returned to his corner to await the bell for the opening round.

"That's the whole story, is it?"
"It is, Your Majesty."
"I don't buy it," King Furthermore said. "This is the heavyweight championship. Lots of people, most people I shouldn't wonder, would be glad to have their faces pounded to a jelly for half a million quid. You are telling me that greed is courage. Report to the chopping block."

£500,000

THE THIRD LEADING STORY TELLER'S STORY

The enemy was throwing everything at our boys to keep them from taking the hill. The hill was in the enemy's country, and they thought we should go home and take our own hills. It was hot as hell. The flies were dropping like soldiers.

Corporal Grubsteak was the last rank left in his company. Captain Parchment, Lieutenant Rump, and Sergeant Bottleneck had exploded. They were taking that big hill in the sky. Grubsteak waved his rifle. "Up and at 'em, men!" he shouted to the private.

The General saw in his telescope that a corporal was about to take the hill. Corporals are forbidden to take hills. The General rode his jeep into the battle and tapped Grubsteak on the shoulder. "You're an officer," he rasped.

Grubsteak caught a bullet with his name on it. It read, "Second Lieutenant Grubsteak".

"Your story," said the King, "does not tell us whether the General survived, but he seems to have believed he would, simply because he was too significant to die. I don't buy it. You are telling me that self-importance is courage. There is an axe outside with your name on it."

THE FOURTH LEADING STORY TELLER'S STORY

It is time for a story about women.

Ms. Shirley Tell was just as obstinate and freedom-loving as her celebrated husband, William, and she was as good a marksperson, too. When Shirley and her tiny daughter Max refused to salute the matching hat, gloves, and handbag of the tyrant Ms. Gessler, she was told to place an apple on the child's head and throw an umbrella through it, or languish ignominiously as a visual object in a centrefold.

Shirley unhesitatingly accepted the challenge, and let fly.

"Applesauce," said King Furthermore. "One should always bow down to tyrants. I speak as a tyrant, of course. Apart from that, you are telling me that overconfidence is courage. You had better see the headsperson."

THE FIFTH LEADING STORY TELLER'S STORY

Let me take you back to the Crusades. Stanley the Wombat-Hearted has been captured by the Saracens. As he is led away, his handsome bearing stirs the heart of the beautiful Queen Hashish.

"Oh, do not kill him," she implores her consort, Sheikh Yamani. "Let me keep him as a pet."

"Very well," says the Sheikh, who is in a good mood. "Here, you—report immediately to Queen Hashish, and try not to foul the footway."

Stanley the Wombat-Hearted tosses his aristocratic head. "I am a Christian and an English gentleman and a queer," he says proudly. "I would not serve an infidel Queen for all the oil in Araby. Execute me."

"You are telling me," said the King, "that a masochistic death wish, probably based on an unhealthy attachment to one's mother, is courage. No sale. Join the queue."

THE SIXTH LEADING STORY TELLER'S STORY

A great King hired some story tellers to instruct and entertain him. The first five told lousy stories in the King's opinion, and he ordered them executed.

When the sixth story teller appeared, he refused to tell a story.

"Your Majesty," he said, "I don't like the working conditions. Since I am soon to meet my Maker, I may as well die a lamb as a sheep. You ain't getting any story."

Now, the easy thing, the popular thing if you will, would have been for the King to have this person executed. But the King was a man of courage, and was not afraid to depart from his usual practice.

He invited the story teller to join him for a drink, and then sent him home to his typewriter.

"So that's what courage is!" the King exclaimed. "Inconsistency. Weakness. Sentimentality and un-Kinglike behaviour. Well, we're not having any of that around here! I will be known henceforth as Furthermore the Pusillanimous. What are you standing around for? Go and get yourself bisected."

The Noble Art of Staying Alive and Well in New York

by CLIVE BARNES

NEW YORK—Impressions grow on one. One notices things gradually. Gradually your hair is falling out, and policemen are getting older. (That is one of New York's most disturbing aspects—the profession is no longer attracting young people.) Or else you slowly come to notice and note New York's latest proliferation of violence. Hand-made death, oriental style.

I knew about unarmed combat. Bulldog Drummond knew that, I think, or maybe it was Biggles. Certainly I can recall an advertisement, probably in *Tit-Bits*, where a frail young man on a beach would have sand callously kicked in his acne-gleaming face by some goliath-brute bully. The girls all laughed. But our hero took a correspondence course, built up his body and the next time sand-drops were falling on his head, he leapt up, grabbed his persecutor by a lesser known muscle and hurled him high in the air, until he landed, with a sickening plop and a ruptured pectoral, in the sea. In America we have gone further now than jujitsu, if that's what that was.

Even judo is passé—a kind of New York children's game on much of a level with black-belt ludo, or killer-shark Monopoly. No, now we are into the martial arts. It seems that the essence of the martial arts is a supreme muscular, emotional and mental discipline that enables you—and very honourably at that—to kill an assailant with a very calculated lift of the left eyebrow.

Almost any night—indeed, if you search for the channel, definitely any night—you can find this special commercial of interest. A man, in a kimono and with Yul Brynner hair, glares at you, at first in a nine-month's pregnant silence. Then he says: "Can you take care of yourself on the street?" By this time you are so intimidated you are wondering whether you can take care of yourself in front of the television set. Don't worry, help is at hand.

Now the man is asking you, with a confidence that can only be described as screamingly quiet: "Are you the kind of guy, or gal, that people just don't mess around with?" Instantly, I realize no. I'm the kind of guy who is even messed around with by box-office officials and proof readers. One of the reasons I left for America was that on deserted English high streets I would be tripped up by old ladies selling flags.

Now this man was offering me a course in Kung-Foo. "It is not just Karate." I should damn well hope not. In America Karate has been reduced to a patented name for an aftershave lotion. Imagine me trying to combat flag-sellers in Cheltenham with a technique based on Aqua-Velva. Not on your life.

Once I thought that Kung-Foo came with egg-roll and was one of the arcane dishes of Szechuan cuisine which, with its spicy Hunam taste, is becoming understandably popular in New York. In fact, as I discussed with my wife, after a particularly heated dinner in our local Chinese hot-house, perhaps you just eat Kung-Foo, breathe on your assailant and he is instantly overcome and, without the proper antidote, dies in two minutes. But this is wrong. You don't eat Kung-Foo, you live it. And you have to be very fit for this kind of stuff, so lay off the egg-rolls.

There are now people in New York who will teach you to kill anyone in seconds. No one kicks sand at

"Cards on the table: I'll admit Harold Shortcliffe didn't exist if you'll say you invented Maisie Dringleton."

"Well, you wanted a typical English pub."

those guys. But even those solid citizens who are taking what are known as the oriental martial arts represent only a fraction of New York's interest in this matter. We are mad about Kung-Foo movies, most of which are made in Hong-Kong. Indeed Kung-Foo movies are only second in popularity in New York to hard-core porno movies, and their great star, the late Bruce Lee, probably, before his untimely death, came only second to Linda Lovelace of *Deep Throat*, as the movie star Mr. and Mrs. New York City would most like to meet in a darkened Shubert Alley.

Films with such attractive titles as *Fists of Steel* make more money than Truffaut ever trifled with. Even on television there is a young man called David Carradine (son of John Carradine) who is appearing in a very successful series of this style, which I never happen to have seen, with a name I happen to have forgotten. But it does terribly well in the ratings, so it may well be absolutely splendid. As I write they are preparing a demonstration of "martial arts" at Madison Square Garden. It is strange.

Easterns, in fact, seem to be the new Westerns. Nor am I entirely joking. The black revolutionary Rap Brown once declared that: "Violence is as American as apple-pie." This seems not impossible. Look at American sport. Those Martian football teams, bearing in on one another like warring buffaloes, baseball with its whirling bats and frantic runs, or most American of all, a curious sport called the Roller Derby which is unconditional war played by two tribes on roller-skates.

America is a land where violence is taken fairly easily. The gun laws are so weak and so antiquated simply because it is a constitutional right of Americans to bear arms—a right that embraced Al Capone as

warmly as Paul Revere. And the concept of the frontier —which with its Go West Young Man ideology still represents America's special romance with itself— encouraged at least an acceptance of violence.

But think how much better it is just to *use* arms rather than bear them. This must be a new American dream—the retiring Superman powerhouse of secretive muscle that at a moment's supply of adrenalin becomes a deadly, personal weapon, always on the side of law, order, justice, boy scouts and little old ladies.

So it seems that today more and more Americans— at least in New York—are eagerly learning inscrutable oriental ways to keep ahead of the battling Jones's. Oh well, it could add variety to bridge games, fairness to golf matches and suspense to lovers' quarrels. (Journey's end, as Shakespeare might have said, in lovers' beating.) It is probably just a fad like pogo-sticks and President Nixon.

Yet certainly the martial arts are with us in New York City. Sometimes around the house, simply for comfort rather than war, I wear a kimono my sister-in-law once kindly bought me in Tokyo. I was wearing it the other day, when the door-bell rang. I went to answer it, and it was a messenger come to collect some copy for my newspaper. He took one look at me, saw the kimono, and looked absolutely terrified. I gave him the package, smiled softly like Charlie Chan's Number One Son, and he scurried up the corridor like a Vespa being chased by the Hell's Angels.

Perhaps I should wear my kimono outside once in a while. Perhaps I should shave my head—after all the hair *is* falling out. And it would be nice to be the kind of guy that people just don't mess around with—and there has just got to be an easier way than taking some form of physical exercise.

107

A Bit on the Short Side

For regular customers of Bill Tidy only

"Stuff your Black Market tickets. We're going to rush the gates!"

"Very well, Anton. You may have my body but please give the baron just a little caviare."

"Give me plenty gold and I will give you the gun which shoots firewater!"

"Tell the captain, 'Situation desperate, we're about forty quid down on 'No. 3 lifeboat!'"

"He laughed at me. Said 'Virgins! You can't even get virgins on the Black Market!' "

"Don't believe them, sir. There is no crucifix and stake shortage in Transylvania, and these are grotesquely overpriced!"

"Genghiz is no fool. He's holding them back till the market's just right."

"He doesn't give a toss, now that he's found that his car runs on chip fat."

THE NEW GREEK CONSTITUTION
Entire text—exclusive

1. From now on Greece is to be a republic, not a monarchy. This will take effect immediately i.e. since two years ago.

2. The Greek Presidency is open to any citizen of the republic who is over twenty-one, has served in the Greek Army to the rank of Colonel, can answer certain questions satisfactorily and owns his own pair of sun-glasses. Anyone who has been King of Greece cannot become President.

3. You may find in the dictionary under Republic: "a democracy where the government is freely elected by the people". This, of course, refers to the old-fashioned concept of republic; the Greek republic is a democracy where the government is freely elected by the government.

4. Why not take your holidays in Greece this year? Cool olive groves, endless sands, starry nights and the magic isles of the Aegean—what more could you want? (advt.)

5. Every citizen shall have the inalienable right to praise the government, enthuse over its policies and defend the new constitution in his own way.

6. The freedom of the press shall be guaranteed to each and every newspaper. If it abuses this freedom, it shall tend not to appear the next morning.

7. The name of the Greek President is George Papadopoulos. *Please note the correct spelling.*

8. At regular intervals there shall be freely held referendums at which the Greek people will be asked to vote on the policies of the present government. The result of the referendum will be an overwhelming Yes.

9. In order to show the millions of foreign tourists that we have a true democracy, it is the duty of every citizen to smile happily in the streets, sit relaxing at pavement cafes and prominently display foreign newspapers.

10. Planning your holidays? Come to sunny Greece, where the cries of the tortured Navy officers in gaol mingle with the no less delicious shrieks of Athenian law students being beaten up for daring to suggest they should elect their own officers! (advt.)

11. The Greek republic shall not apply for membership of the European Economic Community until the E E C has adopted democratic procedures along the Greek lines.

12. It is undemocratic to own records by Melina Mercouri, Theodorakis or ex-King Constantine.

13. A warm welcome awaits you in historic Greece, cradle of democracy, where thousands of years ago the Athenians first evolved the ideal system of government—the creation of a ruthless elite to govern an electorate of slaves. Lots of nice flowers, too. (advt.)

14. Anything not so far covered by the constitution is hereby covered, and made punishable by anything up to ten years in jail, if you last that long.

15. Any queries concerning this Constitution should be made in person to the Head of Police, Athens. Please bring with you identification and the name and address of your next of kin.

Amendments
1. There shall be no amendements to the Constitution.

"Mine too—every week it's 'meat's gone up'—'clothing's gone up'—'rent's going up' . . ."

"But Bangladesh is so passé."

The Best Things in Life are Free

or rather, says VINCENT MULCHRONE, the free things in life are best

WHEN the Indonesian Embassy threw a splendid party at the London Hilton, they actually allowed for one hundred and fifty "uninvited guests". Freeloaders.

Practical, charming and fatalistic, they had cottoned on to the fact that the British will go to extraordinary lengths in pursuit of free booze, food, or rubbing shoulders with the mighty. To their surprise, only about ninety-five freeloaders turned up. Said the Embassy: "It must be the holidays."

Very civilised, the Indonesians. Given that even freeloaders must take a holiday sometime, they had gone too far in laying off the diplomatic bet that freeloaders might account for a good quarter of the Ambassador's entertaining fund. They were working on the experience of the Nepalese Embassy which, in 1969, gave a party for one hundred people. Came the night, one hundred and ninety-five turned up and drank them dry in less than forty minutes. An embarrassed Nepalese is almost indistinguishable from an unembarrassed Nepalese. But they learned another lesson about how low the Sahibs have sunk that night.

The next day, the secret army of freeloaders got their first, official recognition from the Foreign Office which said, in a pained voice, "The trouble is that foreign embassies don't like to demand invitations at the door. We feel the Diplomatic Corps should sort it out themselves." In fact, the current spate of security has more or less sorted it out for them. God's gift to freeloaders, any nation's national day celebrations (from Albania on November 28 to Zambia on October 24), aren't what they were. (God's writ never ran at the Soviet Embassy, where they never had the least compunction in demanding to see your invitation card, and even checking it against a numbered list.)

It is difficult to define the median freeloader. He must be uninvited, of course. He must get in where he's not wanted. He must consume food and drink not intended for him. And he might, as a sort of grace note, hobnob with people he persuades to accept him as an equal. Purists might object, but I would extend the definition to those people who insinuate themselves into subsidised works canteens and get themselves a damned good lunch for 35p. It's not exactly free, but at least they're getting a cheap meal intended for somebody else in a place where they've no right to be.

It's getting away with it that counts among people known as "jibbers". Back in the late 50's a young chap made it his hobby to attend almost every big party (because the bigger they are, the easier they are to crash) attended by Princess Alexandra. He'd no particular crush on her. He just liked having her around. And *he* was a porter at Euston station. Any class of person can play. In the 20's it was young bucks crashing debs' parties. Oddly enough, the actress Mrs. Patrick Campbell was a prodigious freeloader. Challenged by her non-host, so to speak, at a party in New York, she said: "I am Mrs. Patrick Campbell, and your flies are undone." She was deep into his Champagne before he had recovered his composure.

That cheeky chappie, Max Miller, used to indulge in a fairly innocent form of freeloading when he was king of the Moss Empire circuit. Two minutes before the interval he would station himself at the circle bar with a large glass of tonic water into which his fans fairly queued to pour large gins.

But we are drifting away from serious freeloading, best practised in the capital, because that's where all the embassies are. As new nations proliferate, so do the number of national days and the foreigner has come to the conclusion that the best way to make his mark in Britain is to open the Embassy door, jump back, the way they do at sales, and watch the British get sloshed. Embassy receptions are the easiest mark and the easiest of all are the, well, coloured Embassies, still nervous about slinging white men down the Embassy steps in case they're accused of operating a colour bar. The Indians and Pakistanis are particularly susceptible, because they try to out-do each other in numbers, wherein, for the freeloader, lies safety. I shall not break the jibbers' code by giving you their dates. They're easily looked up, anyway. What I will reveal is the *modus operandi*.

I'm taking it that you have the right clothes and supercilious bearing. Next you need a highly embossed visiting card, which might go something like:

M. Vincent Mulchrone, K-G a A, B.C., Dott. Ing., I.C.U.

The initials stand for Kommandit-Gesellschaft auf Aktien (or a private company partly owned as a joint stock company), British Columbia, Dottore in Ingegneria (Doctor of Engineering), and International Communications Union.

You can perm millions of these combinations from the pages of the *International Year Book and States-*

men's Who's Who, available at your friendly neighbourhood library. Place the card before the flustered official at the desk, look over his shoulder at the throng and shout "Ah, François! Ça va, mon pot?" and streak for the bar. Some of the more sophisticated embassies in London have collections of these cards, which they preserve in rueful admiration.

This sort of freeloading was almost kid's stuff until 1968, when the American Embassy decided to work a flanker and switched its Fourth of July reception from the evening to noon, when most of its freeloaders were presumably tied up in the sewers of Bermondsey or at their desks in the Min of Ag. For, as an American Embassy spokesman said, "How's the butler to know when someone arrives and says he's the High Commissioner for somewhere . . .?" Their example was quickly followed, first by the Hungarians, then the Czechs, then—but, again, I think you should in all decency find out for yourself.

Trouble is, the embassies have gone quite crazy about security these days, and the ancient and honourable practice of jibbing has fallen on hard times. In this century, the Press was tut-tutting about freeloaders as far back as 1909, saying they were well known in society but without actually risking a writ by naming them. More recently the well known society hostess (well, that's what it says) Mrs. Bunty Kinsman had a stranger walk into a party, pocket a bottle of Scotch from the sideboard, and walk out again. That she did nothing about it is partly explained by the fact that she was throwing a fancy dress party, and she was bemused by the guest (or was he a freeloader of exceptional talent?), who turned up entirely swathed in bandages as The Invisible Man.

"Don't spend too much time reading it. The first payment is nearly due."

It's not an exclusively British trait, of course. It's on record that, in 1966, the wife of the Finnish Ambassador to Rome came across six women shovelling caviare, smoked salmon and reindeer steaks into big plastic bags from her smorgasbord table. She got rid of them. But when the Swedish Ambassador arrived, there was no food left. And you wonder how diplomatic incidents begin?

But in spite of security at embassies, and hawk-eyed hostesses, the addicted freeloader still has plenty of room for manoeuvre. Go to any big hotel at 1.15 pm and note from the displayed list at least two of the several receptions currently in swing. Watch your timing. They usually start at 12.30. By 1.15 pm the secretary, missing all the fun because she has to take names at the door, will have been slipped three gins by the young executive who is trying to gain her favours on the cheap. By 1.15 pm they'll be so deep into the company's booze and buffet that you'll never be noticed. If you *are*, you say "I thought I didn't recognise anybody. I'm supposed to be at the Silkworm Society's reception." They'll probably think it very funny and press another drink on you before pointing you towards the other reception where, with a bit of aplomb, you can repeat the performance.

Big weddings are a pushover because all you are asked, by groomsmen overawed by their temporary office, is "Bride or Groom?" Take a quick shufti down the nave, and choose the bigger party. Somebody's sure to give you a lift to the reception. The suggestion of a tear at the thought that young Cynthia, whom you've known since she was so high, will stop any awkward questions. *They'll* think you're one of *hers*, and *they'll* think you're one of *his*. Nothing to it.

I can also reveal, for obvious reasons, that some of the best freeloading in the capital is done from 4 pm every Wednesday at the Dorchester and the Waldorf Hotels where, respectively, Littlewoods and Vernons unveil their giant pools winner of the week.

I well remember—well, I half remember—the night when this French waiter ("More Champagne? Certainlee, m'sieur") looked at his watch at 9 pm and said to four dedicated reporters, in pure Bermondsey, "Ain't you got no bleedin' 'omes to go to?"

The pools people are very generous with their hospitality, but experience has given them a keen eye for the freeloader. You could try turning up wearing a flat cap and shouting "Ahm 'is broother", but I wouldn't advise it. They have ways of making you leave.

It's just silly old me, I know, but my favourite freeloader didn't actually qualify as a jibber on account of the fact that she was a barmaid in Chelsea who lived in. She had a lover, who, every night, brought her a single rose, which she would take to bed in a tumbler of water. The landlord was deeply touched until, one night, he smelled the rose. The whiff he got was not from the flower but from the water. Which was gin.

Pity about that. If you run into her at some reception, say hello from the rest of us jibbers.

You don't know where it's been

Prisoner of conscience ALAN BRIEN finds nowhere left to go

THE new Foreign Secretary's decision to cancel Royal Navy visits to Greece and Chile is gunboat diplomacy in reverse. Once upon a time, if a Portuguese-Indian fruit exporter with a British passport had a crate of tomatoes squashed on the quayside at Macao, the fleet would have sailed into port with guns blazing and stayed there until an apology was delivered at our Embassy on a gold platter. Now the fleet steams, or rather oils, by, beyond the horizon, portholes clamped against the siren voices of the native bottlers of imitation Scotch, sellers of archaeological souvenirs made of plastic in Hong Kong, cafe owners with strings of transvestite whores, and "Eth and Rom—A Real Lancashire Hotpot in Our Home from Home."

It's a healthy sign when Governments do not cancel the validity of their consciences at the frontier, when it is not assumed that Ambassadors and Admirals can shake hands and cocktails with thugs and thieves abroad whose hanging and flogging they would be advocating in *The Times* letter columns if they met them at home. But the line is not easy to draw either for politicians or citizens.

The late Fifties were the heyday of the individual boycott of products from foreign countries on ideological grounds. It was a time when dinner guests would be discovered in your kitchen covertly sorting through the garbage bin to satisfy themselves that the tinned pineapple was not from South Africa. You were safe then if you assured them all your fruits originated in Jaffa.

Now with the Arab-Israeli conflicts subdividing the Middle East into goodies, baddies and dubious neutrals, it is wiser to claim that it all fell off the back of a lorry and was sold to you unlabelled in bulk. It was a practice mainly found in the graduate-wife belt of the North London Left, and evoked much exaggerated scorn and hilarity among their opponents. And it is true it bred its own hypocrisies and the suspicion that many of the protesters compounded for goods they were inclined to while damning those they had no mind to. I recall quizzing a prominent activist, shortly after to be Labour Cabinet Minister, on how seriously he took his household's politicisation of their store cupboard. "I have decided to carry it to the extreme of unloading my Bloemfontein gold shares," he announced proudly. Shouldn't he have done that as his first step? I asked. "What? At the bottom of the market?" he said.

Tinned fruit salads have never held a very prominent rank in my cuisine. But, as a drinking man, I did have some problems about my supply of booze. Sometimes it seemed that there was an awkward correlation between the output of alcoholic beverages and the input of authoritarian bureaucracy. Sherry (Franco) and port (Salazar) were clearly beyond the Very Fine Old Pale. Vodka still retained the steely flavour of Stalin. Wines also were tinged with guilt by association. Bordeaux and Burgundy on your table might be tipping the balance of payments in favour of de Gaulle's semi-dictatorship.

Who knew what secret profits might accrue to the Vatican, the largest corporate shareholder in almost all Italian industries, from a switch to Valpolicella and Orvieto? Marsala was a Mafia sideline in Sicily. Might Hocks and Moselles not be bolstering ex-Nazi wine growers still on the list of the Control Commission investigators? Scotch was all right, or all Left, enough before the Thalidomide scandal when I found I couldn't order a large Scotch without consulting a list of all the brand names under which the dreaded Distillers concealed their semi-monopoly.

But looking back, it seems it was easier then to make your gesture and be rewarded by a glow of rectitude out of all proportion to the amount of damage and deprivation inflicted either on you or on the offending nation. You could carry in your head a roll call of politically worthy and unworthy countries and if the regime changed overnight, you only had to wait for next week's *New Statesman* to discover whether the new rulers were on the OK side. Today, almost anything you buy can be faulted as forbidden for reasons which transcend party lines.

Is it the product of cruelty to animals, or perhaps threatens a dying species? Do the manufacturers

"It's a good picture now, George."

discriminate, not just against blacks, but against women, or Catholics, or Tamils, or speakers of Basque, or long hair, or trades unions, or released convicts, or grammar school boys? Does the process pollute the air, or the sea, or the earth, or the lungs of the workers? Does the board of directors contribute to the Conservative Party, or the Festival of Light, or Aims of Industry, or Israel? What interlocking holdings may not the innocent-sounding United Health Foods Inc. possess in other firms which deal in armaments, cigarettes, contraceptives, drugs, second-mortgages, property developing, commodity speculating, or rhino horns and elephant tusks?

Nor are only the profit-makers suspect. How can you tell that the most innocuous charitable body has not been infiltrated by the C.I.A., the K.G.B., the Communist Party, the National Front, the Church of England, the Elders of Zion, El Fatah, the Special Branch, the Scientologists or M.R.A.? Conspiracy rises or descends, depending on what level you enter the structure, ring upon ring, like Dante's Inferno, or the TV Centre at White City. Simply by picking up a magazine, borrowing a fag, collecting a loaf, popping in for a drink, buying a flag, or having your shoes soled, you may be completing a circuit which tortures a man in a Greek dungeon, extinguishes the last iguana in a Malay swamp, returns a Tory MP,

malforms a child in the womb, pulls down an Elizabethan dower house, drives a motorway across your father's grave or doubles the rainfall in Manchester. It would need a computer to keep track of all the small, neutral everyday transactions we enter into, which may end up melting the polar ice caps.

Still, I welcome Mr. Callaghan's move, even if he finds himself at last ordering the entire Navy to scuttle themselves to avoid encouraging some Government of scoundrels and monsters by its presence. The best solution would probably be to allow the Royal Family and the yacht *Britannia* to pay all our calls on those administrations our political rulers dislike. By definition, the Monarch has no politics. To it (a Monarch also has no official sex) all Heads of State are equal whether they be madmen, devil-worshippers, gunmen, drug-addicts, criminals or illiterates. It is not expected to tour the gaols, asylums, slums, brothels, slaughterhouses, opium fields, sweat shops, bacteriological warfare labs or pornographic film studios. It looks its best, and looks at the best, everywhere. It keeps its mouth shut, except for reading out a formal message so designed as to be practically meaningless. This is the Monarch's job. And the Monarch can do it better, without involving the rest of us, than an armada of sailors.

"That's your younger generation today—no sense of social responsibility."

Anyone can become a knight today—Sir John Betjeman, Sir Hugh Cudlipp, Sir Alf Ramsey, Sir Cecil Beaton. What matters is not how you got your knighthood, but how you behave afterwards and, amazingly, there is no set code of behaviour for modern knights. PUNCH answers all your questions

My name is Peter Peterson and I have just been knighted.
Congratulations, Sir Peter.
Thank you.
Careful, now; you should always say "Please call me Peter". Now, what do you want to know?
Lots of companies have written to me asking me to become a director. Should I agree?
That depends. Have a look at the board of directors first. If everyone else is just plain Mr., you're obviously in demand just for your title and they're not interested in you personally. If, on the other hand, there are lots of knights already, even a couple of lords, then they are just compulsive collectors of titles and not interested in you personally.
So I should turn them all down?
No, no. You should ask them twice the money they're offering you.
When I sign in at hotels should I use my full name and title?
That depends who you're staying the night with.
My wife, of course.
Full name and title, then. Your wife will take every opportunity of signing herself Lady Peterson—you're going to look a bit silly if you write "Mr. P. Peterson".
And if, er, I shouldn't be staying with my, er, wife?
Put Mr. X, c/o Old Bailey.
Is there any equivalent for a knight to a peer's maiden speech?
Yes, your maiden letter in The Times.
How do I go about writing that?
You put at the top: "From Sir Peter Peterson".
Yes, then what?
The rest doesn't matter—the easiest thing is to copy out an old *Times* letter. The top line is the important bit because it's a way of telling any friends who may have missed you in the Honours List that your knighthood has finally turned up in the post.
How should I treat women?
Often.
What should I do if they are insulted?
Duck.
I mean, if someone else insults them?
Duck.
But shouldn't I challenge him to mortal combat or a duel or something?
Duels went out of fashion years ago, and quite right too—people sometimes got hurt. If you hear a lady being insulted, leap forward bravely and say to her: "Madam, I am a lawyer and I think I could get you £5,000 for that last remark."
But I'm not a lawyer.
No, but I take it you always have a lawyer with you.

Will I be able to go straight to the head of queues in the Post Office?
No. You write on your letters "From Sir Peter Peterson" and send them without a stamp. Nobody will ever ask for the money back.
Even The Times?
Not even The Times. The Scottish Daily Express might.
What are a knight's main duties as a member of an order devoted to chivalry and courtesy?
To pay final demands in good time, to travel in a chauffeured car so as to make more room in the Tube, to agree gallantly to appear on TV whenever asked, to agree with people richer than himself and to help recapture Jerusalem from the infidels.
What—go on a Crusade? But I haven't got a white shirt with a cross on it
I should hope not—they're very out of fashion. I mean, you should give generously to a Middle East charity. Doesn't matter which side—both sides is best.

TELL SIR HUGH TO GET OFF MY TRAIN

Killing foxes.
That's not nearly so heroic.
The pay's awful these days.
Will I ever be called upon to kill the Archbishop of Canterbury?
You've been reading too many books. Look, the only point in becoming a knight is so that young ladies will open the door for you and you get preferential treatment at restaurants. Anything else money will buy.
You ought to talk to me with more respect. After all, I am a knight.
Some knight. You look more like a stockbroker who was once frightened by a runaway oil boom.
This is no way to talk to me. I am terminating this interview immediately. Out of my way, you insolent wretch.
That's better! At last I've got you behaving like a knight. Twenty guineas, please.
Be so good as to send me your invoice
Better and better! I'll make it twenty-five.

♔ ♔ ♔ ♔ ♔ ♔ ♔ ♔ ♔ ♔ ♔ ♔ ♔ ♔ ♔

A KNIGHT MUST AT ALL TIMES

Give his correct title and address when breathalysed

Not smile and wave at the camera during royal weddings

Believe implicitly that the Queen will not cut his head off

Be prepared at all times to talk to people without titles

Not interfere with the running of companies he is a new director of

Get on with making money. That is what he was knighted for.

Should I sell all I have and give to the poor?
No, there are easier ways of avoiding tax. Ask your accountant.
If I am a property developer, what is my duty to the public?
What do you mean—*if* you are a property developer? Surely you know by now whether you are or not?
Well, I am actually, but isn't it wrong for a knight to be a mere speculator?
For heaven's sake, most knights *are* property men. They only let the others in to give the whole thing a bit of tone.
Well, how should I behave to a damsel in distress?
Evict her. Victimise her. Cut off her gas. Nothing must prevent the erection of new developments.
No, I mean a real damsel in distress. Say I was wandering through Epping Forest and saw a gang of varlets attacking an innocent maiden?
Hmm, tricky. You *could* dash to the nearest phone and get on to William Hickey—something like: "Sir Peter Peterson, recently knighted for his work on social services, and father of debutante Penny Peterson, 23, yesterday heroically broke up a brutal attack in Epping Forest. Leaping from his unassuming Mini, he dashed forward fists flailing (he has recently been attending Kung Fu classes) and," well, and so on. But that's not really worthy of a knight. Far better is to dash to the nearest phone and get the *Times* letter page: "From Sir Peter Peterson, Sir, The problem of violence in our forests seems unsolved. Only yesterday I . . ."
Just one thing. I wasn't knighted for work on social services.
Oh? What for, then?
Property development.
Oh yes, I remember. I don't suppose you have a cheap flat for sale in Mayfair, do you?
No. Tell me, what is the modern equivalent of slaying dragons?

YOU KNOW, BEFORE I WAS KNIGHTED I'D ONLY PLAYED BINGO AT TOP RANK

"Darling—you forgot your Marmite sandwiches."

URBAN
GUERRILLAS

by DE LA NOUGEREDE

"The trick, Garcia, is to keep the pin and throw the grenade . . ."

"Let's move to a town and start again as
urban guerrillas . . ."

"Now, sure you have a nice clean
handkerchief to surrender with?"

"Have a nice time."

All Your Christmas Gift Problems Solved!

by KEITH WATERHOUSE's advice service

UNDERSTANDABLY, in these inflationary times, many of my readers are anxious to get through Christmas on the lowest possible budget. I am afraid I have not much sympathy for those who actually wish to make a profit on the festive season. I think they should be well content to break even, which is what I try to do myself. Here is a selection from my problem post on the subject—and incidentally, in reply to "Worried" of Gloucester, no, I do not deal with my readers' mail on a first-come-first-served basis, I always open the parcels first.

Have you any suggestions what I can give my granny for Christmas, bearing in mind that she is more or less off her chump and always confuses me with my sister Lilian, and furthermore that she is unlikely to remember either of us in her will?

Bath salts. They are the best buy on the market. If you stick to export reject bath salts, which may have got ever so slightly bruised when falling off the back of a lorry, you can get an enormous quanity for practically nothing. Do them up in little plastic packets and the problem of your Christmas presents is solved.

That's granny settled, then. My three-year-old son is my next headache. He is too old for cuddly toys and not old enough for Lego and such. What can I give him for Christmas?

Bath salts.

Don't be ridiculous.

Do as I say and give the lad a plastic packet of bath salts. He will think it is a bean bag.

I have four nephews aged seven, nine, ten and eleven. I honestly can't afford to spend much on them, but I don't want to appear mean. Any suggestions?

Bath salts. Do not forget to enclose a little card with a scribbled note on the lines of: "A few more toy soldiers for your collection" or "I do hope you still play with Plasticine". They will think either that there has been an honest mistake, or that you are following in granny's footsteps and going off your chump.

There is a sweet old lady who takes tea with me sometimes. Unlike granny, she has a bit stashed away and she has no relatives. I would so much like to make her Christmas happier with a little present, and don't say bath salts because that's what I gave her last year.

I have the ideal present for sweet old ladies who have a bit stashed away and who have no relatives. What you will need is a stout cardboard box, about the size of a quarter-pound packet of tea. Sprinkle a little cheap scent in this box—enough to make it reek of the stuff. Now find an empty scent bottle and smash it with a hammer. Put the pieces in the box. Tie the box securely, address it, then jump and up down on it. The silly old fool will think it has been damaged in transit.

"*You swine, McCoy, only good guys ride white horses.*"

"I find it stops them getting too bored."

Can you recommend a strong punch or wassail bowl sufficient to serve two people—a Post Office investigation officer and a big man who says nothing but who I think is a plain-clothes detective?

Not so fast, not so fast. Has this visit of theirs got anything to do with a parcel addressed to a sweet old lady who has a bit stashed away and no relatives?

Well, I don't imagine they're collecting for the orphans' pantomime treat.

You great oaf, you went and registered that parcel, didn't you?

I'm afraid so.

And then you went round the Post Office and tried to claim for a bottle of *Ma Griffe*, didn't you?

Yes. You see, I needed the money to buy some Christmas crackers.

If you wanted Christmas crackers, why didn't you come to me? There's a warehouse down the Mile End Road crammed to the rafters with the things. All you need is a sock filled with bath salts. Crack the night watchman over the head with it and you can have all the Christmas crackers, carnival balloons and novelty place-settings that your heart could desire. Anyway, getting back to those two flat-feet. This is no time for penny-pinching—get out the best scotch and try to look as if you are off your chump, like granny.

Having just had my name and address taken and been told that I may hear more of the matter, I would like to settle my nerves by bucking to and making the Christmas pudding. Can you give me an economical recipe?

Yes. You will need half an ounce of blanched almonds, half an ounce of finely-chopped suet, and a grated nutmeg. Don't buy these ingredients at a soulless supermarket—get yourself along to an old-fashioned, obliging and preferably short-sighted family grocer. While he is busy grating your nutmeg, grab a 16-ounce tinned Christmas pudding (serves four persons) and hide it.

I followed your recipe for an economical Christmas pudding, and also adapted the method to provide an economical turkey, some economical stuffing, a pound of economical butter and a bottle of economical brandy. Now I am serving thirty days in Holloway.

Excellent. Look at what you save on brussels sprouts.

I have been released from Holloway on bail and will be spending Christmas at home after all. Do you have an economical recipe for holly and mistletoe?

With your record, it's rather tricky. Couldn't you have developed a traumatic allergy to evergreens while in the nick? This could also extend to pine needles, unless you want an economical recipe for a Christmas tree?

Does this involve getting down Trafalgar Square with a saw?

Yes.

I think I'll scrub round the decorations and concentrate on sending out a few Christmas cards. Do you know where I can get some cheap?

Well, let's see now. Where does your husband work?

W. H. Smith's.

And you're asking me where to get cheap Christmas cards? The free advice you're getting, you should be giving *me* cheap Christmas cards.

My husband is unemployed, and I am on bail pending my appeal on a trumped-up shoplifting charge; I may also have to pay out some money to two men who have been posing as a Post Office investigations officer and a plain-clothes detective respectively, and who are now blackmailing me. They are spending Christmas with a sweet old lady who has a bit stashed away and who has two nephews. Anyway, what I'm driving at is that my husband and I have not got very much to spare for Christmas presents. What can we buy each other?

Bath salts.

Armchair Offensive

HEATH counter-attacks on the TV front

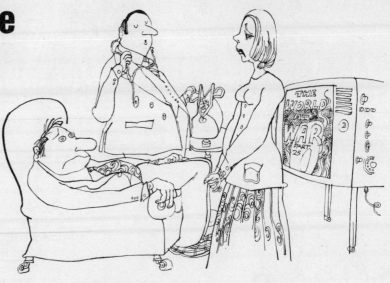

"Shellshock."

"You're too young to remember the First World War series, that was the series to end all series."

"Well, at least we'll be spared watching World War Three."

Owing to circumstances beyond our control 1984 has been unavoidably detained . . . .

Twenty-five years ago George Orwell gave the world a deadline. Some of what he envisaged has already come to pass, some of it was wildly wrong and seems unlikely now to happen. ALAN COREN argues that totalitarianism in Britain could never work. How could it, when nothing else does?

WINSTON SMITH lay on his mean little bed in his mean little room and stared at his mean little telescreen. The screen stared back, blank. Smith eased himself from the side of his mean little blonde, walked across his dun and threadbare carpet, and kicked the silent cathode. A blip lurched unsteadily across it, and disappeared. Smith sighed, and picked up the telephone.

"Would you get me Rentabrother Telehire?" he said.

"They're in the book," said the operator.

"I haven't got a book," said Smith. "They didn't deliver it."

"It's no good blaming me," said the operator. "It's a different department."

"I'm not blaming you," said Smith. "I just thought you might get me the number."

"I was just going off," said the operator, "on account of the snow."

"It's not snowing," said Smith.

"Not *now*, it isn't," said the operator. "I never said it was snowing *now*."

"Perhaps I might have a word with the Supervisor," said Smith.

"She's not here," said the operator. "She gets her hair done Fridays."

"I only need the Rentabrother number," said Smith, "perhaps you could find it for me. You must have a book."

"I'd have to bend," said the operator.

"I'd be awfully grateful," said Smith.

"I've just done me nails."

"Please," said Smith.

There was a long pause, during which a woman came on and began ordering chops, and someone gave Smith a snatch of weather forecast for Heligoland. After that, there was a bit of recipe for sausage toad. Eventually, after two further disconnections, the operator came back.

"It's 706544," she snapped.

Smith put the receiver down, and dialled 706544.

"809113," shouted a voice, "Eastasian Cats Home."

He got a Samoan ironmonger after that, and then a French woman who broke down and screamed. At last "Rentabrother Telehire," said a man.

"Winston Smith here," said Smith, "72a, Osbaldeston Road. I'm afraid my telescreen seems to be out of order."

"What am I supposed to do?" said the man. "We're up to our necks."

"But I'm not being watched," said Smith. "Big Brother is supposed to be monitoring me at all times."

"Ring Big Bleeding Brother, then," said the man. "Maybe he's not suffering from staff shortages, seasonal holidays, people off sick. Maybe he's not awaiting deliveries. Not to mention we had a gull get in the stockroom, there's stuff all over, all the labels come off, broken glass. People ringing up all hours of the day and night. You realise this is my tea-time?"

"I'm terribly sorry," said Smith, "It's just that . . . "

"Might be able to fit you in Thursday fortnight," said the man. "Can't promise nothing, though. Got a screwdriver, have you?"

"I'm not sure," said Smith.

"Expect bleeding miracles, people," said the man, and rang off.

Smith put the phone down, and was about to return to the bed when there was a heavy knocking on the door, and before he or the little blonde could move, it burst from its hinges and two enormous constables of the thought police hurtled into the room. They recovered, and looked around, and took out notebooks.

"Eric Jervis," cried the larger of the two, "we have been monitoring your every action for the past six days, and we have reason to believe that the bicycle standing outside with the worn brake blocks is registered in your name. What have you to say?"

"I'm not Eric Jervis," said Smith.

They stared at him.

"Here's a turn-up," said the shorter officer.

"Ask him if he's got any means of identity," murmured the larger.

"Have you any means of identity?" said the constable.

"I'm waiting for a new identity card," said Smith.

123

"It's in the post."

"I knew he'd say that," said the larger officer.

"We're right in it now," said his colleague. "Think of the paperwork."

They put their notebooks away.

"You wouldn't know where this Eric Jervis is, by any chance?" said the taller.

"I'm afraid not," said Smith.

"Who's that on the bed, then?"

"It's certainly not Eric Jervis," said Smith.

They all looked at the little blonde.

"He's got us there," said the shorter constable.

"I've just had a thought," said the taller, "I don't think people are supposed to, er, do it, are they?"

"Do what?"

"You know, men," the thought policeman looked at his boots, "and women."

"I don't see what that's got to do with worn brake blocks," said his colleague.

They tipped their helmets.

"Mind how you go," they said.

Smith let them out, and came back into the room.

"I'll just nip down the corner," he said to the little blonde, "and pick up an evening paper. Shan't be a tick."

It was crowded on the street. It was actually the time of the two minutes hate, but half the public telescreens were conked out, and anyway the population was largely drunk, or arguing with one another, or smacking kids round the head, or running to get a bet on, or dragging dogs from lamp-posts, or otherwise pre-occupied, so nobody paid much attention to the suspended telescreens, except for the youths throwing stones at them. Smith edged through, and bought a paper, and opened it.

"COME OFF IT BIG BROTHER," screamed the headline, above a story blaming the Government for rising food prices, the shortage of underwear, and the poor showing of the Oceanic football team. It wasn't, Smith knew, the story the Government hacks had given to the printers, but you could never get the printers to listen to anyone, and challenged, they always blamed the shortage of type, claiming that they could only put the words together from the letters available, and who cared, anyhow? The Government, with so much else on its plate, had given up bothering.

It was as Winston Smith turned to go back to his flat, that he felt a frantic plucking at his knee, and heard a soprano scream ring through the street. He looked down, and saw a tiny youth spy jumping up and down below him.

"Winston Smith does dirty things up in Fourteen B," howled the child. "Come and get him, he's got a nude lady up there."

The youth spy might have elaborated on these themes, had its mother not reached out and given it a round arm swipe that sent it flying into the gutter: but, even so, the damage had been done, and before Smith had time to protest, he found himself picked up bodily by a brace of uniformed men and slung into the back of a truck which, siren wailing, bore him rapidly through the evening streets towards the fearful pile of the Ministry of Love.

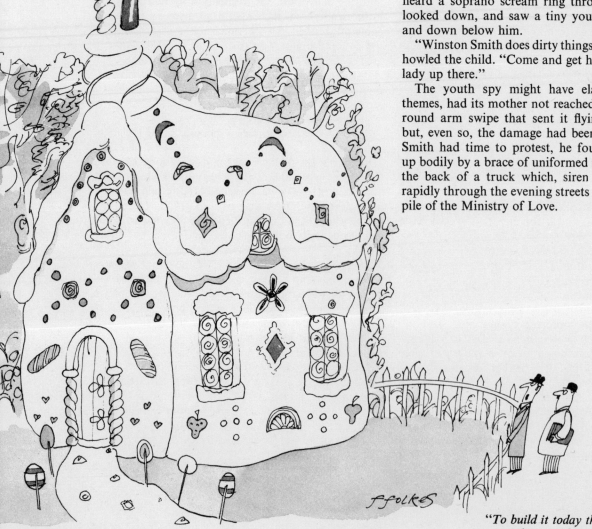

"To build it today the marshmallow alone would cost £1500."

"Of course, nowadays we only keep him around for the tourists."

"Smith, W," barked the uniformed man to whom Smith was manacled, at the desk clerk.

"What's he done?" said the clerk. "I was just off home."

"They caught him at a bit of how's your father," said Smith's captor.

"It's Friday night," said the desk clerk. "I go to bingo Fridays." He turned to Smith. "Don't let it happen again, lad. You can go blind."

"I've written him in me book," said the guard. "It's no good saying go home. I'd have to tear the page out." He put his free hand on Smith's arm. "Sorry about this, son. It'd be different if I had a rubber. We're awaiting deliveries."

"You'd better take him up to Room 101, then," said the clerk.

"NOT ROOM 101," screamed Smith, "NOT THE TORTURE CHAMBER, PLEASE, I NEVER DID ANYTHING, I HARDLY KNOW THE WOMAN, CAN'T ANYONE HELP ME, DON'T SEND ME UP . . ."

"Stop that," said the clerk, sharply. "You'll start the dog off."

Smith was dragged, shrieking, to the lift.

"Ah, Smith, Winston," cried the white-coated man at the door of Room 101. "Won't you come in? Rats I believe, are what you, ha-ha-ha, fear most of all. Big brown rats. Big brown pink-eyed rats . . ."

"NO," screamed Smith, "NOT RATS, ANYTHING BUT RATS, NO, NO, NO."

" . . . Rats with long slithery tails, Smith, fat, hungry rats, rats with sharp little . . ."

"Oh, do shut up, Esmond," interrupted his assistant wearily. "You know we haven't got any rats. We haven't seen a rat since last December's delivery."

"No rats?" gasped Smith.

Esmond sighed, and shook his head. Then he suddenly brightened.

"We've got mice though," he cried. "Big fat, hungry, pink-eyed . . ."

"I don't mind mice," said Smith.

They looked at him.

"You're not making our job any easier, you know," muttered Esmond.

"Try him on toads," said Esmond's assistant. "Can't move in the stockroom for toads."

"That's it!" exclaimed Esmond. "Toads, big, fat, slimy . . ."

"I quite like toads," said Smith.

There was a long pause.

"Spiders?"

"Lovely little things," said Smith. "If it's any help, I can't stand moths."

"Moths," cried Esmond. "Where do you think you are, bloody Harrod's? We can't get moths for love nor money."

"Comes in here, big as you please, asking for moths," said Esmond's assistant.

Smith thought for a while.

"I'm not all that keen on stoats," he said at last.

"At last," said Esmond. "I thought we'd be here all night. Give him a stoat, Dennis."

So they put Winston Smith in Room 101 with a stoat. It was an old stoat, and it just sat on the floor, wheezing, and as far as Smith was concerned, things could have been, all things considered, a lot worse.

FUEL CRISIS! All the News! All the Excuses!

"Who needs petrol?" asks Lord Stokes, Britain's biggest motor manufacturer, here seen going nowhere fast. "Sitting at the wheel is what matters, not getting there."

Why should I go short?

Everyone thinks that rationing's for other people. Look at these letters from the post-bag at the Department of Trade and Industry:

SIR, I am the secretary of a nation-wide motoring fraternity whose members devote most of their leisure to offering lifts to women.

Unlike the average selfish motorist, my members are so constituted that they cannot bear to pass a woman of any age or shape trudging along the pavement without jamming on the brakes and offering her a free excursion to the countryside. Without exception they pride themselves on their winning manners and their ability to establish a quick and pleasurable rapport with their passengers. Occasionally their kindness is ill-rewarded and the passenger elects to walk home, but my members are not the kind to bear a grudge or to be dissuaded from their chosen avocation by one or two failures.

It is unthinkable that such a valuable social service should be hampered by fuel restrictions and I look forward to hearing from you that members of this Association will be exempt from any scheme of rationing. I may say that they regard it as a point of honour to use no more fuel than they can possibly help.

I should add that we also have a Ladies Branch which offers lifts to men. This service, I feel sure, cannot fail to have a strong claim on your indulgence.

> J. C. Gollop, Hon. Sec.,
> National Association of Kerb Crawlers.

SIR, If my chauffeur is unable to drive my dogs each morning to the quiet streets of Chiswick and Acton to "do their business" I dread to think what the Royal Borough of Kensington will soon look like. If this is not a case for a special allocation of petrol, what is?

> (Lady) Alice Pratt-Bunbury
> The Boltons
> Kensington.

SIR, I am a humble student from Kuwait and I need petrol to get about your so beautiful country. Alas, my Cadillac travels only five miles to the gallon. Please mail ten years' supply of petrol coupons to me at once. My uncle, the Shaikh, has asked me to keep him informed of any difficulties I encounter in your so beautiful land.

> Ahmad al-Ahmen al-Kebir
> Hilton Hotel
> London.

SIR, For nearly twenty years, every Sunday, it has been my custom to drive my father from our home at Staines to his favourite car park at Bognor Regis, where he sits quietly for a couple of hours reading the News of the World, completely oblivious to his surroundings. Surely it would be monstrous to deprive him in the twilight of his life of this harmless indulgence for the sake of three or four gallons of petrol? Would it not be far better to cut the ration of those irresponsible young men who take out girls at weekends in vans openly inscribed Singer Sewing Machines and Mother Shipton's Home-Made Pies?

> Arthur Feet
> 1a The Ridgeway
> Staines.

SIR I am frequently invited to take part in a BBC programme called Any Questions? which is held in increasingly remote drill halls and Scout huts. Unless assured of unlimited petrol the panellist runs a grave risk of never finding the locus, which may well be as distant and elusive as Bristol. If the nation wants us to go to the far ends of the earth to answer questions like "Supposing the members of the team were born again, which furry animal would they like to be?" then the nation must provide the fuel, I look to you, Sir, for assistance in my hour of need I enclose my card.

> (Name and address supplied).

SIR, I am bitterly disappointed to hear from you that as sales director of a firm manufacturing high quality budgie mirrors I do not qualify for a special allocation of fuel.

It is with no motive of sour grapes, but from a sense of public duty that I now draw your attention to a spectacle all too familiar to those who travel the roads of this country: that of tipsy farmers roaring home from the public-house on their giant tractors with their equally tipsy wives perched up behind. Such are the new privileged classes of Britain!

It is high time we got our priorities right.

> B. Armstrong-Phipps
> Cage Furnishings Ltd
> Feltham.

Heroes of the motorways:

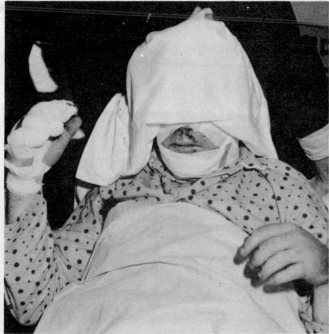

THE ALBERT BROTHERS, of Luton, recently drove from Newport Pagnell to Carlisle, in three cars, in line abreast, at exactly fifty miles an hour, effectively preventing all efforts to overtake, and thus saving the nation an estimated 5,000 gallons of fuel. ''The hooting and flashing behind us were fantastic,'' says John Albert, pictured in hospital after ' something of an argument ' with 1,500 angry truck drivers at Carlisle. ''But I have no hard feelings. It's not every day you get such an opportunity to get Ted Heath out of a hole.''

NICK BUNCE, of the Chelsea Chapter of Hell's Angels, has offered the services of his mates to enforce a 50 mph speed limit on all highways. ''The police say it can't be done,'' says Nick. ''Just stick around and watch us do it.'' Are the Hell's Angels activated by public-spirit? ''Not —— likely,'' declares Nick. It's just that the lads have found they can work up more aggro by making drivers go slow.''

''We've all got to make sacrifices,'' says LEN HOOT, manager of the service station at Little Chiselling. ''They come to me because I offer them Quad Stamps with four gallons, then I tell them 'No more than two gallons for anybody.' You should hear them moan! Some people don't know there's a crisis on.''

How to syphon petrol

This article is for general information only. The instructions should on no account be carried out.

1. Wait until it is dark.
2. Find a car with some petrol still in its tank.
3. Insert a rubber tube into the tank and place a can below the other end of the tube.
4. Extinguish your cigarette.
5. Suck on the rubber tube until your mouth is full of petrol. Do not swallow more than you can help.
6. You fool, you have swallowed the lot.
7. Wait a few moments before lighting another cigarette.
8. Find another car with some petrol in the tank.

How to drive without using petrol

Note: This procedure is perfectly legal.

1. Ensure that you are on good terms with your neighbours, the Huggetts.
2. Hand Sam Huggett a rope with a hook at each end. Tell him to fasten one end to the rear of his car and the other end to the front of yours.
3. Fasten a sign ''ON TOW'' to the rear of your car.
4. Give Huggett the ''thumbs up'' sign. He should now pull you and your family to Great Yarmouth. You will consume no petrol whatever.
5. If you wish, or if Huggett insists, you can reverse the roles and tow him home from Great Yarmouth.

A PRogRESs RePORT on AMERICAN EDUCATION
or How We Get Our Smarts On Nowadays
researched by ARNOLD ROTH

A Horn Book History of American Learning

←This is Jim. He has no EDUCATION. He also has no JOB. He does have a bottle of cheap wine. He drinks it and gets philosophical all over.

←This is Balsam. He is a Ph.D. from Yale. He HAS education. He has NO job though. He gets philosophical. Then he drinks cheap wine.

Contemporary Creative Progressive Free Form

Polytechnics and the Commercial Sciences

Higher Learning

Anti-Intellectual Studies

Liberals Art

Lessons from Real Life

IT TAKES ALL SORTS TO MAKE A PROGRAMME

says WILLIAM HARDCASTLE

I ALWAYS fall for them. They are the singing postmen, the cackling ex-parlour maids, the mad earls and the madder serfs who spend their idle hours making a sun porch out of conkers. Only the other day I collapsed helpless before a professional tree-feller who wrote a letter to *The Lancet* to the effect that hot baths weaken the spine.

He was in the great tradition. He boasted that for twenty years he had eschewed the tub and the result was that, at the age of 64, he stood as straight and as tall as the oaks he keeps chopping down. His theory that to lie in the bath and twiddle the hot water tap with your toes leads to slipped discs may be without any scientific foundation. No matter—he was a character and he was funny with it. When someone like that comes along we in the media tend to turn over on our backs and wave our paws in the air in speechless, nay dumb, gratitude.

It is noteworthy that, in this field of packaged eccentricity, we tend to prefer the extremes of class. A nutty aristocrat whose blood is running blue but thin is particularly acceptable; it is not often that you

"Doris, where are my clean socks?"

get a traditional figure of British comedy who also confirms one's most ingrained prejudices. At the other extreme there are the lower orders. Listen to those old radio archive programmes and you'll be surprised how often they feature some rural oaf making a fool of himself. *But so funny!* Monty Modlin has made a career out of crashing into drawing rooms where angels would fear to tiptoe, and at the same time exploiting the cheerful cockney charladies of which he claims to be a blood brother.

But that is to digress. I am persuaded that the discovery and provision of "Characters" for the media, a hungry market, should be put on a more organised basis. Just as there are talent agencies to spot accordion players, tap dancers, computer programmers and general managers of plastic extrusion factories, so there should be an organisation— O.B.I., standing for Odd Ball Industries, is my first thought—that would, when the news gets too serious, supply the news editor, the programme maker, the talks show producer, with a lady who had the habit of hatching out ducks' eggs in her cleavage. (Where is she now? Hatching out our furry chicks in her brassière with nobody taking a blind bit of notice? I wonder.)

It is delightful, of course, when we hit on the north-western school master who keeps throwing eggs out of aeroplanes and showing that they don't break. There must be something about eggs, because there was the fellow the other day who talked about eggs *fainting* when they were shocked. Which reminds me of Lady Dowding's theory that the real nature-lover can hear a flower scream when it is plucked. It's fine to stumble on these gems but it would be nice if there was the journalistic equivalent of a jewellery shop into which you could stroll and take your pick.

Some of the news agencies try their best. There is the recurring story of the funeral in Naples (it's always Naples) where the mourners suddenly see the coffin lid move. To cut a long and familiar story short the loved one eventually climbs out of the casket and joins the feast. Then there is the 103-year-old wife in Topeka, Kansas (another favourite spot) who sues her 105-year-old husband for divorce on the grounds of his unfaithfulness. "He kept coming in late and

"I can't make up my mind what to wear today."

keeping me awake" is the quote that is always attributed to the offended lady. But there is something shopworn about these whiskery tales. Perhaps it would be better for me to suggest how genuine individuals, hitherto having hidden their off-beatedness under a bushel, can make the grade.

My first advice would be—don't aim too high. Get your name, and oddity, into one of the more obscure publications and be assured that there is many a beady eye in Fleet Street, Broadcasting House and Television Centre scanning them. The tree-feller from Cheadle Hulme who made *The Lancet* is a good case in point. Cries of Excelsior! rose from the news desks of the nation when he surfaced. Even less distinguished medical journals can be of use if you get them to print a piece suggesting that those who blush easily have better sex lives than people who part their hair in the middle. You'll be on *Nationwide* before you can say "and now for something entirely different".

It's one thing to make page three of the *Mail*, *Mirror* or *Sun*—plus two and a half minutes on the *World At One*—but it remains to be seen whether you're a stayer or a flash in the pan. There are those who enjoy fleeting fame—they may have grown a fifteen foot high hollyhock in their garden—and then sink back into obscurity, happy or otherwise. I often wonder about people like the East Anglian Old Age pensioner who makes a habit of vaulting over pillar boxes. Once the *Today* programme had lost interest in him, has life ever been the same again?

By contrast there are the stayers, the Margaret Powells whose early memories and hearty laugh combine into a career and a comfortable bank account. When he first became "Brain of Britain" Ted Moult was the man with straw in his hair and a mind underneath. He might have vanished without trace but the sterner stuff soon showed through. So the off-beat can become the long term. It can also, sadly, be put to professional and political advantage.

The British Association of Ceramic Sanitary Ware manufacturers used to have a Press Officer with a firm grasp on the British penchant for oddity and lavatorial humour. Each year, to coincide with his Association's Annual Report, he would produce some extraordinary revelation about the incidence of bidets in the East Riding of Yorkshire, the style of graffiti in Welsh ladies' conveniences, or the merits of a new silent flush calculated to keep secrets from your neighbours. He was a man with a touch of creativity and a pungent regional accent and he never failed to widen the public awareness of ceramic sanitary ware. Some MPs use the same techniques to enhance their own reputation.

They will put down a question on the Parliamentary Order Paper, not in the hope of eliciting information from the Minister concerned but in the expectation of being interviewed on the point they have raised in such a calculated fashion. Why are imported turnips being used in home-baked Cornish pasties, when crops are rotting in the fields of Lincolnshire? Should women motorists be banned from driving if they wear high heels? They get their names in the papers or on the air and it's supposed to keep the constituents happy. As for me it drives me to taking another hot bath.

My Tour of the North Seas

by Her Majesty the Queen as told to MILES KINGTON

Day 1. Of course, the thing one is worried about, going to these far-off places, is whether one is going to be upset by their strange customs, not to mention their strange food, because if the natives have gone to an awful lot of trouble putting on a show and a big banquet one certainly doesn't want to hurt their feelings by laughing in the wrong place or being seen taking a quick milk of magnesia tablet. And all I really knew about the Isles of Britain—I hope you don't mind if I call me I—was that some of their customs were very strange indeed.

We first visited the main island, which is called England, and were shown some of the natives working in the famous Oxford Street bazaars, which they mostly do by candlelight. I could not help noticing that all these dark and rather cold shops were actually fitted with electrical light fixtures, very few of them being used. It would have been tactless to ask the reason; I suppose either they have very little idea how they work or cannot afford the fuel to work them. It seems a shame to trick these islanders into spending their scarce capital on goods that are no use to them.

I asked if I might see a local factory, but was told it was not a good day. Thursday, Friday, Saturdays were good days. A strange religious survival, this idea of good days.

A native banquet where we feasted on mushroom soup, roast chicken and ice cream, three local specialities.

Day 2. This was the first day on which we were treated to a cultural event. It was called a Royal Command Performance, in my honour, and consisted of the showing of a dull imported American film, which left me no wiser about native art. I enquired what other major art attractions there were in England, and was told of a showing of French impressionist paintings, a German opera conducted by a Hungarian, and a very grand exhibition, now closed, of Chinese art.

"But I would very much like to see some Isles of Britain art," I smiled. "What do you recommend?"

They smiled and discussed among themselves.

"Do you have no native dancing?" I asked.

They promised to find out.

We feasted again on mushroom soup, roast chicken and ice cream. This time the ice cream was not pink but brown. The flavour was the same.

Day 3. I flew to the island known as Wales, inhabited by a people of great warriors of old times who fought constantly against the English; though they are now at peace they have a popular ritual of mock-fighting which I was privileged to see. I must confess privately that I found the violence of the ceremony sickening, unlike the many thousands of natives round the so-called 'rugby field'.

I requested to be allowed to see the famous Welsh coal-miners at work (I had heard of these happy, black-faced folk who spend many hours underground for what would elsewhere seem very little money) but I was told again that it was not a good day.

"Which are the good days for mining?" I smiled, having picked up this phrase by now.

"At the moment, there are no good days for mining," I was told.

An enormous Welsh banquet in the evening, with soup, chicken, ice cream.

*"Actually, we're **not** very together. We thought eating might help."*

132

"On the other hand I don't covet his ox."

Day 4. My smallest island so far, the delightful Isle of Man. This isle is reserved as a kind of haven for those elders among the Britons who have come near the end of their useful life and are rewarded with a small dwelling and exemption from many of the taxes levied on most citizens. Many of them sit at home, contentedly drinking; others venture out so far as the communal hut known as the 'golf club' where they can sit contentedly drinking.

"I suppose our next call will be the Emerald Isle, so called because the grass is green and the folk are so happy?" I smiled.

"We think it is best to avoid Ireland," they smiled.

"It is a bad day for Ireland?" I smiled.

"It is a bad year for Ireland," they told me.

Soup, chicken, ice cream and liver salts.

Day 6. Flew to Scotland, where I was introduced to some of the leading Politicians of the isles. This is the sect which has ruled the nations for as long as anyone can remember, and they speak a kind of dialect not unlike English, though where we would use words, they prefer sacred formulas of their own. I jotted down a few, for interest's sake. "A sense of national purpose, the very real dangers, right across the board, divisive policies and a searching re-examination". At this time of the year it is customary for them to seek the support of their people—as they cannot communicate directly, of course, this is done by a rather primitive method of marking papers with an X which are then counted.

The Scottish Isles are at present in the news because of the vast oil and gas deposits found there. As their technology is quite inadequate to retrieve this oil, the Americans and the Europeans have, as usual, arrived to take over the work and no doubt most of the revenue. The Scots, however, seem quite happy with the attention they are receiving, which is just as well, as this part of the isles seems even poorer than the rest.

Day 7. Back to the main town, London. Did the natives, I enquired, also live entirely on soup, chicken and ice cream? I was informed to the contrary. These dishes are generally too expensive; however, the British have no sense of fine eating and are quite content to eat 'sliced' (a poor copy of bread) and drink 'beer', a kind of flavoured water.

They had not forgotten my request to see some native dancing and I was taken to a hall in Hammersmith to witness the local arts. It was skilful enough, but is the only example of native dancers I have ever seen who seemed to take no pleasure in their art. Perhaps it was a bad day for dancing.

The rain was descending again as we prepared to fly back to civilisation, though it did not prevent a stirring final ceremony by massed airport officials, complete with traditional umbrellas, raincoats, gloves and handshakes. Normally, the British seem an unemotional race, but their reserve broke down at the last and many of them smiled openly as they voiced their traditional farewell: "Well, I hope you've had a pleasant stay and perhaps we may see you again".

A backwater, then, with little to offer the outer world, but not without its own charm. I shall often think of the isles of the North Sea when my eyes fall upon their parting gift, a box of candles and a small can of petrol, which to them represents treasure beyond price.

As the National Book League steps
the printed word and push its sale by any means available, we offer
Apart from being a thundering good read for all the family, it

If a pilot scheme mooted by the National Book League proves as successful as it promises to be, it should soon be possible for you to buy authors as well as books. Here, a customer at W. H. Smith's is shown purchasing five assorted Doctor books and their author Richard Gordon, for an undisclosed sum. Apart from being around to help explain jokes, misprints, and so on, Richard Gordon makes a tasteful addition to any home, and may also bring the fortunate buyer limitless social acclaim by writing, on your very own premises, such instant best sellers as *Doctor At 14 Acacia Crescent Reigate, Doctor Out Shopping With Mrs. Maureen Bigelow, Doctor Just Nipping Down To The Fox And Ferret With His Friend Dennis Quilt*, and many, many more.

The National Book League's answer to the threat of the tranny! Modern youth, Now People of all ages, in fact, need a book that's easy to read, good to feel, and looks smart on a charm bracelet. This one, *The Best of Tolstoy*, contains a full eighty words, many of them different, and gives the complete gist of his most famous novels. It comes with free pill dispenser and bath cube, and is available in Molten Puce, Naughty Gold, and Two-tone Dusk.

Too often in the past, books have been associated with dull, lonely intellectuals incapable of having fun. Now, thanks to modern production methods, this young lady is able to help herself to a large Thackeray-and-tonic whenever she feels like a quick snifter! Of course, expense is still a bug to be ironed out, but at least one bright young London publisher has told us that he's confident of being able to bring out a paperback Campari in time for the Christmas market.

Norman Boone, 53-year-old bachelor sales representative, has perfected a technique of dancing with books. "I started with slow, easy things like waltzes, but now I find even the most intricate tango is possible. Books are nicer than girls, don't tread on your feet, and never ask for large gins," said Mr. Boone. "I am very happy."

up its constant battle to popularise
them this promotional brochure as our contribution to the war effort.
also makes a great paper dart, sun hat and emergency nappy.

◄ Mr. Eric Garamond, tenor, who sings White Papers outside HMSO bookshops, frequently to lute accompaniment. "I find people are very interested in relative fish tonnage, although committee reports on milled steel standards have a surprisingly loyal following, many of whom join in the choruses. Lots of people who would not otherwise count themselves regular readers nevertheless seem to love a book you can whistle."

▲ At Madame Walewska's Fun Palace of All Nations, Frith Street, the inventive lovelies like nothing better than to relax with the latest title from Calder & Boyar's. "We find modern literature keeps us up to scratch," said lissome Pauleen la Thong. "It doesn't do to have a customer come in and spring something he's just memorised in the back room of the premises below. Also, we have a very high standard of clientele, many of whom enjoy being pelted with calf-bound classics, and sometimes I don't know what we'd do without our library."

Klaus von McWhirter and his twin brother Franz testing a claim submitted to their ever-popular *Schnapps Book of Records*. Book-hurling has become a popular German sport, and the national record for throwing Bavaria's largest book over Bavaria's second largest book is now 3.78 metres. "Not since the great days of sweeping them into piles and setting light to them have books been so popular in Germany," Klaus told fact-finding NBL delegates, "although my brother and I had, of course, no idea what was going on. The tallest pyre, by the way, was 16.3 metres, including over a hundred kilos of Heinrich Heine alone." ▼

▲ Why not keep a book as a pet? Railwayman Gerald Wisley has a giant early edition of Benwell's Encyclopaedia of Suffolk, which he finds to be loyal, good with children, and clean about the house. It prefers not to go for walks, but enjoys a good dust, and eats nothing.

Two Generations of Christmas

1. Robert Morley puts up the decorations

I AM always delighted to see the Three Wise Men, they keep themselves so fit. I can't remember how long ago I bought them, or where, but each year I wander from room to room, holding them in my hand and looking for fresh terrain on which to stand them. In the end they always take their accustomed place above the window in the hall. There's a ledge which suits them perfectly, each walking a pace behind the other in the general direction of the golden star, with which I am not so pleased. It becomes increasingly difficult to disguise the tarnish.

I am a clumsy man, not wont, or indeed usually able, to let my fingers do the walking, but the decorations are my special province. If I was honest I would say what I look forward to most each Christmas is the brandy butter and getting my two-hundredth Christmas card. I need two hundred to fix to the

beams in the living room. Without them the room is hopeless. I have tried alternative decorations and failed.

In point of fact I have tried alternative decorations almost everywhere, but each year repeat the pattern with only one or two minor changes. The bandsmen from Tokyo can stand on the mantelpiece and the Holy Family take their places on the window ledge, or vice versa. There are some dilapidated musical instruments which pin either up the stair rail or around the grandfather clock.

I am sick to death of three cardboard angels with feather skirts. Each year they come out of their box and almost at once retire back into it. It is not just that they are common, they are not for instance as common as the Hong Kong plastic mines, or even the Christmas Tree Fairy herself; it's just that I hate them as much as I love the owls, the beautiful white owls who perch in the holly branches, and the golden mobile, the pièce de résistance on the top landing, which only my boundless courage and total disregard of personal danger enables me to fix each Christmas Eve, balancing on the topmost of the folding steps.

I buy my new decorations each August in a shop which sells to the trade. Go in September and it's all over. In September they sell Easter bunnies. I like that very much. I admire people who plan ahead. I revere those who put things behind them. Myself, I hark back. I want this Christmas to be as much like the last as possible. I hold on as a man catapulted into the water will hold on to an upturned keel, surprised at first how easily it helps him to stay afloat, feeling as yet no numbness in his finger tips.

Talking of finger tips, I must try not to be the first this year to pull the cracker, to put on the cap, to read the riddle, to hog the enjoyment. I have had 64 Christmases and enjoyed them all, except possibly my first, and for all I know I may have enjoyed that one too.

On my sixth they gave me the Delhi Durbar. I don't remember what I was given last year or the year before or the year before that. The only Christmas present I ever remember was the Delhi Durbar. It came complete with the King Emperor and his Queen, the elephants and the ceremonial pavilion. It came in a flat red box, the sort of box jigsaws came in, but this was no puzzle. It was what I wanted most in the whole world, it was all I wanted. It was perfection, and I have never, never forgotten the box on the drawing room floor under the Christmas tree at six o'clock on Christmas Eve. It was not done up in idiotic wrapping paper, it was not tied with string. All I had to do was to lift off the lid and start taking the sepoys and the gurkhas, the horses and the tigers out one by one and stand them on the carpet.

So why go on, you ask, why if six was perfect try for 65, why not forget the whole thing this year? Take oneself off to the splendid quiet of an Imperial Hotel at some neglected, out-of-season, watering place, and hole up with an electric blanket on the bed and a "Do not Disturb" sign on the door handle. I have thought of it. I have made a few discreet enquiries. "Are you full at Christmas, and what are your rates?"

To do it properly I suppose I would have to come down to Christmas Dinner and eat my way solemnly through to the mince pies, eyeing the solitary cracker on the table, staring out front, intensely proud, utterly alone—the sort of part Aubrey Smith, or I for that matter, would once have given our eye teeth for.

But no, I have to be home to open the cards, and before anyone else has a chance to read them, impale them with a drawing pin up aloft. Long, short, long, short is the pattern. The picture families I do save for the mantelpiece. There are only a few of those, alas— the Yehudi Menuhins whom I hardly know, and the David Tomlinsons whom I know very well, my niece's family and sometimes the odd godchild or a celebrated photographer out on a spree. I have never had one from the Queen, but then of course she has never had one from me.

I do get one from the Gaekwar of Baroda, but it is almost severely simple and although I sometimes save it for some guest to open up and read His Highness's message, they seldom seem to bother. There was a theatrical manager who used to imagine himself still an officer and gentleman and always sent pictures of

regimental carnage, but these I neither pinned nor planted. They were not, I told myself, the real spirit of Christmas, and I laid them on one side to be used only in dire emergency.

For years the village in which I live used to support a company of bell ringers, and on the appointed evening they would arrive and march into the living room, where we had only just switched off the telly and were hoping they wouldn't notice the fumes. They put their bells on a small portable card table and kept picking them up and putting them down again with a sort of sustained patience, and if you listened very carefully and had an ear for music, it was possible to discover some sort of tune. Then came the moment for which I was waiting, when the head man would enquire whether we had a favourite carol. It was the signal that the performance was about to finish; it was the equivalent of the "and now one final question" on the chat show.

Loudly I would call for Good King Wenceslas.

"Again?" they were wont to enquire.

"Again," I would tell them.

"I can't hear it often enough," I would lie. Then cakes and ale and five pounds in the hat, or possibly a bit less, and God rested the Merry Gentlemen for another year. Now we have carol singers; they don't come in, but I feel just as much of a fool standing in the garden pretending I like being sung at. I would as lief have a Hungarian violinist bending over my crepe suzettes in some ghastly bistro.

So what's it all about, then, you ask, and I can honestly tell you I don't know. Have they spoilt Christmas, and if so, who are They? The butchers, the bakers, the candlestick makers? The poor we cannot forgive or the homeless we will not house or the hungry we have not fed or the prisoners we have not set free?

Are they the ones who announce in the agony columns that they are not sending cards this year, but have made a donation to the Lifeboat Fund, or are they people like you and me, who always want the sort of Christmas we had last year or the year before that, or sixty years ago, who want to stand on the other side of the drawing room door and still be able to reach up and open it when the clock strikes and find the Delhi Durbar under the tree?

138

Two Generations of Christmas

2. Sheridan Morley organises the festivities

W<small>E</small> are not, as my father's preceding article must already have suggested to you, a family who take Christmas lightly: indeed my mother has been known to call in lists of what we would each like sometime during the summer holidays on the principle that the sooner she and Harrods get through with the shopping the sooner they can start planning for Easter.

The first Christmas I can remember was about 1945: there had been some kind of a war on and people were celebrating and I was taken to a pantomime. On the way home we were walking down the Strand and a very old gentleman patted me on the head and my godfather said, "That was George Robey," as if that explained anything.

Then there was the year of the electric trains. By this time we were in New York where Robert was doing a play and there was a firm called Lionel who made trains which, while not exactly lifesize, were about twice the dimensions of anything ever contemplated by our own Triang/Hornby lads. That particular Christmas—it must have been 1948 and there was snow in Central Park and I gave Anna Massey whooping cough (not as a present you understand, it was just that she came to tea and I happened to have it)—was one of Robert's finest. Not a mechanical man, a failing I have alas inherited, he yet managed to rig the trains so that they ran right the way around the living room and out into the dining room and back, a distance of roughly two miles, since American living rooms tend to be large.

The sheer thrill of waiting in the living room while the train made its invisible journey around the dining room and then returned intact was quite something, eclipsing even the thrill of a huge upturned coffin thing in the corner which provided pictures and sound simultaneously at the flick of a mere seven switches.

If there is a prize for good Christmases, I reckon that 1948 gets mine; admittedly being seven helped a lot. Seven is an ideal age for Christmas: you're old enough to enjoy it but young enough not to have to

do much about getting it ready or washing up afterwards. On the Day itself, Robert took my mother and sister and me (my brother, ever dubious about family celebrations, had not yet been born) to Broadway to see Ray Bolger in *Where's Charley?* since it is only the English who are nutty enough to close their theatres on the one day of the year positively made for playgoing. Anyway at the end of the second half Mr. Bolger actually waved to me and I promised myself that I would learn to tap dance and wave to audiences, just two of the promises I have managed to overlook in the intervening quarter-century.

Then there was a Christmas in Australia where it was far too hot and we got sand in the mince pies and one could swim except for the munchies (or sharks as we deep-sea folk like to call them) who fancied a leg or two by way of seasonal chewing. Then we came home to Berkshire where for the last twenty years we have held a series of annual celebrations planned with only slightly more care and attention than the Royal Wedding.

When my grandmother, Gladys Cooper, was alive and had a house in Henley, it was possible to progress through five totally separate households (my cousins, aunt and parents also live within ten miles of us, not intentionally I think—it just happened like that) on a sort of gastronomic tour which could take up to five days depending on whether or not Christmas fell at a weekend. Gladys was at her best doing Christmas teas, sensational affairs since she seldom ate lunch and was therefore always ready for a good tea. At these

Yuletide gatherings she would hand out the presents along with the scones and, as we grand-children got gradually older and more tiresome to shop for, she would pass on to us a selection of her birthday presents, her birthday having fallen conveniently on December 18th (she herself had celebrated more than eighty of these anniversaries by 1970 and was finding she already had most of the things she needed). One year she passed on to me a massive log basket, having failed to notice that its original donor had filled it with all kinds of goodies like smoked salmon and Russian caviare, and for some days afterwards the family debated the ethics of whether or not the contents had technically been a present to me or an oversight on Gladys's part. I need hardly add that by the time the family upheld the latter theory I had eaten most of the salmon.

Then there was the Christmas I brought my fiancée home from America and decided to break it to my parents that they were about to lose their elder son, an event they had I think been keenly awaiting for some years. My mother maintains I began the conversation with "It's, um, about that girl upstairs . . ."

Then there was the year of my sister and the powdered glass. Told by my wife one pre-Christmas night to bring home some cranberry sauce, I drifted into a supermarket and acquired a jar marked down to half price because there was a nasty crack down one side where someone had evidently dropped it. The contents being still intact, and I being ever on the alert for a bargain especially around Christmas, I took it home and decanted it into a dish. Comes Christmas lunch, my sister eating with us, and from her a crunching sound not wholly consistent with cranberries; she, never one to look on the bright side, naturally assumed she was being murdered and the rest of the afternoon was spent in heated discussion of whether Agatha Christie's characters died from powdered or fractured glass. My sister has still not entirely forgiven me, but she's lucky to be alive to carry on complaining, or so I tell her.

From Robert I have inherited a deep fear of not getting enough Christmas cards, an inability to put anything together once my children have taken it to pieces, and a vague feeling that there must be an easier way of doing the whole thing if only one could find it. Still, by careful family planning it is possible to ensure that there's always one child around of mechanical device age, and once you've got him or her on your side there's no limit to the fun: my son has now reached the Hornby Electric age and this year will, if my credit at Harrods holds up, see some refinements to the basic track-and-one-points system that is presently gathering dust on the playroom floor.

Then there is my annual struggle with the Scorpions; this will at some future date be the subject of a five-volume Gothic novel but, for the time being, suffice it to say that one dark and stormy night three Novembers ago I acquired a set of racing cars (named Scorpions for reasons best known to Lesney Products) with a view to giving them to my son for Christmas—admittedly he was then barely three but he is a tolerant child and I thought might be prepared to indulge me. Anyway after six months hard labour I had the track assembled in good time for the summer holidays and then tried to race the cars. They didn't. What followed was a two-year dialogue with a kindly lady at the Harrods toy department who informed me just the other day, with some relief, that as Scorpions were no longer on the market there wasn't much point in my complaining about them any longer. "I think," she said, in one of the most memorable summaries of recent times, "there must have been something wrong with them."

I suppose the most peaceful Christmas I ever had was one pre-marital year when I was in Los Angeles staying with a lovely actor called Richard Haydn who always spends Christmas afternoon at the movies. That year we saw three feature films, two cartoons and a newsreel and still had time for an oven-fresh, hand-prepared, finger-licking good, dinner at a drive-in afterwards.

Things are different now of course, what with the house and the children and the cat and the goldfish (what do you give a goldfish for Christmas?) and the Christmas Tree I carefully replanted last New Year's Eve and which lived all through the summer only to die a week ago, just about the time our local garden centre began selling the new ones—I think they programme them to do that. You'll have to forgive me now, I must just go and find a present for Robert; do Harrods still sell Delhi Durbars, I wonder?

'It's Knight-sign. She's got bad breath, and she's been around."

A Few Rough Knights

BILL TIDY on Medieval Chivalry

"*You said it was a dragon **that** high!*"

"*The Holy Grail I'll look for. The Maltese Falcon—no chance!*"

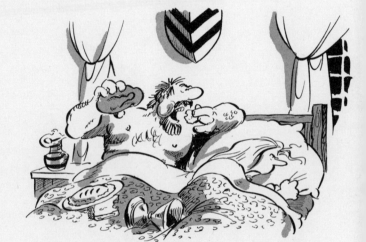

"*I'll tell you why I'm not a gentleman like Sir Gawaine. Sir Gawaine is a big puff!*"

"*Golda, light of my life, tell them I got my Knighthood for welfare and charity work!*"

Where do Bordeaux Wines Really Come From?

Newcomers to wine often suspect that a lot of crude trickery is
involved in its making. Nonsense — it's highly skilled trickery.
Here's a basic guide by MILES KINGTON

I

Bonjour.

II

Many people, you know, seem to think that the supply
of Bordeaux wines is rather like the world supply of
oil—that there is only a limited amount available
each year. But there are big differences between the
wine situation and the oil crisis. For one thing, new
sources of Bordeaux wine are being found every day
in countries all over the world. For another, ordinary
Bordeaux wine has a slightly fruitier taste than oil.

III

Wine-growing can briefly be described as "the art of
mixing and skilfully labelling fermented grape
juice". It is a craft found in many countries, yet
sadly has been surrounded with such secrecy and
snobbery that many newcomers find themselves
confused by the lore attached to it. Will this year's
Bordeaux scandal be a great one or just passable?
How well has the Italian wine scandal of four years
ago lasted? Are the wine labels attached to bottles
in England as good as the French ones they have
replaced? Where does wine marked "Produce of
France" come from? To answer this sort of question
is the task of this little guide. When it has been
mastered the novice should be in a position to choose
for himself, with some confidence, whether he wishes
to drink wine or something far safer like stout or
mineral water.

IV

Red wine has to be nurtured and constantly looked
after if it is to grow from a crude fermentation to a
superb beverage. A really good wine can start life as
a rough vintage in Morocco or Australia, travel
across the sea to France to become a modest local
growth and end life as one of the finest clarets
money can buy. But it must be carefully guarded
during this process in case it is contaminated by the
gaze of the tax inspector or in case it accidentally
ends up as a Spanish red.

(There is nothing wrong with a good Spanish red,
of course, except the profit margin.)

V

There are three great wine-growing areas in the
Bordeaux region:— a huge mixing vat not far from
the city, a lorry depot to the south and a vast tanker
installation near the coast. (Bordeaux, incidentally,
means in French "near water" and has always been
applied to wines from this region.) It is here that
many of the great Château wines come from.

(Château is the French word for the little drawing
of a castle that many firms like to put on the label,
to encourage confidence in the wine. Some of these
Châteaux are very big and important, which means
more money being spent on the ink for the label,
which usually means less money spent on the wine.
By French law the word Château cannot be put on a
wine label unless it is spelled correctly.)

VI

The process of wine-producing starts with the traditional ceremony of treading the invoices. The
invoices, import documents and tax returns are all
put into a large vat and there trodden by several
accountants until the ink has begun to run a juicy blue
colour. The documents are then removed and carefully treated so that the wine begins to mature into
something much better than the rough Tunisian it
may have started as. This is known as the "first

labelling", and by the end of the week the wine should have turned into a respectable mixture of Moroccan red and Chablis, somewhat resembling an immature rosé.

VII

Now comes the long process of fermentation and filtering during which all impure elements must be removed from the label it will eventually bear in the shops (the "second labelling"). It is at this point that the wine is awarded its so-called "cru". Cru, in French, means "thought to be", and it is one of the traditional skills of the French wine-grower that he can judge by tasting the wine, mixing it, tasting it again and sloshing in some rosé to be on the safe side, just how high a cru he can put on it. "Premier cru" is thought to be first class, "grand cru" is thought to be great, "cru exceptionnel" is supposed to be excellent, and so on. The whole point of the word cru, of course, is that it protects the grower against trades description offences.

VIII

But there is much more to a label than this, and a really practised wine expert can tell, merely from sampling the label and rolling it around his mind, exactly where it has come from—a real connoisseur could probably pinpoint the very chain of off-licences. Here is a typical label:

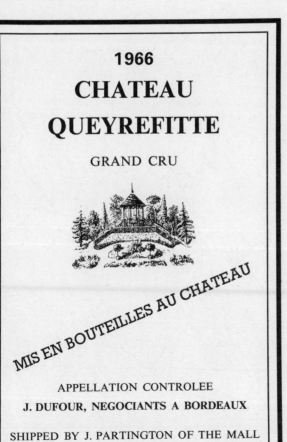

1966

CHATEAU QUEYREFITTE

GRAND CRU

MIS EN BOUTEILLES AU CHATEAU

APPELLATION CONTROLEE
J. DUFOUR, NEGOCIANTS A BORDEAUX

SHIPPED BY J. PARTINGTON OF THE MALL

1966 refers to the date when the label was printed, and

Chateau Queyrefitte means that the drawing on the label is not unlike a castle of the same name, which is a bonus for anyone who collects drawings of castles.

mis en bouteilles means "bottled", and is a guarantee that the wine you are about to buy is not in a tank or a lorry. *Mis en bouteilles au château* means that the wine was bottled and labelled at the same time.

Appellation Contrôlée is a French legal phrase which guarantees that at least part of the wine has come from Africa, Australia or somewhere else. This is a very strict regulation; wine which comes from a non-grape-growing country cannot be so labelled.

J Dufour, négociants à Bordeaux. This is the name under which J. Partington of the Mall likes to be known in France.

Shipped by ... This last line identifies the individual English shipper who has personally, with the experience of generations, supervised the wine at every stage from Bordeaux to England. In this particular case, J. Partington of the Mall is a section of the mammoth United Shoe Polish group.

So, from this label an expert could immediately deduce that the wine in the bottle was grown in France and elsewhere, almost certainly from grapes, and mixed in Bordeaux. From there it was shipped to England, relabelled, bottled and sold in some supermarket or other.

IX

As an additional guide to the prospective wine drinker, many firms add descriptive notes to the label and even, if the history of the wine is very complicated, little booklets hanging from the neck of the bottle. Here is a guide to some of the more common terms, as well as a few other words you will need to know.
Fruity tasting vaguely of strawberries
Young the ink on the label is still wet
Pétillant the French for "sparkling"; some lemonade has been added by accident.
Flinty there is a small deposit of flints at the bottom.
Sediment the accumulation at the bottom of the wine of fragments of torn invoice, twigs, old labels etc.
Full-bodied will stain the table indelibly
Light will not stain the table too badly
Bin place where they throw unusable wine, ready for blending with usable wines.

X

Many of you will no doubt later on want to try your hand at home wine-growing, which is much easier than you think. All you will need is a big bucket, a mixing spoon, a pile of blank labels, a French dictionary and a ball-point pen. With these you could easily produce your own chateau-bottled, top-flight claret. Good luck and au revoir.

Passing Through

Checking the airport and hotels, DAVID TAYLOR and FFOLKES each week fix up a brief encounter to talk to and sketch some of the distinguished, celebrated, glittery or unlikely visitors to London, Passing Through . . .

LIBERACE

EVER since vindictive Cassandra labelled and libelled Liberace with a thesaurus of distasteful opprobrium (and if you think that's prolix you should have heard counsel for the defence) and was obliged to lose face, £8,000 and costs (if not circulation) for the doubtful privilege, correspondents have proved less and less eager to try and take the twinkling pianist and his wardrobe to the cleaners. And personal tastes in bare-faced showmanship aside, there seems to be no good reason that they should. ffolkes and I trudged into the maestro's medium-lavish suite to find a woman from a woman's weekly and a man with a camera in a white umbrella being perfectly sweet. Just what, they would like to know, did a sequinned jump-suit set a man back? Just when might Wladziu Valentino Liberace get married for heaven's sake? The end of a routine gruelling session and he was smiling still. He is blessed with, or at least stuck with, a tireless capacity to reiterate his particular razzamatazz and wholly to convince you that he wants you to know. The cliché of an entertainer coming on honest seems in his case genuinely done and, what's more, he's ineluctably wholesome. There's the charm, in short, to strip the chromium off a candlestick.

What Liberace hopes, he says, is that people will penetrate the bright lights and come to appreciate his person. To this end he has written a book called, and about, *Liberace*. It takes a sweet tooth to complete it, indeed to get past the introductory plea that "If you like this book will you please write and tell me so? It

" . . . and a merger of gin and tonic."

would make me very happy." Never mind. It's a happy and a lucid and an entertaining book and by no means short on wit. "Thank you, thank you," declares the winning author, "I'm so glad that you enjoyed it. Of course it is an intensely personal book, I'm an intensely personal feller. If people once felt that I turned on some magical kind of switch and then turned myself right off afterwards that'd be it. They do really want to know; to start off, all that they know is that I play the piano, wear flamboyant clothes, am nice to my mother, have a brother named George and a candelabra. The book tells some of the rest. I don't mind. I can remember when nobody asked.

"When first I started writing, I fancied myself as an author, you know. Very concerned about style and character and punctuation, all of that. The first six chapters you could call painstaking, as my manager did. He said also he had a feeling that my whole life was going to be over in seventy-five pages. Don't dress it up, he said. Let us worry about the spelling. So I did. You know, I had a very posh English teacher in high school. She was very particular how we spoke, which in my case was Milwaukee English, neither charming nor continental. Well, I thought then it was beautiful to talk the way she did if that was the way you spoke. But it was not if it was put on. Finally, I did attend a speech correction school because I had trouble putting together a sentence without being snickered at." Which is not the kind of story you tell if your singular aim is gushy self-aggrandisement, it seems to me fair to add.

"Thank you, thank you," Liberace beamed. "I've signed a contract, you know, to do another book. Name unknown, subject unknown. How about *Son of*

Liberace? Liberace Rides Again? I have my worries about tackling fiction. And I don't personally enjoy that to the degree that I do biography. Maybe I could just write down a page a day outlining what happens, which is a lot. I'd get 365 pages per annum, right? Or cover some of those mountains of letters? Listen, when I get requests for hand-outs they don't ask me for little amounts, they ask for enormous amounts. They think big. I just had one from a lady, says she's sick and her husband is an invalid. She'd like to borrow £40,000. I mean, she sounds a pretty bad risk . . . And, what's worse, they ask for advice, and credit me with having a lot greater knowledge than I do."

So there we are. A brief snatch of Liberace slightly off familiar ground. Not a word remains to be said on what the world recognises as his act. Clearly it takes a real stamina to sustain the glittering obligations that he does and to have survived a good many celebrated physical and psychological traumas in his time. Because he is the obvious target for the careworn, cynical or purist he has taken some stick. Yet the fact remains that half an hour with Liberace does you good. And as he is quick to point out, his extremes have paled against modern pop-world outrage. Because it is not only affectedly conceited but realistically impossible to decide whether his flamboyance is, at best, affected or, at worst, damaging, don't let's try. Enough to say the book's good, he's damn good company and every mummy loves him. For what it's worth, ffolkes and I liked Liberace and it certainly is awfully nice to know that this will make him very happy. Isn't that nice? Goodnight, everybody. Sweet dreams.

Passing Through

ARTHUR RUBINSTEIN

HE buys his hosiery in France, is taken by the fetching effect of translucent blackness in a quality sock. For ties, no more to be purchased lightly, there is none he considers can match the taste of a London haberdashery. And since, by the by, he must go out this afternoon in search of shaver's requisites, it may be that he'll investigate a fresh tie (nothing too flash), for the saddening news of the Middle East warfare has left him out of sorts, and to be dressed smartly, it uplifts. This, he declares, will be after lunch. Sometimes, he still much anticipates lunch. This morning, we shall sit for an hour beside the buffed-up piano in his room at The Savoy, fine view of the trees he's happy to see, and we shall discuss (in a conversational sequence which only an eighty-six-year-old maestro can sustain without seeming insufferably precious) the pianoforte, wicked William II, Mussolini's turn of phrase, psychic phenomena, the ways of women and of the Israelis, the regrettable demise of a certain politeness in life, life, and socks.

To each, Arthur Rubinstein seems to lend an equal emphasis. In part, it is the blessing of a prodigious memory, one that has allowed him just to complete an autobiography of his early years, in Poland, in Berlin, in England during the First World War, and in astonishing detail throughout. He achieved it without notes or any reference to a journal and has only now come to accept this as anything uncommon as people repeatedly tell him that there are others who cannot recall the days in sequence, seventy-five years or so past. In description, he is wonderfully articulate (in eight languages it turns out) and his tendency to talk in what, by modern standards, is affectedly precise prose comes apparently from a surviving awe for the manners, decency and tone of the Edwardian age. He's an extremely nice old man, in short, who doesn't miss much and who has lived his life, to put it mildly, to the full. For the minute, we have turned from socks and ties to the overall effect of his get-up, in a symphony of browns, and this clearly gives him a mischievous pleasure.

"I was always unhappy to be such an ugly man, it seemed to me. I always was in envy of those pretty men like Cary Grant, Clark Gable, liked to imagine myself seated reading a paper and have all the women kneeling about and kissing my feet. Never worked out. It took work, serenading. Happily, I seemed often to find in any case the sort of girl who did not much care for too much handsomeness. There are always compensations.

"You see, as a child I was accustomed to an age of good-breeding and politeness. Of course, there were wars, with the Boers, in the Balkans, the Dreyfus business, but they were properly conducted. Not now.

146

" Your car will be ready in a couple of weeks, sir. Our senior partner is personally handling the final series of road tests."

But it is not as a result of Hitler or of Mussolini but of the incredible, cruel, nasty son-of-a-bitch, William II. He must conquer the world, because in Germany there is not the space to breathe. Well, now Germany is one-quarter of what they were, they still have the space to breathe and they have more money than the rest of us put together. You know, when I talked to Mussolini he spoke only of money. I got a bit impatient, I am not a banker, after all. I said, rather than win money with my music, I wish to win hearts. Bravo! he cries. Next speech, he is out there—my people, I wish to win hearts . . . I don't know. It sounds a bit banal in English, a bit declamatory, but in Italian, just right. He pinched my phrase. But no, it was from William II that all of warfare turned to extremes. Before then, it was gentlemanly at least.

"I am a great contemplator," Arthur Rubinstein summed up, having been led by way of Mussolini into a reflection on why so many leaders of men are uncommonly short. "It interests me from morning to night: why are we here. The details, no. The moon, what is it for? Some holes, there we hop around instead of walk. It still doesn't answer the question. If they had found beings up there, probably they wouldn't know what they were doing either. You can go crazy thinking about it. You must only reach out to what is here waiting, discover the beauty of life and adore it. I can talk to you like this because I am an old man. People see me with my silver hair in front of the piano, it maybe starts to look like my coffin.

"But! But. It is not like a theatre. They can't expect to see a pretty girl any minute. So I must win them, work on their emotions with this peculiar power, which we don't understand. The same sort of power, in a way, which men like Mussolini must have had. Which clairvoyants have, except they choose to try and explain it with cards, tea-leaves and all that silliness. But that hidden power does exist. We now, we are like the ancient Greeks perhaps—intelligent men, playing about with electricity without understanding what it was. I am not interested in applause. Children applaud a pantomime, even if they have not understood one word. I am interested when the peculiar silence tells me I am getting across, to people's emotions. Because to *listen* to a Mozart Concerto is just sheer happiness. Nothing can match it. Well, enough. But it is a consoling idea, don't you think?"

147

"Yes, sir, I'll tell them as soon as they come back from lunch. You are Captain Hawkins, you're flying a 747, and you want permission to land."

Take a Message

by HANDELSMAN

"This is the 999 recording service. Speaking slowly and distinctly, describe the crime of which you believe yourself to be a victim. Wait for the tone. Peep! Start now."

"So you're a recording? What a coincidence! I, too, am a recording, in a sense."

"A Mr. Handelsman, or Henderson, or Hamilton, wants you to ring back—very urgent. His number seems to have a lot of sevens or fours in it."

"This is not Mr. Martin. This is not even Mr. Martin's tape recorder. This is the machine that takes messages for Mr. Martin's tape recorder when it is broken, which it is."

"We're not here. We've gone out. Try ringing back after 'Star Trek'. This is a recording."

"Dr. Benson's recording device? Please tell Mr. Benson that Mrs. Brown is having a heart attack. Thanks, device."

"Should I begin? I'm not sure whether I heard three pips. Anyway, I hope the tape is rolling, or whatever tapes do. How are you? Silly thing to say to a tape. Here's what I've called about. Well, actually, I don't remember what I've called about. Who do you think you are, forcing your friends to talk to a tape? Does it give you a feeling of importance? Get stuffed."

An Open Letter to Alexander Solzhenitsyn from his Friend Alan Coren

MY DEAR ALEXANDER:

I hope you will forgive me for not having written sooner; but I know that I do not have to explain to you, of all men, how it is sometimes with writers, that clattering of the heart when the sought words elude and you cannot be sure that they will ever come again, that chill greasy fear in the endless waking hours of the night that perhaps it is the mind itself that has gone, that crushing pressure always to anatomise each minutia, each new refraction of the psyche, to place it in its inner context of the soul, and its outer context of society, with unimpeachable precision, always concentrating, always articulating, not to mention where the fence blew down the week before last and neighbour's refusal to restore same, despite arris-rails clearly visible on his side, plus car failing MOT on account of Excessive Play In Front Trunnions, also having to take Percy up the vet for spring worming, while at same time working out Deductible Input Tax For This Period (Partly Exempt Persons Should Also See Box 24) set against Percentage Used To Attribute Input Tax (Box 14 x 100 divided by Box 16), together

"Are you going to talk up to me or shall I talk down to you?"

with small daughter forcing Panda down lav, first sign of which being flushwater turning bathroom into ornamental pond due to stuffed arm stuck in S-bend (with aid of torch, can see glass eye staring back up at me from unreachable depths), and how do you get a plumber Sundays?

Anyway, Alexander Isayevich, every time I switched on the television set during those fraught periods of writer's block that tend to start clogging the mind a few minutes before *Colditz, Match Of The Day, The Pallisers, Colombo, The World At War, Pot Black, Parkinson,* and *Panorama* (not to mention *Jackanory, Farmer's World* and *Nai Zindagi Naya Jeevan*), there was your fraught beloved face staring out of some bulletin or flash, mugging to lensmen across a bald sea of agents and publishers.

Either that, or they were serialising Raymond Massey's *Abraham Lincoln*.

And every time those lugubrious eyes peered out at me from the fringing bristle, guilt welled up within me at my continuing omission. Must dash off a note to old Alexander, I would say to myself, welcome him to the West, extend the hand of literary fraternity, give him a few tips, enclose a couple of quid for nibs and blodge, well, I've been down on my luck myself before now, haven't I?

And now it is probably too late. For I have just caught sight of a tucked-away item in tonight's *Evening Standard*, which runs, in toto: "Exiled Soviet writer Alexander Solzhenitsyn may not settle in Norway because the tax laws would mean he might pay up to fifty per cent tax on his Swiss bank account deposits".

So there it is, Alexander, out of the Communist frying-pan and into the Capitalist fire, and the snow not yet slid from your welts. One moment it's the KGB kicking the doorknobs off in the small hours, the next it's crack teams of Scandinavian revenue men with rimless specs and immaculate clipboards intimating that it's either an immediate fifty pee in the £ or chuck the belongings back into the red-spotted hankie and ring up a mini-cab for Oslo Airport.

It won't improve, either. I gather that your next

150

choice is Switzerland, if they'll let you; and though the tax hammer is, granted, less sledgy, I doubt that the racked Soviet soul is likely to settle snugly among the alpine slopes a-teem with resident millionaire paperback hacks, drunken film-stars, racing drivers, refugee investment analysts, elderly Tory peers, and all the raucous effluvia of less stable European economies, not to mention the Swiss themselves, who tend to blink a lot, if they're the communicative sort, but otherwise constitute an unfertile sod for the authorial rhizome.

There's always Ireland, no tax at all, and a lot of green. But while their total tax concession to writers appears on the face of it generous, they have had some difficulty, as you may know, in determining who is a writer and who not, and are almost certainly, with typical Irish precision, using the rule of thumb which says that if a bloke is lying in a Dublin gutter with a bottle of Guinness in each pocket, no collar, and a four-day growth of stubble, and conducting himself in *The Wild Colonial Boy* with a grubby baton made from the rolled-up manuscript of his unpublished first novel, then he it is who constitutes the literary norm; and, somehow, that is not a part I see you comfortably playing.

France allows resident writers two tax-free years, but the toll exacted, socially, for the financial benefit is heavy: the literary establishment would reject you on the grounds that you had never written a novel entitled *A Rock, A Tree, A Chair* and running to either (a) five thousand words, or (b) five million words; and the intellectual establishment would reject you on the grounds that you knew nothing about (a) Communism, or (b) Alfred Hitchcock.

Spain is clearly out. Nor do I see you, Alexander Isayevich, conforming to the German requirements, which demand either that you live on a derelict farm a hundred miles from anywhere and write about very, very simple things, like hens, or else run for the Bundestag. The tax is murder, too.

Well, yes, all right, so it is in England. But, that aside, the benefits here are limitless, reducing the Inland Revenue's encroachments to negligibility. Pre-eminent among the wonderful advantages is the fact that, whereas these other European sanctuaries will require you to write, will scrutinise each emergent line for signs of growth or decay, will constantly be calling you to account in the slabby pages of their myriad literary magazines and newspapers for any slight deviation from the total commitment expected of you, in England *you will not need to write at all!*

You will only have to *have* written; and with a fair few pages under the belt and a framed Nobel cheque nailed up beside the flying ducks, your qualifications are irreproachable. In England, once he *has* written, the writer's life begins in earnest.

You will never be out of a studio for long, radio or telly: in a dark woollen shirt and a dark woollen tie, you will sit on chromium deck-chairs, semi-circled with a Catholic peer and an articulate musician and a West Indian social worker and a critic who paints a bit or plays the piano a bit, and a pale (but still lovely) girl who has written a virtually unpunctuated trilogy

"Everybody get undressed, grab a spear and stick a bone in your hair! The anthropologists are coming!"

about being a pale (but still lovely) girl, and you will discuss things. All manner of things: the spoliation of the Dorset coastline, the threat of *Deep Throat* to all we hold most dear, supermarkets and the de-humanisation of shopping, battered wives, the initial teaching alphabet, tower blocks, Watergate, What Does The Future Really Hold For The Third World, pets, God, and the licensing laws.

You will generate millions of words, but write none. There will be interviews showing how you have found happiness in a Green Belt executive home, possibly by knocking two internal walls down and converting the loft into a combined darkroom and play-area; and interviews revealing that a life of roulette, elite discos and tall women is no substitute In A Writer's Life for the stability of a happy marriage and your children's continuing wonder at the unfolding world, which you can share; and interviews discussing parking-meters and the concomitant erosion of civil liberties; and interviews At Fifty, At Sixty, and even, if your luck holds, At Sixty-Three and -Four. There will be a lot of money in these interviews, Alexander Isayevich.

There may also be fat contracts to stand beside a dog and sell tasty liver morsels; sip vodka with no more than a silent wink to camera during the pre-Christmas sales-peak; take down from a rose-woodette shelf Volume One of The Complete Winston Churchill bound in rich washable rubbishene.

There will be your name up there in giant capitals: VERY SOLZHENITSYN. VERY SANDERSON.

There will even be wonderful opportunities to act as Script Adviser to the BBC's ninety-eight part serialisation of *Engels In Love*, which means the producer rings you up once a month to enquire whether it's Leningrad that's on the Volga, or is he thinking of Stalingrad, if it's still called that, ha-ha-ha?

There will be wonderful literary parties in Belgrave Square and Gloucester Crescent, where the literary talk will make your very being thrill with its intense and passionate involvement with First Pakistani Serial Rights, and possibilities of adaptation for the Belgian broadcasting services, and a whole chain of speaking engagements in Wisconsin.

So I urge you, Alexander Isayevich, praying that it is still not too late, to reconsider your remaining years: do you really want some bleak and insistent foreign refuge, where you will be compelled to lean across a desk, day in, day out, night in, night out, thinking, thinking, thinking, and scribbling, scribbling, scribbling, page after page, book after book?

Or would you rather not, for the tiny price of a one-way air-ticket, escape to England and become a Writer?

"The typewriter! Lash the typewriter!"

"The sooner these bloody officials start telling us what we are going to be allowed to write and what we can't the better it will be . . ."

That's how Anthony Burgess reacted to the courts' attacks on *A Clockwork Orange.* And this is how the courts have reacted to his challenge . . .

A Wiltshire Magistrate

"Certainly I'll tell Mr. Burgess what he can write. He can write good, decent, family novels, about good, decent, family people, so that people can learn by example. Why do you think the courts of this country are filled with young people who have viciously attacked innocent victims? Because they've read books or seen films full of the most sickening horror. Why do I have in my court every day otherwise decent folk who have succumbed to a moment's temptation and sunk into petty crime? Because they have read books in which the hero has constantly broken the speed limit or broken open the gas meter or parked on a double yellow line. What I want Mr. Burgess to write is novels in which the hero leads a full, exciting and satisfying life without breaking the law. Then, and only then, will the magistrates' courts of the country be full of righteous, upstanding characters without a stain on their reputation."

Another Wiltshire Magistrate

"What Mr. Burgess doesn't seem to realise is that there is violence and violence. There is absolutely no justification for writing a book about a young thug who goes about beating up people for the fun of it. He should turn his attention to the sort of violence which *can* be morally justified. I'm thinking, for example, of actions to which the police can be driven as a last resort. This body of fair-minded, unjustly attacked men have a difficult job to do and one can't blame them if, when they are set upon by masses of Communist-inspired agitators or brutish football supporters, they occasionally have to meet force with force. I'd like to read a novel about that. In fact, I'd like to write a novel about that. I think my hero would be a fearless magistrate

who occasionally had to take the law in his own hands and mete out to these thugs the only sort of treatment they understand. He would probably be expert at karate, fencing, boxing and shooting, and very tough. In Chapter One he would be attacked by three young muggers; with one blow of his calloused hand he would . . ."

Yet Another Wiltshire Magistrate

"We've more than enough novels as it is. Mr. Burgess should use his undoubted talents to fill a gap rather than churn out more fiction. Does he realise, for instance, that there is *no* single good book on the diseases of tomato plants? For the third year running mine have collapsed in a yellow mess and I'm damned if I can find a reference book to tell me why."

A Different Wiltshire Magistrate

"Is this the same Anthony Burgess who was up before me last year for mistreating animals? As I recall, the advice I gave him on that occasion was to take up a hobby like wild flower collecting. Writing books now, is he? Well, that shouldn't give him much time for tying cats to railings. It doesn't really much matter what *kind* of books he wrote, I should have thought, as long as he treats the English language with respect. Had a man in court the other day, used the word 'disinterested' when he clearly meant 'uninterested'. Gave him thirty days without the option."

A Yorkshire Magistrate

"I haven't actually seen *A Clockwork Orange* or read Burgess's book. To be quite honest, I haven't read any of my colleagues' reactions to it, nor indeed have I seen what Mr. Burgess had to say about their reactions. But the whole affair leaves me in no doubt that we are being engulfed in a tidal wave of sex and violence, the like of which we have not seen since the most decadent days of the Roman Empire, which I'm reading a rather interesting book about at the moment, actually."

A Fifth Wiltshire Magistrate

"Mr. Burgess is not the sort of author whose books I would leave lying around my house, to judge from the language he uses. 'Bloody Officials', indeed! This is an irresponsible and reckless attitude to adopt towards the magistrates and judges of this country, who work long hours for not much pay to maintain the fabric of justice and certainly haven't got the time to tell authors what sort of books they should write. My advice to Mr. Burgess is to stop writing books, clean up his language and put his house in order. Thirty days or £50."

The Only Other Wiltshire Magistrate Available

"The sooner these bloody authors stop writing musicals that fold on Broadway and churning out TV serials on Shakespeare's life for Lew Grade, and get back to writing really good imaginative novels like *A Clockwork Orange*, the better it will be."

A Man Claiming To Be A Wiltshire Magistrate

"I thought Clockwork Orange was smashing. I liked the bits where they put the boot in. The blood was very well done and really life-like. No, it didn't give me the idea of doing people over. I was doing that already. But I picked up some points of technique. Shall we show him, lads?"

Fatstock Trials

A thin man struggles out of CLIVE JAMES

IT'S just coming up to the seventeenth month since I quit smoking. I had a real, oil-burning habit. Eighty cigarettes a day. To people who pointed out that I couldn't have smoked that many even if I smoked one every five minutes, the answer was: what do you mean, every five? I could annihilate a full-sized filter cigarette every *three* minutes, yielding a fire-cone slimmer than a red-hot wire. Tallulah Bankhead went through 150 cigarettes a day. Some people have professed their incredulity at this. But considering that she rarely slept, and had a mouth wide enough to smoke four at a time like guns in a turret, there's no mystery. She had the dual psychology of the ideal heavy-duty smoker: i.e., the constitution of a water buffalo and the death-wish of a Zulu regiment. So, in my small way, had I, and still have. But I no longer have a nicotine habit, and what follows is an account of what happened when I kicked it. It is a story less about tobacco, than about blubber.

I started smoking on a regular basis when I was about nine years old, although it was not until my early teens that I climbed above 20 a day. At school and at Sydney university I worked my way towards the forty a day mark without suffering notably in health. My intake of impurities was delicately balanced, the beer which should have made me fat being offset by the tobacco that should have made me thin. As it was, I was the complete surfing hero, with a waist nipped like a bee's and buttocks firm enough to break a needle. As I strode squeakily onto the hot sand of Newport or Avalon (ritzy northern beaches to which the young culturati raced on weekends to rub barn-door shoulders with the bourgeois girls they despised and would one day marry) I was a miracle of finely tempered poise, with nothing to conceal my unearthly beauty except a pair of shades and a weightless pair of blue nylon trunks with a ten-pack of cigarettes and a lighter crammed sexily into the waist band.

When I got to Britain the eco-balance of my body started to come apart in a big way. First of all, I averaged nine quid a week for nearly four years, and needed fags and booze not just as decorations to life but to make life worth living at all. The beer, as Barry Mackenzie so rightly howled when first encountering it, was piss. The cigarettes were Players Weights bought in packets of five. Bumming pennies from my fellow factory-hands in order to score another packet of this archetypal pleb snout still haunts me as one of the most indulgent episodes in a life that has never been exactly rich in forbearance. A diet consisting almost exclusively of starch completed the job of tilting my system over the edge of the slide, and from there on it was downhill all the way for ten long years, until, seventeen months ago, I was thirteen and a half stone—two stone up on the fighting weight that my tanned plates once wafted airily over the fine white sand—had been more than two years at the aforesaid 80 *per diem*, and had a cough like a polar bear with a dum-dum through the throat. I used to wake up with collapsed lungs (it feels like a combination of jactitation—that sudden fall when you're half-sleeping—and choking on a marshmallow) and would have to start my own breathing artificially. Years of bad diet

"You were in Colditz? Well, I've seen every episode and I don't remember you."

154

had done for sixteen of my teeth and 90% of my hair: my clobbered frame was wallowing like the *Scharnhorst* after the British battleships had ceased shelling. The only question was whether I was going to let the cigarette companies box me in and finish me off with torpedoes.

Suddenly, afraid, and with a nod of relieved assent from my brilliantly tolerant wife, who had never nagged but must long since have been worried ill, I got a grip. I quit cigarettes cold turkey. Celebrated for my capacity to get addicted to anything, I was smart enough not to try switching the affection to any substitutes—except food and drink, which I planned to acquire a taste for. Anyway, my motivation was as strong as it could possibly be: stop smoking or get dead. And I had a good idea for a system of rewards: spend *all* the money (which at 80 a day is practically enough to run a Rolls) on something you like—don't try to save it. What I spent it on ensured that I had something to show, every week, for my miracle of self-control: music. I started buying two or three cheap-label records every weekend, and by the end of the first year possessed practically everything in the Turnabout catalogue that Brendel, Frankl and Klien had ever played on. It was good, at the end of six months, to be able to ponder the image of an inspiring line-up of Beethoven sonatas played by Alfred Brendel, instead of an enormous pile of cigarette butts smoked by Clive James. For years I had used the hub-cap off a Bedford van as an ash-tray. I threw it away.

The pang of want never stopped, and probably never will. I still wake up at two o'clock every morning and reach automatically for the cigarettes. To find them missing remains a shock. But on the whole the urge was fairly easily contained—principally, I suppose, because life was on the whole running my way. (It seems to be almost impossible to kick an orally-centred habit when you're on a downer.) It was lucky this part of the job was manageable, because one of the side-effects turned out to be a terror. I mean the weight. Up it went. Two stone overweight already, I thought I would have at the most only half a stone more to contend with before any further increase levelled out. Wrong, baby.

I got unhappy about being heavy and when you're unhappy you eat, thereby getting heavier. I couldn't pass the kitchen without taking a snack. A typical meal on Saturdays was a pound of minced beef divided into 16 mini-burgers fried in butter and eaten between slices of fried bread, the whole deal topped off with two differently flavoured packets of crisps. I would then go to sleep. As my weight edged up past fourteen and a half stone, I bought bigger and bigger pairs of jeans without finding a pair loose enough not to chafe me when I walked: sweating lard onto the central

"Trouser bottoms half an inch wider? Come sir—we don't want to be mistaken for a hippie, do we?"

seam of the trouser is an unbeatable way of slicing your upper thighs to bleeding ribbons, resulting in a walk that looks exactly like piles. I asked a doctor friend why everything I wore smelled like Brie. His answer was, fat stinks.

I had been working on the theory that only a year's indulgence in as much food and booze as I wanted would tide me over the first wave of terror at quitting fags. By the time the year was up, I was $15\frac{1}{2}$ stone and needed a quack. My doctor was a lady who put me on the National Health diet, which at first glance looks like a warrant sequestering everything you have ever loved: it's a bitch. There are two ways to stay on it. The first is to remember that it allows three times as many calories as the ordinary diet in the Soviet Labour camps, and should therefore sustain life, even when it feels like it's going to kill you. The second is faithfully to ingest the accompanying drug, a variety of amphetamine which would drive you crazy with irritable depression if it were not so evident, within the very first week, that the diet *works*.

It really does. I lost a stone and a half in three weeks—call it a pound a day—another stone in the next six weeks, and am now levelling out at a few pounds above twelve stone, which is my medically advisable minimum. And it was all so easy. As with ditching the cigarettes, all I needed to trim the weight was to be afraid. Men, it can be done.

You know the rest: all your old clothes come back to you as a brand new wardrobe, people mistake you for your younger brother, etc. But what needs to be emphasised is that you can *eat* so much better. Steaks as big as your pocket allows, with half a pound of crisp sprouts piled on top. It's expensive—diet is a middle class luxury—but not as expensive as snacking between fatty meals. The only thing I eat between meals now is apples. Can this be the same man who used to wait until his wife wheeled her trolley into the distance of the Marks & Sparks food hall as a prelude to purchasing a packet of jelly babies at the cash-desk and furtively eating them all before she got back? Once again I walk everywhere, and my squash partner—ten years younger than I am and a fanatical athlete—has to break me at deuce in the fifth game instead of blowing me away to nothing in the third. The mirror is my friend again. Imagined sand squeaks beneath my feet. Marble-Bum returns. Time-traveller.

The secret of kicking a habit is to control the side-effects—of that I'm certain. Anti-smoking propaganda ought always to stress this fact: otherwise it's just asking people to quit for a while, get fat, and then get back on the weed, which won't make them slim—all you're doing is turning a thin sick man into a fat sick man. Nor does any man who understands the evil of this world care a damn about living longer. The thing to emphasise is that you'll live *better*. No more Pompeiian ash-clouds when you knock over the hub-cap, or dark-night-of-the-soul encounters at three in the morning with a cigarette machine that charges your last thirty pence for a look at an empty drawer. Instead, you're clean. And if you've been forewarned you can be slim, too. Which is another way of living better. Use my system, designed by an immoderate man for use by immoderate men: if you can't stop getting addicted to things, get addicted to self-control.

"They said they don't want to get involved."

As the Soviet authorities weed out dissident authors, Russian readers can perhaps look forward to the official, expurgated version of their works . . .

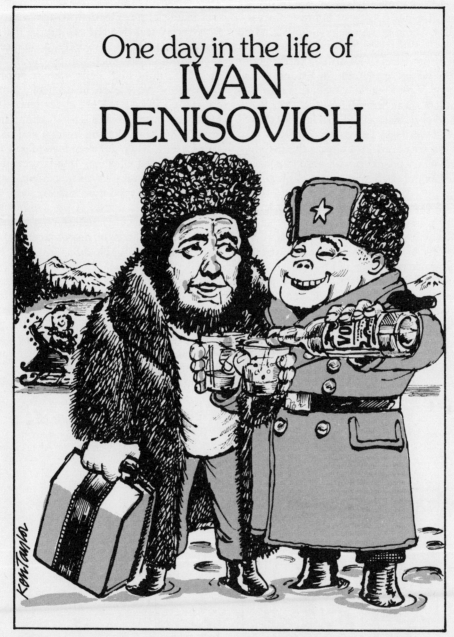

One day in the life of IVAN DENISOVICH

As usual, at five o'clock that morning reveille was sounded by the blows of a hammer on a sawn-off length of rail, hanging up. It was a stirring, pleasantly metallic note, bracing, and filled with anticipation for the day of honest toil ahead. The lanky Shkuropatenko was reminded of his days as a goat-herd in Estonia. It was good. Outside the weather was fresh. Cheliabinsk had sprung from his mattress, shinned up the flag-pole and, buffing the thermometer's glass with his jerkin, hollered that it was -40°C. Ivan Denisovich Shukhov leapt eagerly from the sheets to burnish his teeth in the bucket and to lickspittle his valenki*. He seldom overslept reveille, for the time before they assembled for work was his own; he took pleasure in attending to his chores; to straighten his bunk, wax his over-mittens or rinse out the dog-kennels. Work was like a daffodil —it had two ends. When you worked for the Soviet Socialist Republic you sought after quality and thrift.

* woolly boots available at Gum and all leading stores.

When you worked for selfish capitalist greed and misguided international notoriety you deserved exile and opprobrium. Despite his earlier failings, Shukhov was yet a man for whom human behaviour offered no surprises.

He heard the heavy tread of an orderly carrying out the nightsoil. He was a strong lad, an Estonian, and liked to see the place looking tidy. Well, it is said that nationality doesn't mean everything and that every nation has its bad eggs, often gifted writers who should know better. But amongst Estonians, Shukhov had never encountered a bad one. At evening, the Estonian would regale the weary prisoners with droll laments on a rusty saw. He sang of the Socialist way of life, of the record grain harvest, of a fresh supply of tractor parts and the girls of Omsk and Leningrad. And unlike "one-and-a-half" Alexander, he never short-changed you on the millet or lunchtime kasha†. Once, they had complained to the camp commandant because the nine-hundred-gram loaves were not properly crusty, and the man, a former stonemason, had said Pshaw! and put things right swiftly and with compassion. These were the minor irritations with which Shukhov was learning to live. He had toyed with the foolish notion, once, of leaving Russia, his fatherland. He knew he was free to leave whenever he wished, yet preferred to stay with his comrades and to reform his misguided ideas. At nights, he would read.

† *a wholesome porridge, much prized by hungry workers.*

THE cold made Shukhov gasp. Two powerful searchlights swept the compound from the distant corner, lending to the wintry landscape a Christmasy feel. He felt the nip of the wind beneath his ear-flaps and cried jovially to a guard, "By Jove, it is cold today! Breakfast will be good!" The skilly was bubbling on the hod. Zeks‡ queued for their generous portions of black-eyed beans from Novosibirsk and cutlets. He'd save the bread for later. It often tasted better later on. Where was Tikhon, the carpenter? Some said he was feeling liverish and had reported to the sick-bay, where he would wonder at the spick-and-span decor and efficiency that is typical of the Soviet welfare authorities. Whilst patients waited, artists would touch up the numbers on their warm jackets. There were three artists at the camp. In their leisure, they would execute studies of the authorities and hoped one day to paint many large pictures at Soviet rail termini and the like for the edification of travellers.

Shukhov completed his repast and selected a cigarette. He marvelled at the full rich quality of Balkan tobacco, less than two kopecks from the machine, including tax. And then the gong sounded and they marched quickly from the compound and through the forests where smiling labourers broke off from the hewing and waved, lustily. The view was breathtaking from the steppe. In the clear, crisp

‡ *a friend.*

"As patriots, sir and madam, I'm sure you have noted with approval the absence of central heating."

*"What's this Clockwork Orange that's going to get the
blame for this?"*

weather you could see clean across to the new stove factory at Gopchick. Lorries swept past them on the road, petroleum was plentiful in the Soviet Socialist Republics, and on to the power station where Shukhov and the zeks were to complete the fabrication of an installation that would soon produce untold mega-watts for the benefit of the industry. It was good to work on such a day. The time rolled by before you could say "teaspoon". And there was satisfaction in labouring with the finest tools, such as the mighty concrete-mixer Bolgar which is in its entirety Russian-built using finest materials. Sometimes, he would whistle. On such a day, he felt confident of his imminent release and the day when he would once more find regular work as a caulker. Others boiled asphalt in a pot.

ALREADY it was lunch. Working happily out of doors, my how the hours sped by! Lunch was nothing fancy—the workers had no time for western fol-de-rols which were in any case far beyond the resources of the average working man, he had been told. They supped on broth and plump, smoked whitebait. Shukhov knitted his brows and considered. Looked at the right way, sustaining Russian cuisine was arguably the finest in the world. That afternoon he made good a wall. It was satisfying work, full of interest in the laying of the mortar and grout. There was no small pride in the knowledge that the Soviet building programme was enjoying an unprecedented boom whilst in the imperialist back-waters of the west, anger mounted. In what seemed

the twinkling of an eye, the sun dipped and the steaming workers assembled for the brisk walk home.

There was a delay. Always, it seemed to Shukhov, there was a delay. Someone was dallying, that swine, perhaps, from Rostov-on-Don who would linger over his labour and scratch notes on fragments of paper concealed in his valenki. He would boast that he would one day be writing a book on his adventures at the camp, but the others would scoff at his imagined and ill-founded grousing. The son of a poxy bitch, the cow's udder! Why should he imagine he was the moon? In Shukhov's village, the folk had a saying. It was that God crumbled up the old moon into stars. He would wish that such subversives could be weeded out from the happy comradeship of camp-life and despatched far away overseas and serve them right!

IN groups of three and five, it was somehow chummier that way, the humming inmates of the camp now returned through the spotless streets after their day of toil. They stood eagerly at the Post Office counter for their parcels of luxury goods sent by sympathetic workers from all over the Soviet Union. It had been a good day and one in which they had contributed to the national prosperity and scale of values. The supply of machine tools would be upped by a massive percentage this winter.

There were three thousand, six hundred and fifty-three days like that in Shukhov's vacation at the camp. From the first clang of the rail to the deep, contented slumber. But he was kept so busily occupied, the time seemed just to fly.

Let Myers' Brain Take the Strain

"Please promise you won't be too hard on him—he wants to be an engine driver."

"Come on, be a sport—just **once** more tell me what you did when you stormed the driver's cab."

"Sorry I was so long—it took ages finding something **lewd** to rhyme with ASLEF."

"I'll take a dozen—I reckon they'll stun a driver at fifty yards."

"Then at 18.00 hours exactly we re-formed and took up new positions on this platform here."

"To be precise, I left my umbrella wrapped round the neck of one of your drivers."

If the Cult Fits

WILLIAM DAVIS looks in the wardrobe.

*T*HE *Great Gatsby* hits Britain this week. Well, that's what the publicists say anyway. According to Paramount Pictures "the making of a blockbuster is the newest art form of the 20th century," and this is it, chaps. Forget Picasso, Peckinpah, and Andy Warhol's tribute to baked beans. You are about to experience the spring-time delights of "Gatsbyisation". In America, hit a little earlier, they are peddling Gatsby clothes, hair-cuts, scotch, kitchenware, mansions and, no doubt, Gatsby bath-taps and toothpicks. Here the *Express* has tried to jump the gun with a bold attempt to restore its flagging fortunes: it is giving away Gatsby suits. "Make space in your wardrobe," it says, "for this suit with wide, wide sharply pointed lapels, Oxford-bag-shaped trousers with front pleats at the waist and, of course, turn-ups."

Of course. We may have entered a new age of austerity, but Governments have yet to outlaw turn-ups (as they did during the last war) or, for that matter, to ban collars, lapels and patch pockets.

Making space may, nevertheless, prove a teeny bit more difficult than the *Express* thinks. Before Dastardly Denis became Chancellor it was easy enough for your average trendy couple to throw out all the left-overs from previous blockbusters—the dirndl skirt, the Godfather suit, the caftans, the astrakhan overcoats, the Nehru jackets, the jump suits, the wet-look vinyls, the ranch leathers, the Chinese gear, the evening turtlenecks, the safari outfits, the maxi coats, the hot pants, the paper clothes, the bell-bottoms, the ethnic clothes, the big hats, the clam diggers, the Hawaiian shirts, the Eisenhower jackets, and the Duke of Windsor flannel suits. But the Budget—and the threatened wealth tax —tends to make a chap more careful. And cults change so rapidly these days that it pays to Be Prepared: all or any of these tophole innovations may be in again when Paramount releases its next big sensation.

Do people really fall for these gimmicks? I mean, *really*? A year ago, a much less affluent group of film-makers made a bold attempt to revive the Rudolph Valentino cult. There was a star-studded fashion show, after the premiere of *Blood and Sand*, at which everybody madly—but *madly*—applauded the off-white trench-coats, spats, and bee-sting mouths. And that was it. The film was quickly forgotten, and so were the clothes. The Godfather scene was rather more successful: at least one member of the *Punch* staff, renowned for his frugality, still turns up in his chalk-striped, double-breasted suit, chocolate silk shirt, and wide white tie every Wednesday. (On Mondays and Tuesdays he is Humphrey Bogart, and on Thursdays he represents the people who made *Mayerling*.) But I can't quite see the multitude rushing off to Burtons for their Gatsby fix, even though it would be rather nice to look like Robert Redford.

I do not, of course, pretend to be any kind of authority in this complex field. I'm always at least one cult behind—which perhaps explains the rather sour note of these comments. By the time I get around to some new fad it is invariably heading for the exit. I missed out on baker-boy caps, Lennon cowbells, Maharishi beads, porthole-sized spectacles, the Porkpie hat, unisex, drag, Guards' uniforms and even—if you please—Mao tunics and American Army fatigues. There's nothing more embarrassing than to be taken aside by an old man of nineteen, who is already well into the next cult but one, and politely told to forget it. (The same also goes for underground jargon, especially in the US. As soon as it gets widely known —and well before it reaches this side of the Atlantic —it ceases to be "underground". Your eager attempts to be hip are merely a source of free amusement.)

Well-meaning friends say that I don't take clothes seriously enough—that I ought to devote more time to the fashion pages and less to politics and business. They may be right. But this is one section of the press which neglects the male, except perhaps in his capacity as provider of funds. It isn't much use telling me, as the *Mail*'s Barbara Griggs did the other day, that Kansai the Jap is rocking Paris because the said Kansai does not, apparently, cater for those of us who are condemned to spend our lives in trousers.

Kansai's clothes, says Barbara, "have sizzle, drama, colossal fashion excitement . . . the Kansai girl wears a big full-gathered midi wool skirt in yellow, bright orange, purple or grass green, a wool-crossover blouse tucked into it, a rainbow-pattern knitted jacket on top. Her hair is wrapped up in a scarf, topped by a coloured felt Curé hat. On her feet are the biggest socks ever, and flat childish shoes or thick Japanese boots".

The socks and boots sound all right, but somehow I don't see myself as a Kansai boy. Ever.

Over in Rome Valentino seems a little more obliging. The *Guardian*'s John Hart went quite dotty about his latest effort last week. Sitting through the file-past of Valentino's mammoth ready-to-wear collection, he told the *Guardian*'s fashion-conscious readers, "is like listening to the Goldberg variations. A simple stately theme is, well, stated, then varied, then developed, and so on and on, ad infinitum it seems to some people, until it all gets right back to where it started." Valentino's colours "are his tones; ensembles are his jigs, gavottes and minuets." And when he begins adding maribou, rhinestones, and paillettes, says Mr. Hart, "it's like the virtuoso ornamentation that trills and warbles through key after key to resolve a single final chord."

Yes. I see that. At least I think I do. But what about the clothes themselves? Well, says the intrepid *Guardian* man:

"Purple is his new colour passion, a Parma violet purple which the men leave pretty much alone except in muted orchid stripes on twinsets and scarves. Both sexes get short chocolate waterproofs in poplin studded with brass rings. After purple in solid hues and stripes Valentino likes lap-robe plaids in regulation blue and green. By now her tent coat is below the knee and has a nursemaid's cape to be detached on the afternoon off. He meets her in the park in his modified Sherlock Holmes checked tweed Inverness cape-coat: both will be wearing similar trilby cloches with stitched brims."

And a lovely sight they will make too, I dare say. There seems no reason, though, why one should leave everything to Kansai and Valentino. If there is money in this game! (aha! I'm back, after all, with my favourite subject) then I possess one asset which the experts seem to have overlooked. I refer, of course, to the *Punch* Library. *Punch* has mirrored the changing fashion scene for more than 130 years and the back

*"I'm not in the mood, and if I **was** in the mood we'd both probably fall off."*

volumes are a goldmine for anyone determined to start his own cult.

The magazine was there when cutaways made their debut, when Oscar Wilde was marketing manager for green carnations, when Edward, Prince of Wales made history by introducing the Windsor knot, when golf plus-fours swept the nation, and when some unnamed genius invented the zipper fly. It covered the roaring twenties, thirties and forties and noted the whims of trend-setters like Garbo, Churchill, Astaire, Capone, Dietrich and Carmen Miranda. Its cartoonists recorded a succession of splendid hair-styles—from the cheeky curl favoured by chaps like Disraeli and Charles Keene, the goatee worn by stage Frenchmen, and the flamboyant walrus sported by great figures of our Imperial Past to the Edwardian spade, the neat military moustache, the whizz-bang antenna favoured by the Few, and the Zapata look. It survived padded and puffed shoulders, stocking tops, spats and the British Warm, and was the first magazine to appoint secretaries not because they excelled at shorthand but because they looked good in a mini.

Gatsbyisation, I fear, doesn't command much support in this office—though any attempt to brighten up Spring obviously deserves a welcome. If Paramount would care to get in touch with us, however, we might be prepared to help them launch the next blockbusting art form.

For, of course, an appropriate fee.

THERE'LL BE SOME CHANGES MADE...

says MAHOOD,
when Workers' Participation
becomes a reality

"Sorry luv, I forgot to tell you— I'm lunching at the Mirabelle today!"

"It's not the intellectual pretentiousness of his financial theories that gets me, it's the way he flaunts his Open University tie!"

"Shall I read out to you what the 'Morning Star Business News' has to say **against** this proposed merger?"

"Oh, come on, Dodsworth, it's my turn—your time is up!"

There and Backgammon

SPIKE MILLIGAN disembarks from the QE2 gambling cruise

I ALWAYS thought Backgammon was a side of bacon—but seriously, folks. Dunhills have opted to hire the QE2 while it was going cheap; that is, floundering helplessly off Bermuda. It's a PR man's dream, a Transatlantic backgammon contest. They tell the Press. "Sorry! there's no news value in gambling," says Son of Beaverbrook, sticking "FOR SALE" signs on his Rolls, "I've only got one paper now. what we need are bigger names." From the Dunhill boardroom the cry goes up: "Get star names!"

At three in the morning they phoned Peter Sellers, who was in the Lotus position on the mantelpiece. "PLEASEEE come," whines a director from his coin-operated Bentley. "I'll do my best," says Peter. "That's not good enough," froths the Dunhill Director. "Look, there's a lot of rich old silver-haired ladies on board."

"What are you trying to say?"

"I'm saying, bring *Milligan*, phone him now."

"It won't be easy."

"Why not?"

"He hasn't got a phone."

"Don't stall, Sellers. We'll pay for the call."

Peter does several more Lotus postures, a few "Oms", half a bottle of Blue Nun and falls off. My phone rings at four a.m. "Arghhhh it's-a-lie-officer,-I-thought-she-was-under-sixteen," I say arising from my Tryptazol-induced sleep.

"Peace on you," coos Peter.

". . . and Peace on you too mate."

"Look, Spike, you're getting on in life, you're 56, how'd you like to go to sea FREE, and meet some nice old ladies your own age? It won't cost you a penny. Now the good news, you don't have to tell jokes or wear a funny hat. I'll go if you go." I grope in the dark for the light switch, the radio comes on, "Do we travel first class or Sewerage?"

"First."

"One more thing, is Robin Day on board?"

"No."

"O.K. I'll come."

The instructions from Jon Bradshaw are: "Fly direct to New York, take a taxi to the docks, board the QE2 and come back." A Visa! I send Tanis, my beloved Welsh hysterical receptionist, to the Embassy to a queue a mile long in which she is the only white person. We fill in the form she is given which demands answers from "*When, where, why and how were you born?*" to "*Which side do you dress during an Equinox?*" Every other question is *ARE YOU A MEMBER OF THE COMMUNIST PARTY? HAVE YOU EVER SLEPT WITH A MEMBER OF THE COMMUNIST PARTY? DO YOU KNOW THE DIFFERENCE BETWEEN KARL AND GROUCHO MARX?*

We fill in all the gunge. Norma (my Manager) trudges back to Grosvenor Square but, "No, this is not good enough madame." *I* have to go in person. "What's the trouble?" He points at the entry: *PLACE OF BIRTH* . . . India.

"It's insufficient evidence."

"I'm standing in front of you, a position I could only have got to if I was born, isn't that evidence?"

"We must have the town name."

So. I fill in *PLACE:* Ahmednagar.

"Now," I said. "You know where India is on the map?"

"Yes."

"Do you know where Ahmednagar is?"

"No."

"You see, now you're bloody lost. You should have settled for India."

I was to return the next day for the visa (ha, ha, ha, ha).

Third day of the great visa story: "What's bloody wrong now?"

"It's about your mental condition. In the form against *ANY SERIOUS MENTAL ILLNESS?* you have put: No."

"So?"

"I saw you on the David Dimbleby TV show in which you appeared to be in a Manic Depressive State."

"Of course I was! They only gave me three quid for the show."

"*You should have been firmer with him when he was a puppy!*"

"I've decided to go in for the political and local government market."

"But that condition must be serious."

"Look, if I was seriously Mentally Ill—do you think I'd be appearing on BBC television? My God, it takes enough trouble getting them to accept *sane* people."

"I'm sorry! we need to see a doctor's certificate."

"Look, mister, if it's Richard Nixon you're worried about, the CIA will get him long before I do. If you're not careful I won't go to America."

I go to my physician, the immaculate, precise, intelligent Richard Bell, show him the latest form. (a) *Have any of your parents ever tried to assassinate anyone?* (b) *How many times have you seen "Hair"?* (c) *Are you related to Jack Ruby?* (d) *If you were given the opportunity, who would you kill first; President Nixon/Ronald Regan?* (e) *What time?* (f) *Do you like the United States Marines or Doris Day?* (g) *Did you ever touch Lenny Bruce?*

"I don't think," said Richard, "they will be satisfied with anything less than Spike Milligan is a self-confessed psychopathic homosexual with homicidal paranoia." Richard dictates a lengthy report on my mental condition. "Mr. Spike Milligan has had one nervous breakdown in 1956, he was given Medinal, he is now recovered etc. etc."

"It's still not good enough," says an officious Yankee female in Booth B. "We must know how many milligrams of the drug, how many times a day, etc. etc.!" and walked away like she was the risen Christ. Well, it was goodbye to her. I phoned the Ambassador.

"He's not here, he's in the USA."

"Oh, and his deputy?"

"He's on holiday."

"You know what happened to Israel when they went on holiday?"

"Pardon?"

"Who is looking after the shop? I mean, if the Russians' Atom Bomb dropped on Grosvenor Square, who is in charge?"

"Oh. There's an aide."

"Give me him."

A nice man gets on. I explained all the Crapology that's going on and he solves the problem from the top. Come round tomorrow and you'll have the Visa. So Sucks to Booth B Madonna, and I sent off a secret donation to the Wounded Knee Legal Fund.

THE FLIGHT INTO THE AMERICAS.

16th APRIL: my Birthday, Charlie Chaplin's birthday, Hitler's birthday. I'm picked up by a mini-cab, a lovely sunny day, not too much traffic on the road, we crash into the back of a car. Happy Birthday. The two drivers are slanging each other as the clock ticks dangerously towards take-off. I intervene and get set on by both of them. I transfer to a taxi, and leave them hitting each other. At Heathrow I get a telegram from Sellers. "*Sorry, can't make the trip. Have got to buy a new car on Doctor's orders.*" The swine, I'm wafted to the VIP lounge which is full of the very opposite.

I get a window seat on the Jumbo. I'm joined by Hon. Michael Pearson.

"Peter's not coming," he said. "His Guru told him he had a sense of impending doom."

"Whose?"

"Ours."

"Two brandies, please."

There is a disparity about our time of arrival:

British Airways, London: you'll arrive at 3.30, Sir.

Stewardess: You'll arrive at 2.15, Sir.

Captain: You'll arrive at . . . 40, Sir.

Finally, the Captain announces: "Hello etc. We are half an hour ahead of schedule, we will therefore be landing at 2.00." Ten minutes later—"Sorry that should have been one o'clock because of the hour difference in Summer Time." We land at thirteen minutes past one. The ship doesn't sail till eight. We hired a cab and dropped our luggage at the docks which appeared to be in desperate need of a Government grant.

"Nobody gits on board until after five," says a man like Snozzle Durante.

We mooch around New York, and in four hours see enough to wean me off it for life, I phone Peter Cook, "What are you doing in New York, you naughty fellow?"

"There's a traffic jam at Marble Arch, I detoured."

At five o'clock I am ascending the QE2 gang-plank. A man at the top puts a crappy pink Lei around my meck—"*Welcome to the QE2.*"

"You're welcome to it, too," I say. The cabin is a replica of every modern hotel room built since 1950, and I'm looking for the signature of Richard Seifert. The room is sterile and gives all the glamour of travelling by hospital ward. In my head it's GMT midnight, so I went to bed, so, when the Queen sailed and the decks were crammed with romantic fools, I was ninny byes. I arose at dawn to catch the sunrise. It spilled blood-red lights on to the sleepless sea. I ran around the deserted decks, a lone insomniac appeared.

"Nice day for a sail," he coughed.

"Yes, let me know if you see one," I said, side-stepping him.

The ship's rubbish is getting tipped into the Atlantic. I return sweating to my cabin.

"Brian, for God's sake open the porthole."

"Don't you like air conditioning, Sir?" he says.

"Love it, but outside there's the real thing."

"Is there? Cor fancy that!" he said, and opened it.

I ordered tea and toast, delicious. Arghhhhh! The Musack has started. I turn the knobs to get a classical channel. Ah!, Tchaikovsky's *Nutcracker*, PLUS BBC Overseas News. I wrestle to another channel: Mantovani. O.K. The next ten minutes is spent rushing back and forth to control a volume that goes from complete silence to ear-shattering. The passenger List. My God, Sir Seymour Edgerton, my bank manager, is on board. Where can I hide? I must find a ragged suit and a begging bowl. The old office of Purser has gone now, it's Hotel Manager, so, this is not a ship, it's a hotel. What's wrong with being a ship?

"No sir, that is not a life boat, that is a survival room." My writing is interrupted. Grafted over Barbra Streisand singing *People* is the voice: "Hello, this is the Captain speaking. I'm sorry to say that repairs to the boilers are still going on, and I'm sorry to say that we are under reduced power, we are only making 23 knots (well tie 'em faster damn 'ee) and I'm sorry to say PEOPLE WHO LIKE PEOPLE ARE THE we will be, I'm sorry to say, some hours late in arriving at the LUCKIEST PEOPLE IN THE WORLD thank you." This is the end. Using my breakfast knife, I disconnect the entire communications system and at last I can hear the sea! A swim. The brochure says Heated Pool. I plunge in, the water is freezing. I claw my way out with Angina. "It's-it's freezing," I tell the attendant Lady. "Yes, it is," she grinned. "Why didn't you tell me?" "You didn't ask." I risk going on deck and mixing with the peasants, a ravishing blonde smothered in bosoms approached, giggles, and says, "Here, weren't you Spike Milligan?" "Yes, I weren't," I said. "Shouldn't you be in the milking shed?" Several more asinine enounters drive me to the ship's library. I borrow *The Exorcist*, and end up that night under the bed screaming, "I am possessed by an evil Protestant 2nd Engineer."

Punch have asked me to "Look in and report on the Backgammon." I follow the sound of rattling dice in sporting gloom. I sidle up to contestant Hon. Michael Pearson. "How's it going, Michael?" "Piss off," he says. He was losing.

The tables are alive with Dunhills sporting flags, matches and ashtrays, everything but fags. A film crew are at work, "Look," says the producer, "what we need, Spike, is something to funny the film up."

"Really," I said. "There's a very funny man on the ship."

"Who is he?"

"The Captain."

I'm bored and return to my cabin. The phone is ringing. "Spike, this is Clement Freud, how about lunch?"

"I'm sorry, I haven't got any on me."

"I'll nip down to your cabin and pick you up."

"I'm heavy."

Clement takes me to the Grill Room. He's not happy with the cuisine and, referring to the mayonnaise, says: "My compliments to the Chef and tell him Yuck."

Incident for the increase of blood pressure.

ME (on the phone to the Bureau): Hello, is that the Bureau?

SWEET TWITTERING FEMALE: Yes.

ME: Is it possible to send out a call on your intercom for Mr. Quentin Crewe to come to the phone?

SWEET: Are you a passenger?

ME: No, I'm swimming alongside.

SWEET: Is it an emergency?

ME: Yes, he owes me money.

I give up. I return to writing this article.

APRIL 17, 18, 19: The Backgammon game goes on in a great burst of indifference daily, the ship's paper reports the casualties. CLEMENT FREUD ELIMINATED. HON. MIKE PEARSON DEFEATED AND CRYING IN HIS CABIN.

Now the bad news. I suddenly run a temperature and am confined to my cabin. "I want you to keep Travellers' Cheques handy," says the ship's doctor.

"What have I got?"

"You've got a temperature. That will be five guineas."

So pass the 20th and 21st.

The ship has developed a heavy roll, which they give me for breakfast. Brian, my cabin steward, is a hero. "Anything you want, sir, just press the button, and if I hear it I'll come."

A Backgammon shudder runs through the ship. Victor Lowndes has been eliminated and is selling copies of *Playboy* in the Galley.

SUNDAY 21st: Still groggy in bed. How can you get Malaria on the QE2? Perhaps the doctor's wrong. "Did you have it in the war?" he said, feeling in my pockets for money.

"Well, yes."

"Ah, then it's come back."

"After thirty years?"

"The bug has a strong dormancy factor."

"What's that mean?"

HONEYSETT.

"Another five guineas. Try and keep it going till tomorrow," he says. And exits.

Tonight the finals of the Backgammon—Barclay Cooke (US) vs. Charles Benson (GB), who has been doing the boots at night to keep himself going. The prize: £10,000. After paying his bar bill and tipping the stewards that should leave him with about £2.50.

The form-filling lunacy goes on unchecked. I have written my name, date of birth etc. 25 times, each piece of information identical to the previous form. Who gets these bloody things? I fill one up to get on the plane, I fill one up to get off the plane. I fill one in for the US Immigration authorities, one for the US Customs authorities, I fill one up to get on the boat, I fill another three up while I'm at sea, now I'm filling them up to get off the boat, to give to the Immigration Officers; the Cunard Registration Form, the English Customs Declaration Form. It is a great piece of bureaucratic repetition. I mean, their files must be groaning with my forms, I've been filling them in for the past thirty years. What do they do with them? Why do they need them? Each time I fill the form in I'm still the same person, with the same date of birth. Don't these silly bastards know there is a paper shortage, and an energy shortage, mostly mine? Feel better after that. Now let's see who's won the contest.

Very, very strange. The ship's paper *ignores* the finals and makes absolutely no mention of who the winner is, but the lavatory attendant tells me it's Mr. Charles Benson of England! Thank God, it's all over. Barclays Bank have run out of sterling, and

Cherbourg is off the port bow! Landdddd! the grateful cry goes up.

The last day. Cherbourg: we can have three hours ashore, Barclays Bank has especially closed down so we can't get francs. It's half a mile to the town, no transport. I walk. The pay-off? It's early closing in Cherbourg. Dying for the loo, I find one, am stopped by the Madame.

"M'sieur," she waves three pieces of toilet paper at me, "Dix francs". I only have sterling; have you ever had the indignity of handing back three pieces of toilet paper? Back to the ship. With a bursting bladder, I give a watery farewell to France.

Tomorrow, England. Home and Mortgage! The corridors are turning into great luggage dumps. "Did you know two out of three baggage stewards are ruptured?" said a groaning porter. Dawn! men from Her Majesty's Everything see that you are out of your bed early enough to be unhappy, they collect the bits of paper, and leave. Charles Benson comes down the gangplank, his cases stuffed with money.

Standing at the dockside, his pyjamas showing below his trousers, is the *Punch* courier. "Have you got it?" I hand him the article. The voyage is over. Where's the telly? It's a good ship.

"*If anyone asks, it was a victory for common sense.*"

"Class snob me foot. Just happens it's the only paper in the waste baskets of the offices I clean."

"Now look, son—anyone who isn't sure whether he's upper, upper-middle, middle, lower-middle or working-class is invariably lower-middle."

Touch of Class

by DAVID LANGDON

"Has this fascinating ability to switch accents according to the class of customer."

"On 'Good Morning' terms until I discovered he was a junior executive at BR with a free rail warrant."

"Things **are** changing. Years ago we'd have blackballed you as a property tycoon. Now we just say there's a waiting list."

After Spiro Agnew...
PRESIDENT NIXON'S
FIRST NOVEL

Punch proudly presents an exclusive extract from the novel currently being
written in great secrecy by Richard Nixon. The spelling has been
cleaned up by MILES KINGTON

IT was a very wonderful morning. The dawn had come up over the rooftops of Washington like a stirring version of *Home On The Range* played on the piano. First, a few gleams of gold had appeared, like security officers checking that there were no undesirable elements in the sky. Several clouds had passed slowly as if to test precautions. Finally, when everything was clear, the sun had entered, smiling. Higher and higher it rose, a symbol of American unity and all that was best in, uh, democracy.

The President of the United States opened a window and looked out of the White House. He breathed in the fresh air. He breathed it out again. It tasted good. He felt good breathing in the fresh air.

At the same time, he remembered that any American citizen could breathe in the same air as the President. That made him feel good, too.

When he had finished breathing in the air, he turned and came in. (I don't mean that he then stopped breathing. He went on breathing during everything that happened after that. It's just that I don't mention he's breathing all the time. There are some things that have to be taken for granted about an American President, because if everything had to be explained and justified the whole time, the system would come to a halt. Believe me.)

Not having yet described the President, we shall now proceed to do so. He was tall, handsome, kind, yet strong, also friendly, with a strong growth of hair on his chin which betokens the firm yet compassionate man. His friends sometimes said he was like a cross between Henry Fonda and Paul Newman, and though he accepted this compliment gracefully, he did not fully believe it. For one thing, it ignored his strong resemblance to George C. Scott playing the part of Patton, though he bore no resemblance to the same actor playing the disgraceful caricature in *Dr. Strangelove*. For another thing, he had learnt from experience that people like Henry Fonda and Paul Newman sometimes said tactless things in public, which was something a President could never do. Also, he was breathing all this time, which I won't mention again.

The door of his room opened and in came his wife, whom we shall now proceed to describe. She was the ideal President's wife. She had stuck by him through thick and thin, through all the irresponsible slander and politicking which had made his career so difficult and which we shall describe in detail in chapter three. Suffice it to say now that there had been no truth in any of these rumours. Anyway, a President is above rumours. There is no real need for chapter three. I may not even deliver it to the printers. Or at least, only selected portions of it. The printers do not have the power to force me to deliver chapter three, which in any case has been accidentally lost.

Meanwhile, the President's wife was coming in through the door of his room. She opened her mouth to speak. The President switched on his bedside tape recorder.

"Testing, one, two, three, four . . . " she said. He nodded. The level was good. "How are you this morning?" she asked.

"I am fine," he said gravely. "It is a very wonderful morning. Hold on a moment."

He turned knobs and switched a switch.

"How are you this morning?" asked the tape recorder.

"It is working well," said the President. "Was there something you wished to talk to me about? As you know, the President of the United States should be accessible at all times, even to his wife."

They both laughed at this joke which had gone down so well in his campaigns of 1959, 1963, 1968 and 1976 but not 1975, which was the one they did not talk about. This will be explained in chapter five, but I can reveal now that in that year the President had been exposed to a press campaign of such venom and turpitude that the American public had been temporarily blinded to his statesmanlike qualities.

"There is one thing that puzzles me," said his wife. "On the hall table this morning I found a ten dollar bill. Where did it come from?"

"As you know," said the President to the tape recorder but smiling at his wife to show she was included, "the occupant of the White House is the

*"Just what is it that you people **want**?"*

recipient of many well-intentioned gifts, which it is our custom to return with thanks. This particular gift of money came anonymously. The FBI are working to find out its source; meanwhile I have left it lying around to show that I am not interested in money."

"And yet," said his wife, "we are not rich. Why, even now in my purse I have a bill for nine dollars fifty from the laundry which I am at my wit's end to pay. It would be so tempting to use that banknote to settle the bill."

"But it is out of the question," laughed the President morally.

"Completely," echoed his wife, an ethical smile playing across her features.

*

I wish to state that that asterisk does not represent missing material. *No portion of this novel has been suppressed or withheld.* It is merely a device to denote the passing of time. It has been the privilege of novelists from time immemorial to denote the passing of time. I now call upon that privilege.

After breakfast, the President (a tall, handsome man with a brilliant sense of humour, an ability to see to the heart of problems and an unusually fine touch on the piano) liked to sit for ten minutes reading the newspapers. He did not learn anything from them. It was simply that he found the scurrilous and vicious attacks on his character made him a better and more humble man. Why the newspapers attacked him he had never learnt, but he forgave them. He was big enough to forgive them though he moved with surprising grace as well.

Then it was time to meet his personal advisers. Many people imagine that the American President is cut off from reality by his aides, but I can tell you, my fellow Americans, or rather, gentle readers, that this is not so. Anyone who has ever been the American President will tell you the same. As there are no ex-Presidents alive at this moment in time, the reader will have to take the writer's word for it.

This morning there was a crisis in the Middle East. War had broken out, oil supplies were in danger and Russia was causing trouble. Patiently, the President explained to his aides what had caused the crisis and they agreed with his diagnosis.

"What course of action do you recommend, Mister President?" asked one.

"I am in favour of sending the Secretary of State, Harley Kellinger," said the President. "I feel sure he can successfully negotiate peace and prosperity."

"Do you not think," said another aide, "that Kellinger is in danger of becoming too powerful and self-important? The media love him already."

The President smiled a wise and sad smile.

"My friends," he said. "There is no room in my heart for envy. He is a good man. He is working for America. We are all working for America. I wish him well. I am only sorry that because he was born in Latvia he is not eligible to be President. I think that takes care of that one. Now, is there anything else I should deal with?"

"Would you like to say anything about Congress's move to have you impeached, exiled and stripped of all your belongings?"

"My friends," said the President. "My job is to govern the country. What Congress does is their own affair. I have more important things to do. I must leave you now, for instance, to telephone Zinky Cohn."

"Who is Zinky Cohn?" asked the aides, seemingly unaware that Mr. Cohn had that day broken the all-time American record for holes in one during major golf tournaments, an achievement which made the President proud to be a fellow American, as he said some ten minutes later on the phone to Mr. Cohn who had been waiting for the call since breakfast. The President wiped away a tear of emotion several times for the photographers and went into the morning press conference.

*

It was a very wonderful afternoon. The sun was high in the sky like an American space craft. The President was on the golf course, playing with his close friend, Billy Berozo. Now, there are some people who say that the President is wrong to have close friends who may influence him, but believe me, what they talked about on the golf course was golf. There are other people who say that he is wrong to have very rich, close friends. Have they ever thought that it would look wrong for the President to have poor friends? It would look as if they wanted something from him. Rich friends have all they need and do not ask for favours. They haven't thought of that, have they? They would do well to think of that before they shoot their mouth off.

On the fifteenth tee, a Presidential aide spoke urgently into his ear.

"Sir, there is a revolution in Latin America. You must deal with it."

That's another thing people don't think about. How would they like their leisure spoilt by crises? Do the critics of the President have to break off lunch to counter a Soviet threat in Asia? No, they don't. Not that the President bore them any malice. He just wanted to point it out, that was all.

Having dealt with the crisis, they walked on to the sixteenth tee.

*

That night, as they brushed their teeth, said their prayers and did their exercises, the President's wife asked her husband what sort of day he had had. He smiled.

"It has been a full but satisfying day. I have done my duty honestly and energetically as the President of the United States. No man can do more."

She smiled and kissed him lightly.

"One day you must put all this in a book," she said.

"It might not be very exciting," he smiled.

"No," she said, "but it would set the record straight."

"Of course, we Quakers are totally opposed to divorce."

"I'll miss you too, Oleg."

You'll Die Laughing

by ffolkes

"Ladies and gentlemen. There will follow a short delay while the Execution Committee examine a complaint by the prisoner that the Axe exceeds the statutory width. Meanwhile here is Merrie John and his Madrigalists to entertain. Thank you."

"Do you ever get the feeling you're running out of ideas?"

THE TIMES/SOTHEBY'S SPECIAL OFFER

A limited edition of this extraordinarily moving equestrian keepsake. Equally at home in drawing-room or stable, it can be placed for maximum effect alongside the matching, gem-encrusted heirloom edition of Capt Phillips, flat on his back. "A conversation-stopper"—Willie Hamilton.

ALSO! NEW!! JUST IN!!! FROM SOUVENIR (WESTMINSTER) NOVELTIES: A BOARD GAME ALL KEEN COURTIERS CAN PLAY . . .

ATTRACTIVE STICK-ON FUNNIES FOR YOUR HORSE!

Self-adhesive humorous labels, easily attached to any steaming flank, no need to lick. Available in choice of colours, or in boxes of a gross for gymkhanas etc.

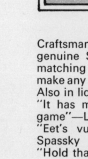

Craftsman-carved by RAOC Joiners in genuine Samoan sapele veneer, these matching **ROYAL CHESSMEN** help make any match a "right royal occasion." Also in liquorice.
"It has made a real difference to my game"—Lord Snowdon
"Eet's vunderfool, vunderfool"—Boris Spassky
"Hold that smile!"—Norman Parkinson

COMING SOON! THE PRINCESS ANNE PIRELLI CALENDAR! THE JUNIOR ARCHBISHOP OF CANTERBURY OUTFIT! A ROYAL YACHT BRITANNIA TO SAIL IN YOUR BATH! A CLOCK STOPPED AT THE EXACT HOUR OF MATRIMONY, AND MANY, MANY MORE!

ART TREASURES YOU WILL WANT TO KEEP FOR YOUR HOME

Stunning, tasteful, simulated alabaster and canvas reminders of the radiant bride, wrought for you by craftsmen who have studied beauty down the ages. Choose between wall or table-top model. Weights and hidden springs tip Venus de Windsor's hat to passers-by on deluxe model. Portrait available in a choice of colours. National Gallery Novelties Ltd.

MACHINE-WASHABLE "ACTION-SOLDIER"–THE MARK ONE; PLUS HIS 'N' HERS TWIN MODEL CARS

Something for the kiddies to treasure. At better toyshops everywhere.

A DAY TO REMEMBER—FOR EVER! THE SOPPY HOUSE-WIVES' FORGET-ME-NOT EVERLASTING ROYAL WEDDING DIARY—

Sumptuously bound in luxurious indigo cardboardette, each embellished with the date that is etched on a whole nation's heart, and printed on every page—both sides.

KISS-ME-QUICK AND SMILIN' THRU' SEW-ON ROYAL WEDDING SOUVENIR PATCHES FOR FADED DENIMS. YOU CAN BE "CHEEK-TO-CHEEK" WITH THE ROYAL PRINCESS'S CAPTIVATING GRIN. ALSO AVAILABLE MOUNTED ON PIECE OF WHITE CARD TO FORM ATTRACTIVE "MODERN" ART LOOK FIRE-SCREEN OR PAINTING FOR YOUR WALLS.

THE "THEY SAID IT COULDN'T BE DONE" GLASS FIBRE STATE-OCCASION GLASS COACH ROD

Be first away from the Abbey in this chrome-moly space-frame mews-hugging roadster. Fuel-injection Blueprinted Rat motor completely supersedes old-fashioned drays. Candy lace or pearl trim, buttoned Thai silk upholstery, Royal Mace gear-shift option. Street models can carry inflatable postilion coachmen in Black Flock Bellstars.

"Can I have a pint of milk and a strawberry yoghurt?"

"Did you ever meet a farmer who **didn't** claim to be ruined?"

The Townies Are Coming!

by THELWELL

"If you keep wanting to see pigs and chickens and things all the time, we'll never get any fresh air."

"I think it's absolutely beautiful—roasted with Yorkshire Pudding."

"Tell us if we're in your way."

"Hello! I think Mrs. Prothero wants us in for lunch."

The Great Summer of
HARRY SECOMBE

ONE swallow may not make a summer, but sometimes just one day can make a summer memorable. A day into which is compressed all the ingredients of my perfect summer—sunshine, good company, freedom from care and a touch of the unexpected to add excitement.

There was one such day just after the end of the North African campaign which makes the summer of 1943 a contender for greatness. Our unit had been withdrawn from the mopping-up operations and we were camped near the beach at Carthage. The relief of not having to fight anybody, at least for a while, was remarkably heady and I found myself on that first day with time on my hands, a sandy beach, plenty of sunshine, free fags and permission to stand up on the skyline.

So, stuffing my German phrase book into my kitbag, making sure to turn down the corner of the page containing the declension of the verb "to surrender"—I was obsessed by the idea that if I were to find myself in a tight spot I might say "I am about to surrender" rather than the more urgent "I surrender", which could have meant the difference between life in a Stalag and a paragraph in the *Swansea Evening Post*

"*We're thinking of sending away for brochures on Morocco this year.*"

obituary column—I headed towards the sea, wearing my drawers cellular short in lieu of a bathing costume.

As I approached the beach I was surprised to hear the sound of a military band. To my astonishment, there on the sands of Carthage stood a complete German Regimental Band in a roped-off enclosure guarded by military police and surrounded by various members of the British First Army, most of whom were completely nude. They stood in the blazing sunshine for more than an hour playing selections from operettas, tunes of the 'thirties and even *Tipperary* and *Pack Up Your Troubles*, all the time encouraged by cheers, applause and cries of "Good old Jerry!". There was no animosity on either side, and apart from some good-humoured attempts by some naked lads to conduct the band with improvised batons, the whole dream-like incident passed off peacefully.

The sensation of utter contentment as I lay back in the sand smoking free cigarettes, shorn of responsibility, secure in the knowledge of a job well done, and being serenaded by the end-product of that task, is something which has remained with me all my life. So much so that whenever I hear a military band I have an urge to strip off my trousers and lie down in my underpants to recapture that magic moment. If one day you read "Ex-Goon hustled away in blanket from Horse Guards Parade during Trooping of Colour" you can rest assured that it won't be Spike Milligan—he's kinky about string quartets. But that's another story altogether.

I suppose it is the relief from responsibility which goes to make a Great Summer. There's not much enjoyment to be had from lying in a deckchair at the seaside, wearing your knotted handkerchief, if you have to sit up sharply every five minutes or so to count the kids. Perhaps that is why some of my best summers were the ones of childhood when I had no responsibilities. However, I find I have difficulty in remembering those golden days of my youth. They lie scattered like amber beads over the floor of the disordered bed-sitting-room which is my mind. Some lie trapped in the fluff under my subconscious, whilst others wink tantalisingly from behind the libido. It seems as if nothing short of a frontal lobotomy will get this piece finished.

Then I remember an old trick which is usually successful in springing the lock of my memory bank—

I look for scars on my person. My legs, in particular, are to me what the walls of the Olduvai Gorge were to Professor Leakey—on them are chronicled the history of my childhood. A crescent-shaped lump of scar tissue on my left knee records the time when I fell over in the school playground and cried so much that the headmistress gave me a biscuit with a butterfly made of icing on it. A number of associated marks show of subsequent falls in the hope of another biscuit, which never materialised. Here and there various indentations tell of the hazards of playing school soccer without my spectacles.

Then I rediscover a series of cicatrices on my right shin, and it all comes flooding back to me—the Summer of the Bicycle! It must have been about 1935, when I was fourteen. All my life I had wanted a bike, and after a determined campaign of sighing over Raleigh and BSA catalogues, and threatening to run away to sea—an idea which seemed to appeal to my father—parental resistance collapsed about June. I was handed a second-hand Hercules with some considerable misgivings and shakings of the head.

At last I was free to conquer fresh horizons; the whole world from Kilvey Hill to Skewen Oil Works was mine. I pedalled furiously up and down the hills of our neighbourhood. I paid unexpected visits to remote members of the family, descending on them trouser-clipped and sweating, stopping only for a cup of tea and a few slabs of cake, and then off to go swooping away down steep streets named after Crimean battles, leaving behind bewildered third cousins on my mother's side who usually only saw me at funerals.

In a very short time I knew more about St. Thomas, Swansea, than the Borough Surveyor. Then, when the school holidays came that summer, I was off exploring the coves and bays of the nearby Gower Peninsula with my towel and costume strapped to the crossbar, and the addresses of distant relatives as a hedge against hunger. It was becoming increasingly difficult to get people to answer the door when I called—the screech of my brakes was a signal for whole families to lie on the floor until I had gone. My appetite has always been legendary in our family.

But I was content with the sense of freedom that glorious summer, drunk on the wind that filled my lungs; though a little sore in the crutch with the rubbing of the saddle. I didn't need company that summer, I had my bike. I have never been as fit as I was then, with calf muscles bulging and my face and arms tanned by constant exposure to wind and sun. I had taken on the identity of my bike—I was a twenty-two-inch Hercules with glasses.

All great summers must turn into average autumns, and that year was no exception. I got over-confident in my cycling prowess, and one day, attempting to pedal backwards down St. Leger Crescent, I misjudged the sharp turn past the church and finished up in the allotments, having somersaulted backwards over the railings. The bike was a write-off, my shin was badly cut, and to add the bizarre touch which was needed to finish off a truly memorable summer, the only witness to my misfortune was the parrot in its cage outside the McKenzies' back door. It laughed so loudly and so hysterically that even I was forced to join in as I lay bleeding amongst the cabbages.

So it appears that, in my experience anyway, the ideal great summer should contain a German military band, a secondhand bicycle, plenty of sunshine, a parrot, and, of course, a scar to remember it by.

"*Seventeen years old and he still loves chasing cars.*"

179

"I must say, Mr. Baskerville, we had expected something larger."

Another Chance to Read this Article

by BASIL BOOTHROYD

YOU may have missed this article the last time it came round. Or even the time before. That would have been its first appearance, making this the third. I think. The programme planners aren't sure. Naturally, when they see a thousand-word blank space looming ahead, they keep stuffing this piece into it. I suppose they go on the old stand-up comic's principle, viz., that even at "That was no lady, that was my wife," there's always someone in the audience who will laugh.

Then they have their own principles, admittedly a bit inward-looking. As a performer, I get a small repeat fee, but there's nothing to pay out in studio or technicians' time, because the thing's all here ready to slap on the screen—the page, sorry—and once the mighty transmitters, or presses if you prefer, get churning, you don't need anybody around but a machine-minder. And bored, at that. And no wonder. If all he has to do is doze over an old *Radio Times*, betting himself he can't find an original programme tucked away somewhere among the adverts, pull-outs

and success stories of hostesses on *The Golden Shot*, it's hard to blame him for not realising he's five minutes late pressing the FAULT ON VISION button.

If you think it signifies my deep contempt for readers, constantly pumping out this dog-eared material, then I reply (a) that that's true enough, but (b) it's irrelevant, because you don't suppose the editorial planners consult *me* about it? and (c) let's be fair to them, there's usually a clue in the fine print, if your eyes are up to it. Sometimes this comes right out and says, "First printed on p. 91", though it's true you don't usually look at that without first having been intolerably teased by a creeping sensation of *déjà lu*. "Funny," you say to yourself, or anyone else present not sleeping—"I just knew, before he did it, that he was going to do that bit of French word-play about *déjà lu*." And just as you fear you're about to go down with a bout of precognition, out he comes with this bit about going down with a bout of precognition.

Then you turn to the fine print, noting with a

180

muffled cry of "Bloody twisters!" that they haven't, in fact, admitted the deception in so many words, but just given you a devious hint and left the rest to your deductive powers:

"A sparkling excursion into the by-ways of history. Was Queen Victoria really a man? Utterly gripping. Humorous journalism's finest hour."—*The Accountant*
"Highly bewitching."—*The Grocer*

As it's well known that *Radio Times* goes to press three months before publication, hence the continued billing of late-night attractions during that 10.30 pm closedown period, it dawns on you that the humour critics of these papers must obviously have already enjoyed this rubbish about a pre-Aztec civilisation that worshipped the buzzard, and their proclaimed entrancement—totally baffling in your view, but what the hell, since your sole function is to keep handing over your mirth money at the bookstall or sit reading behind thick-drawn curtains lest the terror detector van comes rolling up with its detachment of humour police—their remarks, I repeat (if the word gives no offence), can only have been induced by earlier exposure(s).

I don't quarrel, let me say, with the planners' assumption that these present words passed you by at their previous printings: only with the motivation for such an assumption. They take the view, as far as it can be discerned, that owing to powerfully adverse circumstances at the time, the funeral, say, of a loved one, or your copy of the magazine getting overheated and going up in flames, you were cruelly cheated of a unique (as it then seemed) experience. Planners of printed entertainment are stuck with this conviction. That's how they live with themselves, and in saying so I may be clearing up a mystery that's bugged you from way back.

But another reason for your not having read this before, or before that, and one which they would beat back with knouts rather than recognise, is that you missed this article the last time it came round because the moment you saw its opening sequence, beginning "You may have missed this article the last time it came round," you said, "Oh, God," and went out in the garden to kick back all the horse manure the blackbirds had dragged out of the rose-bed on to the lawn.

In those circumstances, and they are widely prevalent, the cheap cynicism of re-presenting this same old scratched, stale, creased and marmalade-stained programme under the generic title of "A Second Chance to Read" is an exercise in universal, not to say self-, deception, whose implicit enticements of another-treat-in-store, you-lucky-people and our-whole-intent-is-all-for-your-delight only makes the reader want to tear it out and wrap fish in it.

Don't do that. Yet. I haven't finished. You wouldn't expect this article, knowing it as you do like the back of your hand, to pose a problem shared by millions without suggesting a solution?

Kick the habit, is the answer. Give up reading this muck. There's a risk, of course, that you could miss actual items of original material elsewhere in this magazine, appearing for the first, and even the last, time on any page.

That's too bad. But just think, as I've said many times before, but you could have missed it, of the money you're saving. You'd be surprised how it mounts up. And I can only conclude, in the words I always use to conclude, since they're set up in type already, that after a few years you not only won't miss me, you'll have enough loot piled up to get a TV set.

And then, oh, boy! Michael Parkinson again, interviewing Peter O'Toole again! Great British films of the twenties, that you haven't seen since—oh, I don't know—was it Thursday? You won't regret it. It's the nearest you'll get to eternity without actually going there.

"*We've solved our conscience for holidaying in Greece. We've found a little restaurant in the Plaka whose owner voted No in the Referendum.*"

181

FROM THE CRADLE TO THE

Much of British life is still untouched by the Welfare State.
PUNCH spotlights some of the most neglected areas

OMBUDSMAN

Some years ago it was proposed that we should have an Ombudsman to deal with the private subject's complaints. What happened instead was that we got a Parliamentary Commissioner, whose job it is to explain to private subjects that their complaint does not fall within his province. What we now need is an Ombudsman to deal with all the complaints outside that province. One of his first clients would be the Parliamentary Commissioner, who could complain that nobody knew his name or what he did. The Ombudsman could then give him a real job, like dealing with the complaints that the Ombudsman suddenly found he was ineligible to deal with. This is called democracy.

THE PRESS

One of man's inalienable rights is access to free, unbiased information, or, if it isn't, it should be. None of the privately run newspapers provides this. What we need is a government newspaper which, free from the pressures of political and financial bias, would be able to explain to us in great depth the real facts behind the sale of slag heaps, Chilean naval policy and the urgency of the need to get out of Europe. To balance this, there would have to be an Opposition newspaper presenting the *real* facts behind the real facts. There would also have to be a Liberal, a moderate, a militant and an extremist newspaper. After a few months of this, nobody would grumble about the capitalist press any more.

WEDDINGS

It seems incredible that in this democratic age, there is still a place in our society for private weddings. The disproportion between lavish upper income ceremonies and small token weddings at the lower end of the scale is too heartbreaking and tragic for me to point out. All wedding services must immediately be nationalised. I propose that they are paid for by a small increase in Social Security payments, in the same way that pensions are secured by regular payments. In the case of a payer who decides to get married early in life, he would be able to pay off his wedding expenses over the next ten years. People who decided never to get married would be allowed to opt out, with stiff penalties if they then changed their mind or are adjudged by an inspector to be living with someone merely to avoid wedding payments.

SCHOOL

Everyone except the politicians are now convinced that the extra school year is a bad mistake, causing resentment, frustration and even violence among those forced to stay on. Unless the government decides to cancel the extra year, it should set up a nationwide service of psychiatric help and care to deal with the problems caused by it. This would include medical aid for teachers who had been vandalised.

LEGAL AID

We already have a small measure of legal aid for defendants in court and financial compensation for victims of violence or accident. What we do not have is any form of restitution for those most seriously affected by crime: the criminal himself. Crippled by years of living in prisons which are over-crowded and mentally contaminating, he should receive ample compensation from the State which has inflicted this ineradicable damage on him. The prisoners of this country, many of them perfectly respectable ex-policemen, stockbrokers, architects and Old Etonians, deserve a better deal from a society which has never known what it is like to live in such conditions unless they happen to be one of the millions living in sub-standard housing.

HOUSING

Every day thousands of people are locked out of their own homes simply because they have lost their keys or can't remember where they last put them. This seems incredible in our democratic age. There should be a National Office for

GRAVE?

the Replacement of Lost Keys (NORLK, or NOUGHT if that's easier to say). Victims of this common domestic accident would be able to apply in writing to NOUGHT, submitting their birth certificate, rent book and/or lease, a £50 deposit and letters of reference from two respectable people, or lawyers. Within a matter of weeks, an official would be round to let the unfortunate sufferers in. Even if it did not allay the problems immediately, it would be an excellent excuse to build a new unwieldy Civil Service complex in Swansea or Sunderland.

POLICE

It seems incredible in our democratic age that our under-manned police force should be harassed and overworked by having to deal with so many complaints about police behaviour. Instead of having them dealt with by civilian authorties, which would only increase bureaucracy and officialdom, this load of work could immediately be lightened by decreeing that complaints could only be filed by police officers who are, after all, the only ones who really know the field.

TITLES

Some are born with titles, some thrust them upon themselves, but the vast majority go through life without the slightest hope of ever owning their own titles. This is obviously unjust. But instead of doing away with titles, let us simply make them freely available through Social Security so that anyone who wants them (and there will be a minority who would rather stay common) can have them, on the same principle that the only way to rid the railways of inequality is not to get rid of First Class, but to do away with Second Class.

SPORT

It seems etc in our etc that football should be dominated by the boring, system-ridden teams produced by capitalistic investment. To nationalise the entire Football League is probably beyond even Tony Benn's dreams, but it seems imperative at this moment to sponsor a Government-backed football team which could bring adventurous play and entertainment to the public. The money spent on the air sickness bags in Concorde would suffice to form a team worthy of the First Division. They might not be able to beat Leeds every time but at least they could thrash anything Alf Ramsey put into the field. At the very worst, the government might consider nationalising West Ham and Hans Keller.

FOOD

There is nothing wrong with British cooking that a complete rethink could not put right. If it has any faults at the moment, they are a total lack of imagination and a tendency to regard eating as a duty rather than a pleasure. Now, to institute a chain of British National Restaurants, in an attempt to restore the erstwhile grandeur of our cuisine, or at least eatable food, might seem an unromantic move. But as the quality is so scarce and as the great days of British cooking are so far removed, it might prove possible to sneak it in under the banner of regional culinary museums in which the traditions of our past glories could be revived and tasted on the spot. If nothing else, it would be a good excuse to build a new unwieldy government employment centre in Leeds or Glasgow.

DEATH

The cradle is well looked after, but what about the grave? It seems incredible in this d.a. that state funerals should be lavished on people who could perfectly well afford their own state funeral, but nothing given to those who could hardly afford to die—at this moment thousands of old people are kept alive merely by the thought of what their funeral will cost. A tiny addition to Social Security payments would ensure that, when the moment comes, the late deceased would not simply be a name on a gravestone but also a proud number in a State Death Scheme, would be able to choose from a range of three simply worded epitaphs and could rest comfortable in the knowledge that he was safely interred in an unwieldy new tower block in Birmingham, Carlisle or East Kilbride.

PARLIAMENTARY GOVERNMENT

It seems incredible in this democratic age.

Please Give Generously

LARRY in the land of the free

NATIONAL HEALTH DENTURES

Country Life

Not everything that happens in Britain gets into the national press. This feature, to which readers contribute, presents some of the news which never made it.

The town clock at Conisby chimes forty times at 2 a.m. daily and never at any other time. The town council says it is considering replacing it.

F. J. Davis (*Straits Times*)

"It is about time we all got our shoulders to the wheel and pulled the same way, instead of the county, in its ivory tower at Exeter, heaping coals on top of us and squashing us flat. Unless we do something now, we will never get from under," he said.

R. C. Leventhorpe
(*Western Morning News*)

As a biologist, Dr. Jones studies many fish. "But the salmon is my first love. It's such an interesting creature and there is so little known about it. I wrote a book on it a few years back that consisted mainly of things I didn't know."

K. P. M. Williams
(*Liverpool Daily Post*)

Beccles ended its 390-year history as a borough with a weekend of events which contained the contrasting elements of hilarity, apathy, sadness, civic dignity and hope for the future. The contrasting emotions were most evident on Friday evening when a planned torchlight procession suffered the misfortune of taking place in daylight and attracting only about eight people in fancy dress, plus a pantomime cow.

I. Yarham
(*Beccles and Bungay Journal*)

It seems that cremation is a dying trade, perhaps the ultimate in dead-end jobs.

W. Scott (*Glasgow Herald*)

"*As far as I'm concerned he could stay out all night.*"

The "Horam" sign at the entrance to the village from Heathfield direction has been knocked down by vehicles many times but its future should now be more secure, the Parish Council heard at their meeting last week. Mr. C. Heath said that previously cars had hit the sign and then bounced off against a nearby oak tree but now they would have to hit the tree first as the sign had been re-sited behind it.

E. Band (*Sussex Express*)

A 20-year-old Cambridge bus conductor says he was forced to resign because he arranged for tea and biscuits to be served on his bus to cheer up the passengers.

A. M. Bailey
(*Cambridge Evening News*)

The programme, which is about the development of number systems, will include an interview with Dr. David Fowler, of Warwick University, on the historical crises associated with the square root of two.

M. Carter (*Leamington Spa Courier*)

"*I don't know much about art but I know what it's OK to talk about.*"

When a police constable asked Michael Maloney why he had 22 packets of ham under his jacket, the Irishman told him it was for sandwiches. His mate, he added, was just buying an onion and some bread to go with it. But the Constable did not believe him.

P. Browne (*Southern Evening Echo*)

A remarkable achievement and one by which they had reversed the direction of flow of Bournemouth's sewage. That was how Cllr. Richard Judd, chairman of the council's works and transportation committee described the £6¾m scheme.

H. K. Mills
(*Bournemouth Evening Echo*)

A 15-year-old Cambridge boy, who smashed a street-lamp by shooting at it with an air gun, told the police he was trying to save electricity.

N. Sellers (*Cambridge Evening News*)

Dungeness nuclear power station lost half its production this week because engineer Mr. Peter Hobbis tried to stop a horse from eating a rose bush. The horse trod on his foot, putting him off work. And under the engineers' restrictions, he could not be replaced. As a result, one of the two reactors was shut down.

A. Szmelter
(*Folkestone, Hythe & District Herald*)

As a result of her riding prowess, Mrs. Gillon will travel to Newcastle on Sunday to take part in Hughie Green's television programme, The Sky's the Limit. She will answer questions on spelling.

J. Mitson (*Sevenoaks Chronicle*)

A man who was arrested in Sutton Coldfield for being drunk and disorderly told the police his name was Enid Blyton. Not until he was put in a cell did he realise he was not the famous authoress of children's stories, Sutton magistrates were told last Thursday.

S. J. Foster (*Sutton Coldfield News*)

STANLEY by Murray Ball

Continuing the adventures of the Great Palaeolithic Hero

The Madder they Are, the Harder they Try

BARRY TOOK roams the wilder regions of showbiz

THE customers at Bournemouth's Maison Royale certainly got their money's worth recently when contortionist Eric Jarvis, as the high point of his cabaret act, coated himself with butter and slipped into a 12 in. diameter, 5 ft. long concrete pipe. Alas, poor Eric! Having got in he couldn't get out and was eventually released some hours later at Boscombe's Royal Victoria Hospital with the help of six pints of detergent, two ambulance men, and a nurse.

Reading the news item started a small noisy memory that has been rushing round in my mind giggling ever since. Now—hands up all those who remember Carroll Levis and his discoveries. For those of you who don't remember, Carroll Levis ran what I suppose was the first of the nationwide amateur talent contests which hit Britain back in the thirties.

His slogan was—"Remember, the discoveries of today are truly the stars of tomorrow." Although it would have been more accurate to say "the oddities of today are truly the oddities of tomorrow." But not that many of them ever did become stars. Off-hand I can think of only one Carroll Levis discovery who has become by definition a star. He unearthed a lot of talent, it's true, but there's a mysterious chemistry at work where stardom is concerned and it hasn't much to do with "local boy makes good."

I worked for Carroll for a time as road manager holding auditions in every town we visited, staging mini talent contests and passing the more promising discoveries up the line to Carroll for national exposure on radio or at least a spot on his big shows at the number one variety theatres.

I don't know what the rest of the world was singing in 1952, but at those auditions everyone sang either *Bless This House* or *Oh, My Beloved Father*. (There was another unspeakable version—*Oh, My Beloved Daddy*. Either way it made *Deck Of Cards* sound like Tom Lehrer at his most jaundiced.) Auditioning on average 100 hopefuls a week you develop a callousness towards aspiring talent that verges on the brutal. Many poor singers never got further than "Bless this . . ." or "Oh My Beloved . . ." before the traditional "Thank you—we'll let you know." On bad days the poor wretches wouldn't get further than "Bless . . ." or "Oh . . ." before their hopes were dashed by the heartless villain in the stalls.

But the joy that sprang in my heart when someone produced a novelty item or a new idea was enormous. I've sat watching an aspiring acrobat clambering on and falling off a Unicycle for twenty minutes on end—with a sensation of pure pleasure. A dog act where the dog was overcome by stage fright and just stood on the stage shivering was nectar—and one red letter day a contortionist (to the strains of *A Pretty Girl Is Like A Melody*) became locked in an extremely bizarre position and had to be carried to the local cottage hospital to be unravelled. These made up for the hours of *Oh, My Beloved Father*, but were all too rare.

The high watermark from the point of view of the student of the esoteric was when a comedian in Darlington, at the end of each joke, pressed a button concealed in his trouser pocket and his eye lit up. Truly. He had a glass eye into which he'd put a small light bulb, wired it up to a pocket battery and hey presto! The sheer horror of his grisly partially illuminated skull still gives me shudders when I think of it.

I suppose it could be argued that he'd made a practical and sensible adaptation and harnessed his disability for his own benefit and others' pleasure, but you need to have an advanced taste for Kitsch before

GET-RID-OF-THE-STEEPLE FUND NOW AT: £705

NickBaker

188

the illuminated eye socket can be truly said to give deep enjoyment.

Why go to these lengths to get into Show Business? I suppose it's the desire not only to be different but to be seen to be special. Is it yet another aspect of the ascent of man? Some people do the football pools or study the F.T. Index. Others pull themselves together and go out and become fire eaters or clog dancers. Take Kardomah—a variety artist of great skill and spectacular originality. His bill matter was Kardomah—"fills the stage with flags"—and that was exactly and precisely what he did. His costume was a maze of hidden pockets in which were concealed flags of all nations—every batten in the flies had more flags attached to them, and in a ground cloth, a sort of carpet covering the stage, there were more hidden pockets also packed with flags. Kardomah, to the appropriate music, then produced flags. Hundreds and thousands of them, until quite literally the stage was full of flags. Curtain!

In twice nightly variety Kardomah, having done it once, would have to do it again and it took him the entire two hours between one appearance and the next to collect, refold and secrete these multifarious flags. Day in, day out, year in, year out. He made Sisyphus look like a dilettante.

Then there was a one-legged tightrope walker, whose name I forget, who turned his disability to advantage by dressing as a pirate—you could hear the crash when he fell off the wire—as he frequently did—all over the theatre. He was a New Zealander and as cheerful a man as I'd ever met and as his good humour was only equalled by his lack of balance, he needed to be cheerful.

My favourite one-legged entertainer was a negro tap dancer who rejoiced in the name of Peg Leg Bates. A tap was fitted to the bottom of his peg and he would hammer out dance routines that were the envy of his fellow dancers. His biggest hazard was knot holes in the stage. If he wasn't careful he'd disappear up to the knee and the pit orchestra would have to vamp until he'd extricated himself. These men were pros. I cherish a memory of a week spent at Llanelli with, among others, a spoon basher. Playing the spoons is an engaging, if limited, entertainment and he was scheduled for five minutes tapping his anatomy with a pair of dessert spoons while the orchestra rattled through the Savoy American Medley.

Unfortunately a combination of circumstances had decimated the local talent who were to be the Koh-i-nor in the crown of our week's presentation and having to provide a two hour show twice nightly with only four acts proved a bit of a headache. The spoonologist, however, came to my rescue and volunteered to lengthen his act. I asked how? He told me, and I agreed. I had no option really—but have you ever heard *Oh, My Beloved Father* played on the spoons?

"He's scared of heights."

When I next ran into him some years later, he'd become a road-sweeper and seemed fairly content. He explained that he'd given up Show Business as it was too chancy. "But," he confessed, "I miss the glamour."

I'm sure that Hughie Green would bear me out when I say the world is full of apparently sane, rational people who at the slightest sign of encouragement will burst like the opening title sequence of *Monty Python's Flying Circus* into a triffid world of eccentric—let's not fool about—lunatic activity, just to get into Show Business. Mother, fetch me a five-foot pipe and a pound of the very best butter. I feel an act coming on.

"*I am head of secret intelligence. To disclose my identity would endanger the national security.*"

Alla da Compliments of da Season

BILL TIDY
in Old Napoli

"Thank God Enrico's doing so well in America. Here, these tapes must be for the kids to play with."

"They're simple decent people, if somewhat communist inclined!"

"The Mafia are being a bit blatant this year!"